TAX EXPENDITURES

TAX EXPENDITURES

Stanley S. Surrey and Paul R. McDaniel

Harvard University Press
Cambridge, Massachusetts, and London, England   1985

RECEIVED

SEP 1 6 1985

MSU - LIBRARY

Copyright © 1985 by the President and Fellows of Harvard College
All rights reserved
Printed in the United States of America
10 9 8 7 6 5 4 3 2 1

This book is printed on acid-free paper, and its binding materials
have been chosen for strength and durability.

LIBRARY OF CONGRESS CATALOGING IN PUBLICATION DATA

Surrey, Stanley S.
  Tax expenditures.

  Bibliography: p.
  Includes index.
  1. Tax expenditures.   2. Tax expenditures—United States.
I. McDaniel, Paul R.   II. Title.
HJ2305.S88 1985   336.2   84-19718
ISBN 0-674-86832-3 (alk. paper)

HJ
2305
.S88
1985

1111 3238   11.22.85 Ae

PREFACE

AFTER the concept of tax expenditures was introduced in the United States by the Treasury Department in 1968, it was scrupulously analyzed by government personnel and fiscal scholars. In 1973 the late Stanley S. Surrey's book *Pathways to Tax Reform* provided a comprehensive exposition and summary of developments to that date.

Since 1973, applications of the concept have proliferated and new perceptions of possible further uses have emerged. The concept was incorporated into the budget process by the Congressional Budget Act of 1974, and use in government fiscal and budgetary policy analyses of both the concept and the data generated by it has grown steadily. The interchangeability of spending through the tax system and spending through direct appropriations has been increasingly recognized. That recognition in turn has led to closer examination of budget policies and processes and of the design and implementation of federal subsidy programs run through the tax system. Tax expenditures have also been scrutinized more carefully in the courts, although formal recognition and application of the concept by litigants and judges is still only in the formative stage. Other countries have grasped the necessity for developing tax expenditure budgets to control their overall budget and fiscal policies effectively. As a result, in recent years many countries have prepared tax expenditure lists. Inevitably this process has led to a need for comparative studies, and development of uniform guidelines for identification and measurement of tax expenditures has begun.

This book traces the development since 1973 of uses of the tax expenditure concept. It considers the impact on budget policy, on tax

601976

policy and administration, and on government decisions between using tax expenditures or direct spending to implement subsidy programs. And it examines the use of the tax expenditure concept in the courts and its implementation in other countries.

Chapter 1 provides an overview of the issues to be considered. Chapters 2 through 6 focus on the uses to which tax expenditure analysis has been put, and chapter 7 is a detailed exposition of the conceptual framework of tax expenditure analysis. Readers who are not familiar with tax expenditure analysis may find it useful to refer to chapter 7 before turning to chapters 2 through 6.

We have benefited greatly from the research and editorial assistance of Paulette Furness, Joseph Hamilton, Robert Roth, Cynthia Shupe, and A. D. Spitzer. We also appreciate the invaluable work of Katherine A. Dangora and Donna Marie Teehan in preparing the manuscript.

CONTENTS

TABLES

TAX EXPENDITURES

1

THE TAX EXPENDITURE CONCEPT

MOST PEOPLE probably regard the Internal Revenue Code as the revenue-raising instrument of the U.S. government. Many are surprised to learn that it is also a vehicle by which the government *spends* hundreds of billions of dollars each year. A clear understanding of this fact is essential if an informed public is to be able to consider intelligently the total impact of government spending both on the economy and on particular groups of people or businesses. The spending programs embedded in the Internal Revenue Code are termed "tax expenditures." Because the tax expenditure provisions look like other parts of the code, many have traditionally viewed them as weaknesses of the tax system—as "loopholes" or "escapes from tax"—and as objects of needed tax reform.

In 1968 the Treasury Department published the first tax expenditure budget for the United States. Since then, the concept of tax expenditures has expanded rapidly in scope and uses. The Congressional Budget Act of 1974, for example, made the concept an integral part of a new congressional budget process. Accordingly, all budgets after 1975 have contained a special analysis titled "Tax Expenditures" describing the tax expenditure concept and providing a detailed tabulation of income tax expenditures. In 1976 both the House and the Senate budget committees specified a reduction in tax expenditures as a goal of tax reform legislation; this step was a material factor in the passage of the Tax Reform Act of 1976. In 1977 the President asked the Treasury for a detailed report on the continued desirability of each item listed as a tax expenditure. Starting in 1977 the

Congress, in its continuing effort to make the ever-growing federal budget more manageable, again recognized, as it had in 1974, that it must grapple with the impact of tax expenditures. In this period Congress focused principally on proposals for "sunset" reviews of federal programs and on various possible statutory limitations on federal spending.

The concept also began to attract international attention. In 1976 and 1977 the two major international tax organizations—the International Fiscal Association and the International Institute of Public Finance—made the concept of tax expenditures a principal subject of their annual meetings. In 1979 the Canadian government published a comprehensive list and conceptual analysis of tax preferences in its federal income and commodity tax systems. In the same year the government of the United Kingdom included a table of tax expenditures in its *Expenditure Plans Paper*. Between 1980 and 1982 a number of other countries adopted formal tax expenditure budgets, and several countries launched preliminary studies both in and out of government. In 1984 fiscal scholars from six countries in the Organization for Economic Cooperation and Development (OECD) completed the first comparative study of their tax expenditures.

These events demonstrate a rapidly growing recognition of the role of the tax expenditure concept both in budget policy issues and in tax policy issues. Once a country focuses on the presence of tax expenditures in its tax system, it becomes aware that only through attention to those expenditures can it control its budget policy and its tax policy. This awareness in turn leads to new insights into the ways in which the concept affects both the substance of fiscal policy and the political processes by which that policy is formulated.

General Description

The U.S. Treasury Department developed and applied the tax expenditure concept in 1967–68.[1] In the 1960s the Treasury had taken a general position against the use of tax incentives to advance particular social policy goals and had instead urged the use of direct programs to provide the needed assistance. Its study of tax incentives disclosed that nowhere in government was there any comprehensive analysis of the existing tax incentives or of the amounts they involved. As a result, the Treasury compiled a list cf tax expenditures together with an estimate of the revenue lost—that is, the amount spent—for each item. The items in the list corresponded with direct budget categories to permit comparison between direct programs and tax expenditure programs.

The tax expenditure concept posits that an income tax is composed of two distinct elements. The first element consists of structural provisions necessary to implement a normal income tax, such as the definition of net income, the specification of accounting rules, the determination of the entities subject to tax, the determination of the rate schedule and exemption levels, and the application of the tax to international transactions. These provisions compose the revenue-raising aspects of the tax. The second element consists of the special preferences found in every income tax. These provisions, often called tax incentives or tax subsidies, are departures from the normal tax structure and are designed to favor a particular industry, activity, or class of persons. They take many forms, such as permanent exclusions from income, deductions, deferrals of tax liabilities, credits against tax, or special rates. Whatever their form, these departures from the normative tax structure represent government spending for favored activities or groups, effected through the tax system rather than through direct grants, loans, or other forms of government assistance.

Put differently, whenever government decides to grant monetary assistance to an activity or group, it may choose from a wide range of methods, such as a direct government grant or subsidy; a government loan, perhaps at a below-market interest rate; or a private loan guaranteed by the government. Or the government may use the tax system and reduce the tax liability otherwise applicable by adopting a special exclusion, deduction, or the like for the favored activity or group. Examples under the income tax are investment credits, exclusions of certain types of income, accelerated depreciation deductions, deductions for particular forms of consumption, and low rates of tax for certain activities. These tax reductions in effect represent monetary assistance provided by the government.

Tax expenditure analysis is based on the concept of a normative tax of the type under consideration. The Treasury Department focused on income tax, but the analysis is appropriate also to any broad-based tax intended to have a general application, such as a consumption tax (examples are a retail sales tax, a value-added tax, and a progressive expenditure tax), a wealth transfer tax, a general property tax, or a wealth tax.[2] Tax expenditure analysis, as applied to a particular tax, requires an understanding of the normative structure of that tax in order to determine whether a provision is a part of the structural or the tax expenditure component. In the U.S. analysis of income tax expenditures, the normative concept of net income is based on the Schanz-Haig-Simons (S-H-S) economic definition of income, that is, an increase in net economic wealth between two points of time plus consumption during that period.[3] "Consumption" in effect covers all expenditures except those incurred as a cost in the earning or production of income (which are proper offsets to gross income to arrive at taxable net income). Because the S-H-S approach does not specify which accounting techniques are to be used, in establishing a normal structure the Treasury employs widely accepted standards of business accounting. The application of these economic and accounting norms is tempered by reference to "the generally accepted structure of an income tax."[4] This last standard considers as normative the exclusion from income of unrealized appreciation in asset values and of imputed income from homes or other assets, since in the United States those items have not been commonly regarded as income for tax purposes even though they fall within the economic definition of income.

The taxable unit is not specified by the S-H-S definition, nor is there a normative concept of that unit. Rather, the choice of taxable unit— for example, how to tax single persons versus married persons, and the family in general—is regarded as a policy issue wider than tax policy per se, embracing a country's attitudes toward marriage, women in general, women in the work force, and so on. Nor is the rate schedule itself a normative concept. Instead, such matters as how progressive the rates should be or at what minimum point in the income scale the rates should apply are regarded as issues to be determined by fiscal policy and political goals. Once the taxable unit and a general rate schedule are decided upon as matters of fiscal policy, variations from those decisions intended to confer a special tax benefit become departures from the normal structure. Thus a general reduction of tax rates would not be a tax expenditure—though it would be relief from taxes. Likewise, the norm does not specify any particular relationship between the corporate and individual income taxes, and thus does not specify as normative a classical corporate tax structure, a completely integrated corporate tax, or a partially integrated corporate tax. However, once a government decides what the relationship between the corporate tax and the individual income tax is to be, then special departures from that choice constitute tax expenditures. In the United States, the current context for tax expenditure analysis is the classical separation of corporate and individual income taxes.

The norm also does not specify whether the determination of the tax base is to involve nominal amounts or inflation-adjusted amounts. In this case also, once a clear choice is made, any special departure can be a tax expenditure. Thus an approach that would adjust the cost of an asset for inflation in computing gain or depreciation but fail to make an adjustment in the real cost of funds borrowed to acquire the asset would effect only a partial or preferential change to reflect inflation and would therefore be a tax expenditure. In the United States, the context for tax expenditure analysis is the current nominal dollar determination of the base. Indexing of the rate schedule for inflation is not a tax expenditure, since the shape of the rate schedule itself is not involved in the normative structure; hence a decision to change rate brackets because of inflation is also outside tax expenditure analysis.

The essential feature of the definition of a normal income tax is the determination of the net income base allocated to the particular yearly accounting period used to compute tax liabilities. Generally speaking, in countries using a broad-based modern income tax, the determination of that base is not a matter on which informed fiscal experts would significantly disagree if their sole function were to establish a normative structure. As stated earlier, the S-H-S definition of net income is the accepted norm. But that definition covers only basic aspects and a few details. Since the inception of the income tax, its widespread application and changes in patterns of employment, business, government, and many other activities have produced numerous questions of detail, some of them involving quite difficult classification questions. The construction of a tax expenditure budget therefore requires an extension of the S-H-S analysis to many issues that have arisen since its initial explication; bringing the application of the S-H-S definition up to date involves determining the normative base of the income tax in the light of more recent developments. Application of the tax expenditure concept thus requires an intellectually consistent, thorough analysis of the normative structure of an income tax in today's world. It is a unique but necessary task not attempted by any other fiscal concept.

The classification of an item as a tax expenditure does not in itself make that item either a desirable or an undesirable provision; nor does it indicate whether the inclusion of the item in the tax system is good or bad fiscal policy. The classification of an item as a tax expenditure is purely informative, just as the presence of an item in the direct budget of a government is informative; it is simply a way of announcing that the item is not part of the normative tax structure. This being so, it is appropriate to ask whether the presence of those items in the tax system is desirable or undesirable, given the existing budget policy, tax policy, and other relevant criteria.

Along with the definitional task of determining the normative base for a tax so that a list of the tax expenditures under that tax may be developed, tax expenditure analysis requires a technique for estimating the amount spent through the tax expenditures. Under the customary approach, the amount spent under a particular tax expenditure is the revenue loss associated with that item. The technique used to determine the loss is precisely the same as the one used by the Treasury to estimate revenue loss or gain when any change in tax law is proposed, whether it involves a structural provision or a tax incentive subsidy.

Table 1 lists the estimated tax expenditures for corporate and individual income tax for fiscal 1983–1988, by budget category and subcategory.[5]

Uses of Tax Expenditure Concept, List, and Estimates
BUDGET POLICY

A brief review of the list of tax expenditures reveals several important aspects. The total amount of "spending"—revenue loss—by the government through tax expenditures estimated for fiscal 1984 was over $259 billion. The estimated direct expenditures listed in the 1984 budget came to $880.3 billion. Tax spending was thus 22.8 percent of an estimated total of $1,139.8 billion. These very substantial figures would be lost in an analysis of government spending were it not for the use of the tax expenditure concept. Obviously the real amount of government spending for 1984 was $1,139.8 billion. Hence any sensible discussion of government expenditures should start from that basis and not relate solely to the direct outlays of $880.3 billion.

Those who are concerned with the growth in federal spending must also take into account the trend in tax spending. The amount of government spending through tax expenditures increased by 179 percent from fiscal year 1974 to fiscal 1981, compared with an increase of 145 percent in direct outlays. Moreover, the Congressional Budget Office projected that between fiscal 1981 and fiscal 1987 tax expenditures would increase by 92 percent, as against a 71 percent increase for direct outlays. Thus tax expenditures in fiscal 1987 will equal 28 percent

Table 1. Tax expenditures by function and subfunction, fiscal years 1983–1988 (millions of dollars)[a]

Function and subfunction	Corporations						Individuals					
	1983	1984	1985	1986	1987	1988	1983	1984	1985	1986	1987	1988
050 NATIONAL DEFENSE												
051 *Department of Defense—Military*												
Exclusion of benefits and allowances to armed forces personnel	—	—	—	—	—	—	2,205	2,250	2,380	2,520	2,670	2,820
Exclusion of military disability pensions	—	—	—	—	—	—	165	160	165	175	185	195
150 INTERNATIONAL AFFAIRS												
155 *International Finance Programs*												
Exclusion of income earned abroad by United States citizens	—	—	—	—	—	—	1,285	1,300	1,365	1,435	1,505	1,580
Deferral of income of domestic international sales corporations (DISCs)	1,390	1,185	1,075	1,050	1,075	1,110	—	—	—	—	—	—

Table 1. (Continued)

Function and subfunction	Corporations						Individuals					
	1983	1984	1985	1986	1987	1988	1983	1984	1985	1986	1987	1988
Deferral of income of controlled foreign corporations	430	345	375	390	420	455	—	—	—	—	—	—
250 GENERAL SCIENCE, SPACE, AND TECHNOLOGY												
251 *General Science and Basic Research*												
Expensing of research and development expenditures	2,165	2,370	2,360	2,425	2,485	2,535	105	120	125	125	130	135
Credit for increasing research activities	615	650	660	305	65	25	30	35	40	30	5	b
Suspension of regulations relating to allocation under section 861 of research and experimental expenditures	120	60	b	—	—	—	—	—	—	—	—	—

271 *Energy Supply*

Expensing of exploration and development costs												
Oil and gas	660	440	590	740	835	895	875	800	815	855	900	950
Other fuels	30	30	35	35	40	40	—	—	—	—	—	—
Excess of percentage over cost depletion												
Oil and gas	375	430	445	465	510	555	1,425	1,275	1,305	1,410	1,505	1,625
Other fuels	325	350	355	380	410	440	15	15	15	15	15	20
Capital gains treatment of royalties from coal	35	40	40	45	50	55	140	145	160	175	190	205
Alternative fuel production credit	5	20	25	40	105	285	—	—	—	—	—	—
Alcohol fuel credit[c]	5	5	5	5	5	5	—	—	—	—	—	—
Exclusion of interest on state and local government industrial development bonds for energy production facilities	15	20	30	40	55	70	5	10	15	20	20	25
Residential energy credits	—	—	—	—	—	—	340	450	610	700	20	25
Supply incentives	—	—	—	—	—	—	—	—	—	—	70	—

Table 1. (*Continued*)

Function and subfunction	Corporations						Individuals					
	1983	1984	1985	1986	1987	1988	1983	1984	1985	1986	1987	1988
Alternative conservation and new technology credits												
Supply incentives	215	200	175	100	35	20	10	10	5	—	—	—
272 Energy Conservation												
Residential energy credits												
Conservation incentives	—	—	—	—	—	—	330	305	305	260	—	—
Alternative conservation and new technology credits												
Conservation incentives	135	35	15	5	b	—	b	b	b	—	—	—
Energy credit for intercity buses	5	5	5	b	—	—	—	—	—	—	—	—

300 NATURAL RESOURCES AND ENVIRONMENT												
302 *Conservation and Land Management*												
Capital gains treatment of certain timber income	275	390	430	500	575	595	95	125	150	175	205	230
Investment credit and seven-year amortization for reforestation expenditures	b	b	b	b	b	b	10	10	10	10	10	10
303 *Recreational Resources*												
Tax incentives for preservation of historic structures	65	90	110	140	185	240	130	165	215	275	355	460
304 *Pollution Control and Abatement*												
Exclusion of interest on state and local government pollution control bonds	900	1,025	1,140	1,255	1,375	1,510	440	505	565	620	680	745
Exclusion of payments in aid of construction of water, sewage, gas and electric utilities	45	75	75	80	75	70	—	—	—	—	—	—

Table 1. (Continued)

Function and subfunction	Corporations						Individuals					
	1983	1984	1985	1986	1987	1988	1983	1984	1985	1986	1987	1988
306 *Other Natural Resources*												
Expensing of exploration and development costs, nonfuel minerals	55	60	65	75	80	85	b	b	b	b	b	b
Excess of percentage over cost depletion, nonfuel minerals	270	295	310	335	355	380	10	10	15	15	15	15
Capital gains treatment of iron ore	5	5	5	5	5	10	5	5	5	5	5	10
350 Agriculture												
351 *Farm Income Stabilization*												
Expensing of certain capital outlays	85	90	95	100	100	105	475	495	510	530	545	565
Capital gains treatment of certain income	30	35	35	40	40	45	455	475	500	530	545	565
Deductibility of patronage dividends and certain other items of cooperatives	950	980	1,010	1,040	1,075	1,110	−390	−400	−410	−425	−435	−450

Exclusion of certain cost-sharing payments	25	25	30	40	45	50	—	—	—	—	—	—
370 COMMERCE AND HOUSING CREDIT												
371 Mortgage Credit and Thrift Insurance												
Excess bad-debt reserves of financial institutions	—	—	—	—	—	—	1,030	1,060	930	785	575	335
Deductibility of mortgage interest on owner-occupied homes	37,950	35,305	32,785	30,130	27,945	25,065	—	—	—	—	—	—
Deductibility of property tax on owner-occupied homes	14,980	13,215	11,710	10,480	9,535	8,765	—	—	—	—	—	—
Exclusion of interest on state and local government housing bonds for owner-occupied housing	385	415	445	475	485	450	1,070	1,105	1,145	1,190	1,190	1,060
Exclusion of interest on state and local government housing bonds for rental housing	665	585	510	430	355	285	1,345	1,185	1,035	880	735	585

Table 1. (Continued)

Function and subfunction	Corporations						Individuals					
	1983	1984	1985	1986	1987	1988	1983	1984	1985	1986	1987	1988
Deferral of capital gains on home sales	—	—	—	—	—	—	3,770	4,895	5,625	6,000	6,480	7,030
Exclusion of capital gains on home sales for persons age 55 and over	—	—	—	—	—	—	1,255	1,630	1,875	2,000	2,160	2,345
376 *Other Advancement and Regulation of Commerce*												
Exclusion of interest on state and local industrial development bonds	2,355	2,790	3,265	3,875	4,385	4,615	570	675	800	985	1,180	1,310
Exemption of credit union income	170	185	200	220	240	260	—	—	—	—	—	—
Exclusion of interest on life insurance savings	—	—	—	—	—	—	4,805	5,170	5,805	6,640	7,590	8,675
Deductibility of non-mortgage interest in excess of investment income	—	—	—	—	—	—	7,735	8,160	8,815	9,590	10,550	11,645

Expensing of construction period interest and taxes	505	610	735	855	975	1,110	275	320	390	455	515	590
Depreciation on rental housing in excess of straight-line	120	155	165	170	180	185	575	665	720	760	795	820
Depreciation on building (other than rental housing) in excess of straight-line	175	200	215	240	265	295	150	165	185	210	230	250
Reinvestment of dividends in stock of public utilities	—	—	—	—	—	—	365	415	450	230	—	—
Net interest exclusion	—	—	—	—	—	—	—	—	1,110	3,095	3,480	3,945
Exclusion of interest on certain savings certificates	—	—	—	—	—	—	2,335	550	—	—	—	—
Accelerated depreciation on equipment other than leased property	9,510	15,865	18,860	17,445	14,110	13,890	1,015	2,460	2,845	2,825	2,225	1,915
Safe-harbor leasing Accelerated depreciation and deferral	1,745	1,885	1,635	1,285	1,040	525	—	—	—	—	—	—
Investment credit	1,625	915	705	710	515	280	—	—	—	—	—	—

Table 1. (Continued)

Function and subfunction	Corporations						Individuals					
	1983	1984	1985	1986	1987	1988	1983	1984	1985	1986	1987	1988
Amortization of business start-up costs	15	20	25	30	35	40	105	160	230	285	315	355
Capital gains other than agriculture, timber, iron ore, and coal	1,770	2,075	2,130	2,305	2,475	2,695	14,955	14,320	15,365	16,440	17,590	18,820
Capital gains at death	—	—	—	—	—	—	3,975	3,565	3,665	3,920	4,195	4,490
Dividend exclusion	—	—	—	—	—	—	445	435	440	450	460	480
Reduced rates on the first $100,000 of corporate income	5,690	6,525	7,025	8,060	8,765	9,090	—	—	—	—	—	—
Investment credit, other than for employee stock ownership plans (ESOPs), rehabilitation of structures, reforestation, and leasing	9,965	12,315	16,075	19,870	21,650	22,860	3,220	3,350	3,615	3,945	4,245	4,595
400 TRANSPORTATION												
401 Ground Transportation Amortization of motor-carrier operating rights	70	70	50	15	5	b	5	5	5	5	b	—

Exclusion of interest on state and local government mass transit bonds	45	65	75	75	65	75	15	25	20	15	10	20
403 *Water Transporation*												
Deferral of tax on shipping companies	30	40	40	40	45	45	45	—	—	—	—	—
450 COMMUNITY AND REGIONAL DEVELOPMENT												
451 *Community Development*												
Five-year amortization for housing rehabilitation	20	25	25	25	25	25	30	35	35	35	35	35
Investment credit for rehabilitation of structures other than historic structures	175	200	185	195	215	235	160	165	160	165	180	200
500 EDUCATION, TRAINING, EMPLOYMENT AND SOCIAL SERVICES												
502 *Higher Education*												
Exclusion of scholarship and fellowship income	—	—	—	—	—	—	415	375	395	410	435	460

Table 1. (*Continued*)

Function and subfunction	Corporations						Individuals					
	1983	1984	1985	1986	1987	1988	1983	1984	1985	1986	1987	1988
Employer educational assistance	—	—	—	—	—	—	40	20	—	—	—	—
Exclusion of interest on state and local government student loan bonds	150	200	260	320	390	460	70	100	125	155	190	225
Parental personal exemption for students age 19 or over	—	—	—	—	—	—	995	950	885	895	905	920
Deductibility of charitable contributions (education)	280	345	360	415	480	525	495	495	580	735	660	615
504 Training and Employment Services												
Credit for child and dependent care expenses	—	—	—	—	—	—	1,520	1,765	2,190	2,465	2,765	3,160
Targeted jobs credit	215	395	355	155	30	5	75	70	30	[b]	—	5
505 Other Labor Services												
Exclusion of employee meals and lodging (other than military)	—	—	—	—	—	—	680	725	795	870	945	1,030

Tax credit for employee stock ownership plans (ESOPs)	1,250	1,375	1,875	2,235	2,330	950	—	—	—	—	—	—
Exclusion for employer-provided child care	—	—	—	—	—	—	10	25	55	85	120	155
506 *Social Services*												
Deductibility of charitable contributions, other than education and health	350	425	445	515	590	645	6,795	6,765	7,930	10,030	9,030	8,370
Exclusion of contributions to prepaid legal services plans	—	—	—	—	—	—	25	25	10	—	—	—
Deduction for two-earner married couples	—	—	—	—	—	—	3,555	5,835	6,350	6,935	7,600	8,460
Deduction for adoption expenses	—	—	—	—	—	—	10	10	10	10	15	15
550 HEALTH												
551 *Health Care Services*												
Exclusion of employer contributions for medical insurance premiums and medical care	—	—	—	—	—	—	18,645	21,300	24,280	27,680	31,555	35,975

Table 1. (Continued)

Function and subfunction	Corporations						Individuals					
	1983	1984	1985	1986	1987	1988	1983	1984	1985	1986	1987	1988
Deductibility of medical expenses	—	—	—	—	—	—	3,105	2,630	3,070	3,370	3,740	4,165
Exclusion of interest on state and local government hospital bonds	795	960	1,115	1,265	1,420	1,580	385	470	545	625	700	780
Deductibility of charitable contributions (health)	175	215	225	255	295	325	995	990	1,160	1,470	1,320	1,225
Tax credit for orphan drug research	10	15	15	10	—	—	—	—	—	—	—	—
600 INCOME SECURITY												
601 General Retirement and Disability Insurance												
Exclusion of Social Security benefits												
Disability insurance benefits							1,690	1,660	1,695	1,755	1,840	1,930
OASI benefits for retired workers							15,685	16,680	18,070	19,640	21,275	23,045
Benefits for dependents and survivors							3,765	3,870	4,095	4,355	4,630	4,920

Exclusion of railroad retirement system benefits	—	—	—	—	—	—	780	765	765	745	755	775
Exclusion of workmen's compensation benefits	—	—	—	—	—	—	1,870	2,090	2,395	2,755	3,170	3,645
Exclusion of special benefits for disabled coal miners	—	—	—	—	—	—	170	165	165	160	160	165
Exclusion of disability pay	—	—	—	—	—	—	145	135	130	130	130	130
Net exclusion of pension contributions and earnings	—	—	—	—	—	—	49,700	56,560	66,365	78,310	92,405	109,035
Employer plans												
Plans for self-employed	—	—	—	—	—	—	1,065	1,050	1,070	1,115	1,165	1,220
Individual retirement plans	—	—	—	—	—	—	2,695	3,180	3,705	4,240	4,745	5,360
Exclusion of other employee benefits												
Premiums on group term life insurance	—	—	—	—	—	—	2,100	2,250	2,465	2,715	2,985	3,285
Premiums on accident and disability insurance	—	—	—	—	—	—	115	120	125	130	135	140

Table 1. (Continued)

Function and subfunction	Corporations						Individuals					
	1983	1984	1985	1986	1987	1988	1983	1984	1985	1986	1987	1988
Additional exemption for the blind	—	—	—	—	—	—	35	35	35	35	35	35
Additional exemption for the elderly	—	—	—	—	—	—	2,365	2,410	2,570	2,720	2,410	3,130
Tax credit for the elderly	—	—	—	—	—	—	135	135	135	135	135	135
603 *Unemployment Compensation*												
Exclusion of untaxed unemployment insurance benefits	—	—	—	—	—	—	3,260	3,020	2,585	2,405	2,265	2,120
609 *Other Income Security*												
Exclusion of public assistance benefits	—	—	—	—	—	—	430	430	440	455	470	485
Deductibility of casualty and theft losses	—	—	—	—	—	—	575	380	470	520	590	670
Earned income credit[d]	—	—	—	—	—	—	385	330	290	215	155	210
700 VETERANS' BENEFITS AND SERVICES												
701 *Income Security for Veterans*												
Exclusion of veterans' disability compensation	—	—	—	—	—	—	1,820	1,830	1,950	1,995	2,070	2,145

Exclusion of veterans' pensions	—	—	—	—	—	—	310	290	280	275	275	275
702 *Veterans' Education, Training and Rehabilitation*												
Exclusion of GI bill benefits	—	—	—	—	—	—	130	130	115	100	90	65
800 GENERAL GOVERNMENT												
806 *Other General Government*												
Credits and deductions for political contributions	—	—	—	—	—	—	190	200	220	220	230	240
850 GENERAL-PURPOSE FISCAL ASSISTANCE												
851 *General Revenue Sharing*												
Exclusion of interest on general purpose state and local debt	6,985	7,850	8,695	9,530	10,370	11,280	3,435	3,870	4,295	4,715	5,130	5,580
Deductibility of nonbusiness state and local taxes (other than on owner-occupied homes)	—	—	—	—	—	—	20,060	21,770	26,605	29,970	34,125	39,010

Table 1. (Continued)

Function and subfunction	Corporations						Individuals					
	1983	1984	1985	1986	1987	1988	1983	1984	1985	1986	1987	1988
852 *Other General-Purpose Fiscal Assistance*												
Tax credit for corporations receiving income from doing business in United States possessions	1,350	1,075	1,135	1,240	1,375	1,525	—	—	—	—	—	—
900 INTEREST												
901 *Interest on the Public Debt*												
Deferral of interest on savings bonds	—	—	—	—	—	—	50	160	225	290	355	410

Source: Congressional Joint Committee on Taxation, *Estimates of Federal Tax Expenditures for Fiscal Years 1983–1988* (March 7, 1983), 10–18.
a. All estimates are based on the tax law enacted through the ninety-seventh Congress.
b. Less than $2.5 million.
c. In addition, the exemption from the excise tax for alcohol fuels results in a reduction in excise tax receipts, net of the income tax effect, of approximately $40 million for 1983, $60 million for 1984, $80 million for 1985, $95 million for 1986, and $110 million for 1987 and 1988.
d. The figures in the table indicate the effect of the earned income credit on receipts. The increase in outlays is $1,197 million in 1983, $1,119 million in 1984, $1,032 million in 1985, $1,004 million in 1986, $968 million in 1987, and $910 million in 1988.

of total federal outlays.[6] Clearly, any discussion concerning the growth of federal spending must take into account not only direct outlays but also the amount of "spending" in the tax system, through tax expenditures.

TAX POLICY

For a considerable time since the inception of the income tax a number of provisions in the tax law were described as "tax loopholes"—for example, the exemption of the interest on state and local government bonds. This term connoted a tax escape route not foreseen by Congress but discovered by astute tax lawyers. When it was recognized that most of these provisions had been deliberately adopted by Congress, and thus did not represent unforeseen escapes, they were referred to instead as "tax preferences." The tax expenditure concept takes the next step of recognizing that these "tax preferences" are really government spending programs and hence government assistance, run through the tax system. According to the tax expenditure concept, the beneficiary of a tax expenditure has paid the tax due under the normative structure, absent the tax expenditures, and then is paid the amount of the tax reduction effected by the special tax provisions ("tax preferences" under the former terminology). Although the use of tax expenditures short-circuits the direct spending process by involving only one net payment by the taxpayer—the tax actually paid—analysis indicates that in effect there are two transactions involved. One is the payment of normative tax liabilities and the other a government appropriation of funds to the taxpayers benefited by the tax expenditure programs.

The tax expenditure concept has cast a new light on tax reform efforts. In the past, most tax reform proposals aimed at achieving "horizontal tax equity"; that is, two taxpayers with the same amount of income should pay the same amount of tax. Other tax reform proposals were designed to achieve more "vertical tax equity," making taxpayers in upper brackets relatively higher taxpayers through a more progressive rate structure. However, less vertical tax equity—a less progressive rate structure—would constitute tax reform in the eyes of some. "Tax reform" is thus an imprecise term that can cover a number of goals.

The tax expenditure concept informs us that the tax preferences that have been the targets of traditional tax reform efforts are really spending programs. Thus the traditional tax reformers were really seeking to reduce or terminate particular spending programs and thereby cut or end government assistance to particular activities or groups. Once this fact is recognized the basic question then becomes whether or not government assistance should be provided. This question must be answered in terms of criteria applied to government spending programs. In seeking to eliminate a particular preference in the interest of horizontal tax equity, tax reformers have rarely faced that issue and have rarely justified adequately—in spending terms—the appropriateness of government assistance for the activity or group. For if such assistance was appropriate, then tax reform had to encompass a wider scope. It had to consider how government could provide that needed assistance through a direct spending program. It also had to consider whether direct spending or tax expenditure was a better framework in which to provide the assistance.

The tax expenditure concept also casts in a different context the constant efforts over the years to achieve "tax simplification," or at least less complexity. The goals may be regarded as desirable. But tax expenditure analysis reveals that in 1983 the income tax, inevitably a complex mechanism itself in its normative form, contained 105 spending programs. Any tax saddled with carrying this huge load of government assistance through so many diverse measures involves enormous complexities. Tax simplification will be impossible if these tax expenditures persist.

The same kinds of problems apply to tax administration. The administration of a normative income tax is a difficult task, involving both proper interpretation of the tax laws and maintenance of as high a degree of compliance as is possible in the real world. The income tax sweeps across all human and corporate activities (and trusts and partnerships as well). It must classify *all receipts* as included or excluded from gross income and *all expenditures* as deductible or not in determining taxable net income; and if the expenditures are deductible, it must determine whether they are to be taken currently or capitalized and taken over a period of years. This task must be performed anew each year and the work kept as current as possible. The classification must be done as fairly as possible, and both the Internal Revenue Service and the judiciary must play their part in seeking that fairness. But if the task of administering 105 spending programs is then added to this enormously difficult and complex task of normative income tax administration, the load becomes too great. Both the administration of the normative income tax and the administration of those spending programs must suffer. The Commissioner of Internal Revenue cannot also serve as the Secretary of Health and Human Services (HHS), the Secretary of Housing and Urban Development (HUD), the Secretary of Commerce, and as every other cabinet official and properly perform either his or her prescribed role as Commissioner or these added roles. The tax expenditure concept thus reveals the problems of administration—both of the normative tax and of the tax expenditure items themselves—that a system of tax expenditures involves. The obvious questions raised are whether it would be administratively more efficient to recast the various tax expenditures as direct programs, which would be administered by the departments regularly responsible for direct spending in the various areas, or, if the spending is to remain in the tax system, whether its administration can be improved so as to ensure the programs' effectiveness and to lighten the burden on the Commissioner, perhaps through combined administration.

Choosing between Tax Expenditures and Direct Programs

It does not appear that any government has consciously attempted to develop criteria to govern the choice between tax and direct expenditures or to approach the matter in any other organized way. The reason has been the failure until recently to recognize that tax expenditures exist and to understand that they are spending programs.

Once this fact becomes evident, it is clear that orderly government requires both the development of criteria to determine the choice between tax and direct expenditures, and an analysis of the possible consequences of each choice.

The Tax Expenditure Concept in the Courts

The tax expenditure concept has begun to come under the scrutiny of constitutional law. Under constitutional doctrines, the U.S. government may in general not engage in discriminatory activities, for example with regard to race or sex, or act without due regard for fair procedures and process. Hence, direct government spending programs that may involve such practices can be challenged in the courts. Private entities significantly supported by government funds and engaging in such practices are also subject to challenge. The question now being raised is whether these constitutional doctrines apply to special tax benefits and to private entities receiving those benefits. Thus the grant of direct government aid to a private school or other entity that practices racial discrimination would be unconstitutional. This being so, is the income tax exemption granted to that school or entity as a charitable organization, or the grant of a charitable deduction to individuals contributing to the school or entity, similarly subject to challenge? A direct grant of state funds to parents who send their children to parochial schools is unconstitutional as state aid to religion. Does the granting of an income tax credit to those parents also violate the Constitution?

In addition to constitutional issues, the courts must determine whether federal legislation regulating direct government assistance applies to tax expenditures. Thus, Title VI of the Civil Rights Act of 1964 prohibits grants of financial assistance to organizations that discriminate on grounds of race, color, or national origin. Would the allowance of a charitable deduction for a contribution to an organization that discriminates contrary to that act, so that direct government assistance would not be given to the organization, likewise be prohibited?

The underlying issue in both kinds of questions is whether tax assistance is legally equivalent to direct assistance.

International Aspects

Other countries have swiftly followed the United States in systematically applying the tax expenditure concept. These developments have revealed the need for comparative studies of tax systems and budgetary expenditures. For such comparisons to be meaningful, it is necessary to identify the tax expenditures in the tax systems and to associate the amounts involved with the amounts in the regular budgets.

The tax expenditure concept also is helpful in resolving substantive issues that arise in an international context.

Conceptual Issues

Like any other dynamic concept, tax expenditure analysis has revealed a number of issues with important implications for tax theory and fiscal policy. For example, just as special tax provisions provide government assistance, other provisions that depart from a normative income tax penalize the taxpayer by requiring a greater tax payment than would occur under the normative net income base. These tax penalty provisions frequently have counterparts in direct governmental regulatory or penalty provisions. The effect of the tax penalty is to increase the cost a taxpayer incurs to engage in a particular activity. One example of a tax penalty is the disallowance of gambling losses in excess of gambling gains even if the gambling is entered into on a "for profit" basis. Other examples are found in the various "public policy" provisions that deny deductions for certain business expenses involving lobbying, bribes, or fines.

In addition to the tax penalty provisions, and not to be confused with the tax penalties, is another group of provisions adverse to taxpayers, consisting of limits on the use of the tax expenditures themselves. Thus the restriction on the deductibility of capital losses is a concomitant limit on the tax expenditure treatment of capital gains. Superficially, some may see such limitations as tax penalties. But such provisions limiting existing tax expenditures perform a function quite different from that of the tax penalties.

Those concerned with state and local taxes are gradually coming to apply tax expenditure analysis. Beginning with the 1975–76 budget, for example, the governor of California has included in the annual budget a list of major tax expenditures effected through the state's principal taxes. Apart from special tax expenditures written in by the states themselves, states that base their income tax on the federal income tax have automatically adopted all or parts of federal tax expenditures. This automatic adoption may, of course, have marked effects on a state's own fiscal policy and may result in expenditures of state funds for purposes or in amounts that would never be approved for direct support by its legislature.

In sum, the tax expenditure concept when first announced in 1968 represented a new approach to both budget policy and tax policy. A Canadian public finance economist and former cabinet minister, Eric Kierans, has designated the concept "the major innovation in tax and public finance during the last twenty or thirty years."[7] Congress's adoption of the concept in its budget legislation in 1974 and the movement by other countries to apply the concept to their tax systems—all occurring within less than two decades—indicate that the concept does indeed have a useful role to play in budget policy and tax policy.

Alongside this expanding use both in the United States and internationally, there has been a steady growth in the theoretical understanding and implications of the concept. This progressive implementation requires continued study by tax and budget experts in and out of government. The task of educating the taxpaying public and its elected representatives about the tax expenditure concept and the effects of those expenditures on budget efficiency and tax equity is both necessary and ongoing.

2

BUDGET POLICY

THE TAX EXPENDITURE CONCEPT received its first concrete expression in the form of a budget. Since 1968, both budget policy and budget processes have been influenced by increased study and understanding of the implications of analyzing special tax provisions as functional equivalents of direct spending programs.

In the decades before 1974, formulation of the federal budget had become almost the exclusive province of the executive branch. The document submitted by the President each January for the following fiscal year was the only formal presentation of estimated receipts and expenditures by the government. With the enactment of the Congressional Budget and Impoundment Control Act of 1974, Congress reasserted its role in the budget process. The 1974 act gave Congress greater influence over the budget itself and specified procedures that potentially enabled it to exercise more effective control over federal spending.[1]

The 1974 act also reflected a clear understanding by Congress that the revised budget process must be applied to tax expenditures as well as to direct federal spending. The President was required to include a list of tax expenditures in the annual budget submitted to Congress. The newly established House and Senate budget committees were required, as part of their overall responsibilities to develop and manage the congressional budget process, to include the projected levels of tax expenditures in their reports accompanying the first concurrent resolutions on the budget for the coming fiscal year. The act applied procedures to tax expenditures similar to those adopted to give Congress greater power over direct spending.

Both the executive branch and Congress have made progress in integrating tax with direct spending programs, in terms of both budget development and budget presentation. But significant differences remain in the budget treatment of the two forms of spending. Those responsible for the budget must still develop and implement budgetary policies and processes to integrate fully all forms of federal spending.

Tax Expenditures and the President's Budget

The budget document submitted each January serves multiple purposes. It sets forth the President's priorities for expending the resources committed to the federal government. It plays an important role as a tool to stabilize, stimulate, or slow down economic growth and/or to affect the nation's balance of payments. It sets forth the aggregate of the nation's resources that are to be devoted to the federal share of the public sector through taxes collected, and it sets the level of aggregate federal spending. The budget and the budget process also provide tools for evaluation, coordination, and control of federal programs. In sum, the central functions of budget policy are (1) to establish spending priorities; (2) to set the level and control the aggregate of federal spending; and (3) to evaluate, coordinate, and control spending for particular programs within the budget. Before passage of the 1974 Budget Act, these functions were carried out only with respect to direct federal spending. Beginning in 1975, the budget included a list of tax expenditure items as required by the 1974 legislation. Let us now consider the extent to which tax expenditures have been integrated into the central functions of budget policy.

ESTABLISHING SPENDING PRIORITIES

Even under the 1974 Budget Act, a tax expenditure program has one major advantage over a direct spending program: *every* tax expenditure automatically has a higher budget priority than *any* direct spending program. In the vigorous debates over direct spending priorities between, for example, national defense and social welfare, policymakers often lose sight of this fact. Thus national defense currently has a lower priority than funds expended through the tax system for motels, motion pictures, luxury housing, cattle feeding programs, and the like. This automatic priority status undoubtedly contributes much to the popularity of tax expenditures with their beneficiaries. Perhaps a majority in Congress and their constituents would agree with these priorities. But it seems unlikely that *all* tax expenditure items would be accorded priority over *all* direct outlay programs if tax expenditures had to compete with direct expenditures in the normal budget process. Given the existing lack of coordination in that process, lobbyists for a particular interest group clearly have a strong incentive to try to get their subsidy programs treated as tax expenditures rather than as direct outlays. In fiscal 1985 tax expenditure programs accounted for some $370 billion, with direct spending programs competing for the remaining estimated $745 billion in federal revenues.

The current practice of granting automatic priority to tax spending items over direct spending ones is not inevitable. Closer coordination of the two methods of spending during preparation of the President's budget could ensure that priorities are established that take both types of spending into account. The Office of Management and Budget (OMB) could fix an overall spending limit for each department that would include both tax and direct spending programs in that department's area of responsibility. During preparation of the 1985 budget, for example, OMB could have advised HHS that a *total* of $60 billion in direct outlays and tax expenditures would be expended for health care (the 1985 budget actually called for $32.9 billion in outlays and $35.7 billion in tax expenditures). HHS could then have been required to establish priorities for health care programs in both spending categories. If it wanted to spend more than $32.9 billion in direct programs, it could have been required to recommend changes that would reduce tax spending by a corresponding amount. Applying the same scrutiny and review to all the nation's health care programs would ensure that priorities for federal health care spending were properly established and pursued. This procedure, implemented on a governmentwide basis, would ensure that neither form of federal spending enjoyed a preferred budget status over the other.[2]

CONTROLLING FEDERAL SPENDING

The procedure described above would also help achieve control of federal spending. Under existing budget procedures, tax expenditures are largely uncontrolled—many would say, out of control. In 1968 there were fewer than 50 tax expenditure programs, involving about $36.6 billion. For fiscal 1985, the OMB tax expenditure list contained more than 100 separate items, with aggregate revenue costs of almost $370 billion. Even taking into account that part of the increase in the number of items and revenues was the result of more refined budget presentation techniques and of inflation, there has obviously been an enormous increase in the use of tax expenditures. Moreover, the rate of growth in tax spending has been quite rapid even since the introduction of the 1974 Budget Act procedure. In fiscal 1976 tax expenditures totaled $98.5 billion. The growth to over $228 billion in fiscal 1981 represented more than a doubling of tax expenditure costs in five years, and the 1976 figure had almost tripled by fiscal 1985.

Tax expenditures have also grown at a much faster rate than direct outlays since 1967, both in terms of relative percentages and as a percentage of gross national product (GNP). The 1982 Congressional Budget Office tax expenditure study revealed that tax expenditures had risen ninefold, from $36.6 billion in 1967 to $228.6 billion in 1981. In contrast, in the same period direct outlays rose from $178.8 billion to $660.5 billion, not quite a fourfold increase. Thus tax expenditures grew at more than double the rate of direct outlays from 1967 to 1981.[3] In 1967 tax expenditures represented 4.14 percent of GNP, in 1981 8 percent. In contrast, federal outlays as a percentage of GNP were 21.4 percent in 1967 and 23.1 percent in 1981. Thus, while tax expenditures almost doubled as a percentage of GNP, direct outlays as a percentage of GNP rose by only 10 percent. Table 2 presents the trends discussed above.

During the past two decades, in many budget areas tax expenditures began to assume far greater importance than direct outlays both relatively and absolutely. In the budget category "National Resources and Environment," for example, tax expenditures grew by more than 800 percent from 1974 to 1981 while direct outlays grew by just over 140 percent. In "Commerce and Housing Credit," tax expenditures rose by more than 800 percent from 1967 to 1981 while direct outlays actually declined. Indeed, 1981 tax expenditures in this budget category were nearly twenty-five times as great as direct outlays ($98.2 billion in tax expenditures versus $4.0 billion in direct outlays).[4]

The executive branch has largely ignored tax expenditures in its efforts to attain budgetary objectives. President Carter's anti-inflationary 1980 budget, for example, called for a sharply lower federal deficit, achieved by a combination of increased revenues and reduced federal spending. The expenditure reductions, however, targeted only direct programs. No reductions in tax spending were proposed. Had the two

Table 2. Tax expenditure growth, selected calendar years 1967–1973 and fiscal years 1975–1982[a]

	1967	1969	1971	1973	1975	1977	1979	1981	1982
Tax expenditures									
Totals (billions of dollars)	36.6	46.6	51.7	65.4	92.9	113.5	149.8	228.6	253.5
Percentage of federal outlays	20.5	23.7	22.3	24.3	28.5	28.2	30.3	34.6	34.6
Percentage of federal revenues	23.8	24.1	24.8	24.7	33.1	31.7	32.3	37.9	40.8
Percentage of total federal "spending" (outlays plus tax expenditures)	18.8	20.3	19.7	21.0	22.3	22.1	23.4	25.7	25.7
Percentage of GNP	4.4	4.8	4.6	4.7	6.3	6.1	6.4	8.0	8.4
Federal outlays as a percentage of GNP	21.4	20.3	20.6	19.5	22.0	21.6	20.9	23.1	24.2
GNP (billions of dollars)	777.3	910.6	1,031.5	1,252.0	1,479.9	1,864.1	2,417.8	2,937.7	3,033.8

Source: Congressional Budget Office, Tax Expenditures: Budget Control Options and Five-Year Budget Projections for Fiscal Years 1983–1987 (1982), 14–15.

a. Tax expenditure estimates were prepared only on a calendar year basis for the years 1967–1973. These estimates correspond roughly to fiscal years 1968–1974 and are thus compared with the GNP, outlay, and revenue figures for those fiscal years.

forms of spending been subjected to the same kind of scrutiny, it seems highly improbable that direct spending programs would have been required to bear the entire brunt of the tighter budget. Senator Kennedy made this point as follows:

> For fiscal year 1980, Federal revenues spent through the tax laws will total approximately $150 billion, while direct expenditures will total approximately $550 billion under the so-called current services budget. Total Federal spending in 1980, therefore—counting both tax spending and direct spending—will reach $700 billion, with tax spending representing over 20 percent of the total.
>
> As a matter of budget policy, therefore, it would be appropriate for any necessary budget cuts to be allocated in a 4-to-1 ratio between direct spending programs and tax spending programs. For example, to reach the administration's target of a deficit of $30 billion for 1980, it is likely that total spending will have to be reduced by approximately $15 to $20 billion. If the cuts are allocated properly, then $12 to $16 billion of the cuts should come from direct spending programs, and $3 to $4 billion of the cuts should come from tax spending programs. Clearly, direct spending programs should not be required to bear the full brunt of any spending cuts that may be necessary.[5]

In 1979 and 1980 Congress exerted increasing pressure for a balanced budget. President Carter's initial budget for fiscal 1981 called for a $16 billion deficit. Bowing to congressional pressure, the President submitted a revised budget that purportedly eliminated the deficit. But again the proposed reductions in spending affected only direct programs.[6] Obviously, reductions in tax expenditures could have contributed to the balanced budget objective. But OMB does not appear to have implemented any systematic, coordinated approach. For example, in the original 1981 budget, the administration discussed, as required by Public Law 96–5, alternative budget proposals that would have achieved a balanced budget for fiscal 1981. The discussion focused exclusively on reductions in direct spending programs; no mention was made of the fact that a balanced budget could also have been achieved by cuts in tax expenditure programs, nor was a list of possible cuts included.[7] Of course, since the budget is a political document of the President, it does not set forth the options considered by the administration, only those finally chosen. It is therefore possible that in preparing the budget, the administration considered but rejected a reduction in tax expenditures.

Similarly, President Reagan's rhetorical attacks on excessive government spending have not appeared to include tax spending. He has never publicly addressed the fact that the new and larger tax expenditures included in the Economic Recovery Tax Act of 1981 had precisely the same effect on the deficit as did increased defense spending.

A procedure requiring integrated departmental consideration of tax and direct spending could provide the needed balance between the two forms of spending. Another beneficial result would be that nontax departments in the executive branch would no longer tend to support indiscriminately the use of tax expenditures for programs in their areas of interest. As things stand now, a department or agency that has reached its limit for direct spending tends to favor new or expanded tax expenditures rather uncritically. However inefficient, inequitable, or ineffective the tax program may be, the nontax departments appear to take the view that some spending for their program areas is better than none. The result, however, is increased federal spending.

Whether the objective is control of the aggregate level of federal spending or a balanced budget, failure to include tax expenditures fully in the budget process means that only 75 percent of total federal spending will be considered. As long as this practice persists, federal spending will be under no meaningful control.

EVALUATING, COORDINATING, AND CONTROLLING SPECIFIC TAX EXPENDITURES

The task of evaluating, coordinating, and controlling spending for specific programs is also an important element of budget policy and procedure. The techniques for evaluating particular tax expenditure programs and coordinating them with direct programs are discussed more fully below in connection with congressional proposals, and in chapter 4.

INTEGRATING TAX EXPENDITURES INTO THE BUDGET DOCUMENT

Initially the tax expenditure list was presented in a new section in the *Special Analyses* volume submitted each year with the budget.[8] The

1976 Special Analysis F, following the pattern of earlier, less formal lists, set forth for fiscal 1975 and 1976 the tax expenditure programs and estimated costs under the budget categories used for direct expenditure programs.[9] Also included were estimates of changes in tax expenditures that would result from proposals submitted by the President in the overall budget recommendations. No attempt was made, however, to integrate the information contained in Special Analysis F with the material contained in the basic budget document itself.

The special analysis of tax expenditures (now Special Analysis G) has continued to be the principal method of presenting the tax expenditure budget. Since 1976, however, OMB has increasingly integrated tax and direct expenditure data in the various aspects of the budget. Thus, beginning with the fiscal 1981 budget, each discussion of the separate budget program categories has included a description and cost estimate for associated tax expenditure items. As the following examples indicate, however, integration of the two forms of spending is still in the formative stage.

Special Analysis F of the 1981 budget contained an extended discussion called "Federal Credit Programs."[10] In many respects, budgetary problems created by off-budget federal credit programs parallel those created by tax expenditures. The 1981 budget reflected an increased effort to bring the credit programs under greater control. Consideration of federal credit programs must also include tax expenditures, because a number of tax expenditure programs constitute loans or interest subsidies or affect credit markets by lowering interest rates and increasing credit demands. As the 1981 Special Analysis F stated: "Tax expenditures have important and direct effects on the credit markets in at least four ways. These effects arise from (1) the exemption of interest on State and local debt from being subject to Federal income taxation, (2) investment tax credits, (3) personal deductions for mortgage interest and property taxes, and (4) various depreciation methods."[11] Because items 1 and 3 are functional equivalents of interest subsidies, it would be possible to substitute direct interest subsidy programs for them. Item 2 is the equivalent of a direct government grant to businesses to subsidize their purchases of machinery and equipment, with a resulting decrease in the borrowing costs for the acquisition; a direct grant system could be substituted for the tax credit. Item 4 includes programs that are equivalents of interest-free loans by the government; again, those loans could be effected directly rather than through the tax system.

The 1981 Special Analysis F did include some data concerning the subsidy granted through the exemption for state and local bond interest.[12] However, more information on tax expenditure credit programs is needed for a complete picture of federal credit programs. Specifically, those compiling the budget document need to identify and present each tax expenditure credit program now in Special Analysis G with the associated direct credit program in Special Analysis F.

Other special analyses also reflect increasing integration of tax expenditures with direct programs. Special Analysis H, for example, provides extensive discussion of the budget category "Federal Aid to State and Local Governments."[13] For 1981 this analysis mentioned the associated tax expenditures,[14] but it did not integrate the $25 billion in aid through the tax system with the $96 billion in direct program assistance to give a complete presentation of total federal aid to lower government levels. In 1985, however, Special Analysis H included discussion of the aid provided to state and local governments through tax expenditures.[15] On the other hand, the 1985 Special Analysis K, "Research and Development," discussed direct federal programs but omitted the $1.4 billion program provided by the immediate deduction and tax credit for research and development costs incurred by business.[16]

The lack of integration of the tax expenditure and "regular" budgets has caused some technical problems for those who must develop the tax expenditure budget. The following discussion examines the current treatment of several of these items by OMB and, when applicable, by the Congressional Budget Office (CBO).

Treatment of refundable credits. One budget presentation issue to be resolved is whether the revenue associated with the refunded portion of refundable tax credits should be included in direct budget outlays or whether the entire credit should be placed in the tax expenditure budget, with separate estimates for the portion that offsets tax liabilities and for the portion that is refunded. The existing example in this category is the refundable earned income credit. The earned income credit is so structured that if an individual's tax liability is not sufficient to absorb the full credit, any excess credit is refunded to the individual. Differences of opinion existed for some time over the appropriate budget presentation of the refunded portion. OMB originally included the refundable portion in direct budget outlays but placed the portion that offset tax liabilities in the tax expenditure budget.[17] In contrast, CBO included the entire credit in the tax expenditure budget, with separate estimates for the two portions.[18]

The choice between the two treatments turns on whether the important budgetary distinction is the issuance of checks by the Treasury, as in the original OMB approach, or the inclusion, in a single place in the budget, of all the funds expended for a particular program, as in the CBO approach. The original OMB approach divided a tax expenditure program into one part producing a tax reduction and one producing an outright grant of Treasury funds. Under this approach, the principal function of the direct budget is to show all Treasury outlays. Hence proper budgetary practice requires inclusion of the refundable portion of a tax expenditure in the direct budget. Since tax expenditures are not fully integrated into the regular budget, the tax expenditure program must be split into two parts and shown in different parts of the budget presentation. The justification for the CBO approach, on the other hand, is that a clear budget presentation should reflect the total costs of each program, both those incurred through tax reductions and those incurred through refundability. The crucial budgetary emphasis is on the program rather than on whether a Treasury check is issued for all or part of the tax credit.

In 1977 OMB accepted the CBO approach for the earned income credit and placed the entire item in the tax expenditure budget, with separate estimates for the two parts.[19] Then in the First Concurrent Resolution on the Budget for Fiscal Year 1979, Congress changed its approach and treated the refundable portion of the earned income credit as a direct budget outlay.[20] CBO subsequently revised its tax expenditure budgets to correspond to the congressional procedure, and OMB followed suit. As a result the tax expenditure budget currently includes only the nonrefundable portion of the earned income credit; the refundable portion appears in the direct budget under the category "Income Security."[21]

From the standpoint of the executive branch, given the existing practice of preparing separate tax and direct expenditure budgets, neither of the two approaches to treating refundable credits appears inherently superior to the other.[22] In the congressional context, however, there are important practical consequences in the tax, budget, and appropriations processes that depend on which of the two methods is used.[23]

Treatment of taxable tax credits. A tax credit intended to provide financial assistance for a particular economic or social objective is the equivalent of a government direct grant program. When the direct grant approach is adopted, the question arises whether the grant should constitute taxable income to its recipients. If a direct grant would represent taxable income under normative income tax principles, so too should a tax credit for the same purpose.

Recognition of this fact has begun to be reflected in the Internal Revenue Code. Taxpayers claiming the alcohol fuel tax credit must include the amount of the credit in their gross income. The targeted jobs tax credit is in effect a taxable credit, achieved indirectly by the requirement that taxpayers reduce the deduction for wages by the amount of the credit claimed. Similarly, the tax credit for rehabilitating older business structures is in effect taxable over the life of the structure because the taxpayer must reduce the basis of the building by the amount of the credit and hence take reduced depreciation deductions, pay tax on a greater amount of gain if the structure is sold at a gain, or take a reduced capital loss deduction if the structure is sold at a loss. The investment credit for machinery and equipment and for rehabilitation of certified historic structures is partially taxable; the basis of the asset must be reduced by one half of the tax credit.

The budget presentation issue is how tax expenditures that are themselves treated correctly under normative tax principles should be reflected in the tax and direct expenditure budgets. Apparently OMB in its "revenue loss" computation shows the net revenue effect of the taxable tax credit in the tax expenditure budget. That is, the total amount of the credit claimed is reduced by the taxes that will be paid on the credits. Presumably, the estimate of receipts in the direct budget reflects the revenues resulting from subjecting the credits to tax.

If the tax credit program were instead a taxable direct grant program, the direct budget outlay figure would be the gross (pretax) amount of the program outlays (comparable to the gross amount of the tax credits), unreduced by the revenues to be collected from taxation of the outlays. Use of the "outlay equivalent" approach to tax expenditure estimates makes it inappropriate to reduce the cost of the tax credit program by the revenues that would be collected from taxation of the credit.

Provisions that phase out tax expenditures by adopting the correct normative rule. Another budget presentation issue involves the effect of phasing out a tax expenditure. This issue has arisen in the context of legislative actions to repeal accelerated deduction (tax deferral) items. Tax deferral is the functional equivalent of an interest-free loan. The revenue estimate for an existing tax deferral item in the tax expenditure budget is the difference between (1) the tax payments that would have been made for the year in question had the deferral provision never been enacted and (2) the tax payments actually made. Under the five-year accelerated cost recovery system (ACRS) class for depreciation, for example, the tax loan on any given investment with a fifteen-year useful life is paid off in the sixth through the fifteenth years, during which time new assets qualifying for the tax deferral are being acquired. Hence the revenue loss shown in the tax expenditure budget for deferral items in any given year represents the net of the tax loan repayments and the new tax loans being made for the next year in question.[24]

Suppose, however, that Congress repeals a provision granting accelerated deduction, as it did in 1976 in the case of the five-year rapid amortization for railroad rolling stock. After the effective date of the repeal, no new tax loans are made; hence only taxpayers who have invested previously in the qualifying property make tax loan repayments. The issue for resolution is whether the increased revenues from these provisions as they are phased out should be reflected only in direct budget receipts, with a corresponding reduction in and ultimate elimination of the item from the tax expenditure budget, or whether a negative figure should be included in the tax expenditure budget during phaseout.

In resolving this issue, OMB and CBO showed negative figures for certain terminating five-year amortization provisions.[25] The negative figures reflected the increased taxes from the repayment of the tax loans that were due as the availability of new tax loans ceased. The increased federal receipts, however, should be reflected in the direct budget revenue estimates, in which case it is improper to show a negative figure in the tax expenditure budget (just as it is improper to show the refundable portion of a tax credit as a direct budget outlay *and* as an item in the tax expenditure budget).[26] Eliminating from the direct budget the increased receipts that result from repeal of a tax expenditure item and showing the revenue effect solely in the tax expenditure budget would be consistent with the prior treatment of refundable credits; that is, all revenue effects associated with tax expenditures appear in the tax expenditure budget and are shown nowhere in the direct budget.

Provisions that reduce or limit the scope of a specific tax expenditure. As was discussed in chapter 1, Congress may impose limits on specific tax expenditure items. The 1976 action to deny domestic international sales corporation (DISC) benefits to taxpayers who cooperate in international boycotts is an example. Although the issue was not discussed in Special Analysis G or in the CBO budget presentation, presumably the revenue loss associated with these tax expenditure items was simply reduced and direct budget receipts reflected a corresponding increase in revenue. Alternatively, as in the case of the 1976 congressional reduction of DISC benefits (viewing DISC as a tax deferral provision), the budget effects could have been reflected entirely in the tax expenditure budget; that is, the revenue loss from DISC apart from the 1976 changes could have been shown and a separate negative figure employed to reflect the reduction in funds expended through DISC after the 1976 changes.

The approach adopted in the OMB budget is not unexpected, but it does not seem consistent with the CBO practice described above with respect to the elimination of tax expenditures.

Provisions that reduce or limit the scope of more than one tax expenditure. Provisions such as the minimum tax, the "at risk" rules, and the limitations on the deduction for investment interest affect indirectly several tax expenditures. The result of each provision is to increase direct budget receipts and thus to reduce the revenue expended through the affected tax expenditures. In the case of the minimum tax, the tax expenditure budgets of both OMB and CBO reduce the revenue loss for each affected tax expenditure by the minimum tax revenue associated with that expenditure.[27]

In contrast, in the cases of the limitation on investment interest and the "at risk" rules, the difficulty of matching a portion of the revenue gain with a particular tax expenditure and the fact that the rules apply to nontax expenditure items have required that the revenue effects of such provisions be reflected only in increased direct budget receipts. Accordingly, the tax expenditure figures for specific items affected by the limitation have not been correspondingly reduced.[28]

Tax penalties. Under current practice, the revenue derived from tax penalty provisions is shown in direct budget revenue receipts. The persons involved in these penalty situations are paying amounts in excess of their normative tax liability to the government. Instead of being included as direct budget revenue receipts, these amounts could be excluded from the income tax total shown in direct budget receipts and then classified separately in the tax expenditure budget as receipts from tax penalty provisions.

Clearly, current budget practices are inconsistent in presenting revenues and outlays associated with tax expenditures and tax penalties. One solution to these problems would be to develop a single unified budget that fully integrates tax expenditures and tax penalties with direct budget receipts and outlays. With regard to the income tax, a unified budget would reflect the following items:

Receipts
   Cash receipts derived from the normal income tax system
   Receipts associated with tax expenditures and tax penalties
      Imputed revenue receipts associated with tax expenditures
      Cash receipts from special provisions that limit tax expenditures
      Cash receipts from tax penalties
Outlays
   Direct cash outlays
   Outlays associated with tax expenditures
      Imputed outlays from tax expenditures
      Cash outlays associated with tax expenditures (that is, refundable tax credits)

This unified presentation, by showing all program receipts and outlays, actual or imputed, in a single place, would produce a rational and comprehensive document for use by policymakers.

Short of adopting a fully unified budget, another solution would be to expand and refine Special Analysis G to mitigate some of the current presentational problems. Retitled "Tax Expenditures and Tax Penalties," Special Analysis G would consist of two parts: (1) Imputed receipts and outlays associated with tax expenditures,[29] and (2) direct receipts and outlays associated with tax expenditures and tax penalties. Receipts under part 2 would include the minimum tax, the "at risk" rules, the limitation on the deduction for investment interest, and tax penalties; outlays would reflect the refundable portion of tax credits. If desired, the effects of parts 1 and 2 could then be combined to demonstrate the net revenue result of using the tax system to expend funds in excess of the amount reflected in direct outlays and of collecting funds in excess of the amount normal income tax rules would produce. This expansion does not achieve all the benefits of a fully unified budget. But refinement along these lines would result in a more complete budget presentation of the extent to which the tax system is used to achieve nontax objectives.

Tax Expenditures in the Congressional Budget Process
THE 1974 BUDGET ACT

The Congressional Budget Act of 1974 and the structure and process it created for consideration of budgetary matters focused increased congressional attention on the tax expenditure concept. The act established a Senate and a House Budget Committee whose essential function is to develop an overall congressional approach to the annual budget process.[30] One duty specifically assigned to these committees is "to request and evaluate continuing studies of tax expenditures, to devise methods of coordinating tax expenditures, policies and programs with direct budget outlays, and to report the results of such studies to the Senate (House) on a recurring basis."[31] Each budget committee initially established a task force relating to tax expenditures.[32] The budget committees and staffs have held hearings intermittently and issued ad hoc reports on some proposed and existing tax expenditures. In some cases they have joined with legislative committees having jurisdiction over direct programs and with the tax-writing committees to study the interrelationships between tax expenditures and direct programs.

The act also created the Congressional Budget Office, with a director and a staff of lawyers and economists.[33] One of the CBO's assigned duties is to provide congressional committees with information on bills that include tax expenditures and related general information on tax expenditures.[34] One unit of the Congressional Budget Office, headed by an Assistant Director for Tax Policy, is responsible among other things for analyzing tax expenditures.

Every January the budget committees begin preparing a First Concurrent Resolution on the budget for the next fiscal year (commencing October 1). To assist in the preparation, each standing committee of Congress, including the tax-writing committees, must submit to the budget committees, by March 15, information concerning programs under their respective jurisdictions that can effect increases or decreases in the level of federal revenues.[35] The reports by the tax-writing committees include information on tax expenditures.[36] Each budget committee must report its First Concurrent Resolution by April 15. The accompanying committee reports must state the projected levels of tax expenditures. The committee reports and recommendations are then debated on the floor of each house, and the resolution is to be adopted by May 15. Until adoption of the First Concurrent Resolution, no bill can be considered that would decrease revenues (increase tax expenditures). This resolution establishes revenue and expenditure targets against which to measure appropriations and tax bills as they are considered by Congress. By the seventh day after Labor Day, Congress is to have completed action on all appropriate bills. By September 15, Congress is to adopt the Second Concurrent Resolution on the budget. This resolution establishes *binding* revenue and outlay figures; thereafter no measure can be considered that would increase outlays above or reduce revenues below the figures specified in the resolution.[37]

By the terms of the Budget Act the treatment of tax expenditures constitutes an important element in the congressional budget process. Increases in tax expenditures reduce amounts available for direct outlays; reductions in tax expenditures increase revenues available for direct outlays or provide funds for general tax cuts. Accordingly, during floor consideration of various budget resolutions there are proposals to increase or reduce tax expenditures, proposals that formerly would have been labeled tax reform or tax revision measures. In turn, the budget resolutions have played an important role in the consideration of tax legislation. The inclusion of tax expenditures in the overall budget process also has inevitably led to conflicts between the Senate Appropriations and Finance Committees as to which committee should control tax expenditures. So far, Congress has not produced definitive principles or procedures.[38]

THE CONGRESSIONAL TAX EXPENDITURE LISTS

The Congressional Budget Act of 1974 requires the Congressional Budget Office to submit annual projections of tax expenditures for the five succeeding fiscal years.[39] The budget committees use the basic CBO list in preparing their respective reports on the First Budget Resolution. By March 15 of each year, the staff of the Joint Committee on Taxation likewise issues a tax expenditure list, primarily for use by the tax-writing committees.[40] This list, prepared in cooperation with CBO, OMB, and the Treasury, is identical to the CBO list. In a number of respects, the annual CBO reports have provided Congress with more information on the relationship between the tax and direct spending budgets than have the OMB budget documents. The data from the 1982 study, discussed earlier in conjunction with table 2, reflect this fact.[41]

TAX EXPENDITURES IN BUDGET COMMITTEE REPORTS AND RESOLUTIONS

The concurrent resolutions by which Congress establishes the budget are themselves rather brief documents. Under the Budget Act, the First Concurrent Resolution sets forth for the fiscal year:

1. The recommended level of federal revenues and the amount by which the aggregate level of revenues should be increased or decreased

2. The level of "total budget authority"

3. The level of "total budget outlays"

4. The amount of deficit or surplus

5. The level of public debt and the amount by which it should be increased or decreased

6. Such other matters as may be appropriate[42]

In addition, the resolution specifies the amounts of "new budget authority" and "outlays" for each major budget category (such as "National Defense" and "Energy").[43] Neither the budget resolutions nor the accompanying committee reports specify how the amounts allocated to each budget category are to be spent. Those decisions are within the jurisdiction of the appropriations committees.

To date, the budget resolutions have not specified any ceiling for tax expenditures, as is done for direct outlays. Instead the aggregate revenue to be raised is established, and within this figure the tax-writing committees are free to raise or lower tax expenditures, constrained only by the revenue level figures established by the budget resolutions. This relative freedom from budgetary restraint has inevitably led to jurisdictional disputes, particularly in the Senate, whose Budget Committee has sometimes attempted to apply the spirit if not the letter of the Budget Act to tax expenditures.[44]

Both the Senate and House budget committee reports accompanying the First Concurrent Resolution include the tax expenditure lists prepared by CBO and a brief explanation of the tax expenditure concept. With the discussion of each major budget category they also list the tax expenditures associated with it. In general, however, the reports do not integrate the tax and direct expenditure budgets to any greater degree than the budget submitted by the President.

ESTABLISHING SPENDING PRIORITIES

One result of the failure of the 1974 Budget Act to integrate tax expenditures fully into the congressional budget process is that the spending priorities of the tax-writing committees are automatically higher than the direct outlays under control of the appropriations committees. The same is true of any tax expenditure that a senator or representative succeeds in attaching to a tax bill. Under this process, tax expenditures have the same automatic priority as under the executive branch process.

CONTROLLING FEDERAL SPENDING

Members of Congress have advanced several proposals to place more rigorous controls on federal spending than those provided in the Budget Act. Some urge a mandatory balanced budget; others would limit government spending to a specified percentage of GNP or national income; others would limit the growth in government spending to the growth in GNP for the previous year.

In 1980 the House Rules Committee established a Task Force on Federal Spending Limitations to consider, among others, three bills to limit federal spending: H.R. 6021 (Congressman Giaimo), H.R. 5771 (Congressman Jones), and H.R. 6056 (Congressman Holt).[45] A comparison of these bills illustrates the need to cover tax expenditures in such proposals.

Title I of H.R. 6021 (Giaimo) would have limited "the sum of total budget outlays and total tax expenditures" to 28.5 percent of the estimated gross national product for fiscal 1981, 28 percent of GNP in fiscal 1982, and 27.5 percent of GNP thereafter. These limits were to be implemented by changes in existing Budget Act procedures. Congress could not adopt the First Concurrent Resolution on the Budget if the sum of direct and tax expenditures exceeded the applicable limit in the fiscal year. It could, however, suspend the limits by approving specified actions of the President and/or the budget committees. After adoption of the Second Concurrent Budget Resolution, any bill, amendment, or resolution that would cause the "total budget outlays and total tax expenditures" to exceed the applicable limit would be subject to a point of order.

H.R. 5771 (Jones) and H.R. 6056 (Holt) would have used procedures like those outlined in Title I of H.R. 6021, but these bills covered only direct outlays and not tax expenditures. Accordingly, the limits were set at 21 percent of GNP in fiscal 1981 and 20 percent of GNP thereafter.

As stated in section 102(a)(3) of H.R. 6021, "curtailment of Federal spending in the future will only be meaningful with an accompanying limitation on the growth of tax expenditures since, absent this, tax expenditures might be favored as a way to circumvent the direct spending limitations." Indeed, this feared eventuality would become a near certainty if a spending limitation covered only direct outlays, as in the Jones and Holt bills. Any direct spending program to provide financial assistance or incentives—whether it is a grant or a loan program—can be redrafted as a tax expenditure program, producing the same revenue loss, same economic benefits, and incentive or relief from hardship as its direct spending counterpart. The tax expenditure has precisely the same effect on the budget deficit or surplus as an identically structured direct spending program. However, because the Budget Act treats tax expenditures generally not as outlays but as tax reductions, tax expenditures would be exempt from the spending limit in the Jones and Holt bills.

Nothing in the Jones-Holt approach would prevent a budget deficit. An administration, representative, or senator with a favored spending program that could not be enacted as a direct outlay measure because the spending limit had been reached would simply propose the same measure as a tax expenditure. The program objective would be achieved and federal spending would have increased unhindered by the limit. A spending limitation procedure that fails to cover tax expenditures is no limitation at all.

Indeed, the Jones-Holt approach seems likely to guarantee the increased use of tax expenditures. If budget surpluses did result from the limitations, the excess revenue might be used for general tax reductions. More likely, however, special interest groups would mount pressure to see that excess revenues were used to fund new or expanded tax expenditures to provide federal funds for purposes such as savings incentives or capital investment.[46] Moreover, the desire by some to use federal spending to provide economic stimulus in slowdown periods presumably would not be affected by enactment of direct spending limits. Again, if the use of direct spending to achieve this objective were blocked by the applicable limit, tax expenditures would present a ready solution.

Some past, current, and proposed measures demonstrate the potential to use tax expenditures to avoid spending limitations such as those in the Jones and Holt bills.

President Carter's 1979 proposal for real wage insurance was in fact a program to provide governmental wage supplements for workers who accepted wage increases below a 7 percent guideline figure. The wage supplements could have been paid directly through a Department of Labor program. Instead they were to be provided through a tax credit mechanism. Under the Jones-Holt approach, the minimum $2.3 billion cost of the program would have been completely exempt from the spending limit.

Under the Crude Oil Windfall Profit Tax Act of 1980, an estimated $16.3 billion in revenues from the tax between 1980 and 1990 will be expended via new and enlarged tax expenditures.[47] These billions would be unaffected by the spending limitations outlined in the Jones and Holt bills. Correspondingly, direct outlays could be $16.3 billion higher between 1980 and 1990 than would be possible if tax expenditures were included in the limitation figure.

The windfall profit tax legislation contained a new and expanded special exemption for interest earned from savings accounts and for dividends. This tax expenditure could have been drafted as a direct program to provide interest supplements to savings account depositors and dividend recipients. But if a spending limit applicable only to direct outlays had been in effect the $4.3 billion expenditure[48] could have been made even if direct outlays had reached their limit.

Some proposals have been advanced to implement a national health insurance program entirely through tax credits.[49] If such a system were adopted, under the Jones and Holt bills the rather strange result would be that a program whose implementation has been delayed in part because of feared costs would be completely unaffected by the federal spending limitation.

The accelerated cost recovery system for depreciation, adopted in 1981, provided the equivalent of a direct system of interest-free loans to encourage investment in new buildings, machinery, and equipment. This program involved an estimated revenue cost of over $27 billion in fiscal 1985.[50] Again, failure to include tax expenditures in a spending limit would allow funding of a huge federal program even though no comparable direct outlay program would be permissible.

Table 3, prepared by CBO, buttresses the point. As table 3 shows, direct expenditures under 1980 law were projected to decline as a percentage of GNP between fiscal 1981 and 1985 and, by the latter date, to be lower than in 1975. Tax expenditures, on the other hand, were projected to increase, so that total federal spending would actually increase from 27.4 percent of GNP in 1975 to 27.7 percent of GNP in 1985. And this increase would be completely unaffected by a spending limitation that applied only to direct outlays.

The examples and data show clearly that if a spending limit is desirable, it must extend to tax expenditures. Otherwise there is simply no effective control on overall federal spending, only on direct outlays.

There are some technical issues to be considered if tax expenditures are included in spending limitation procedures. The Giaimo bill would have applied its limits to "total tax expenditures" and "total outlays." Though not defined in the bill, presumably total tax expenditures would be the total revenue cost of the items in the tax expenditure budget published annually by the Congressional Budget Office. As is discussed in chapter 7, there is an interaction effect in totaling tax expenditures that needs to be taken into account. The revenue estimate for each tax expenditure is based on an assumption that it alone is repealed and that all other provisions remain constant. But as 1981 Special Analysis G stated: "In general, elimination of several itemized

Table 3. Tax expenditures and direct expenditures as percentages of gross national product, fiscal years 1975–1985

Year	Tax expenditures	Direct expenditures
1975	6.1	21.3
1976	5.7	21.5
1977	6.0	21.2
1978	5.8	21.2
1979	6.5	21.3
1980	7.2	22.1
1981	7.4	22.2
1982	7.4	22.0
1983	7.5	21.3
1984	7.6	20.6
1985	7.7	20.0

Source: 1980 CBO study, 12–13.

deductions would increase revenue by less than the sum of the revenue gains measured by eliminating each item separately because more taxpayers would use the standard deduction. Conversely, elimination of multiple items that are exclusions from adjusted gross income would increase revenue by more than the sum of the individual gains because taxpayers would be pushed into higher tax brackets."[51] Special Analysis G does not indicate whether the net of the two countereffects would produce a larger or smaller tax expenditure budget total than that achieved through a straightforward totaling of estimates for individual tax expenditures.[52]

This interaction effect should not preclude the use of the sum of individual tax expenditure items as the total tax expenditures amount. The same interaction effect occurs in totaling estimated direct outlay costs. Repeal of one welfare program, for example, may not reduce total outlays by the amount associated with the repealed program. This result occurs if benefits under the repealed welfare program must be counted in determining an individual's eligibility under another welfare program. Repeal of one program could cause more people to become eligible for the other, and total government outlays would increase for the program continued.

No one asserts that budget outlays cannot be added to produce a total outlay figure even though the interaction effect described above exists. Nor should this interaction effect prevent tax expenditure items from being totaled. If one assumes that outlay estimates can be totaled despite interaction effects, then so can tax expenditure estimates.

More broadly, it must be recognized that spending limit proposals described above involved relying on two other numbers that are simply estimates. GNP is an estimated number that can change significantly within a few months. The estimates of such changes may or may not be produced in time to be reflected in a revised spending limit. Likewise, estimates for outlays may be affected by changes in economic conditions, by actions that affect the timing of actual outlays of previously authorized funds that are yet to be spent, and by changes in conditions that increase or decrease outlays under entitlement programs. Thus, in the context of these proposals, establishing spending limits by reference to gross national product, outlays, and tax expenditures involves reliance on three estimates. It is quite likely that none of those estimates will prove to be accurate. Accordingly, a decision to adopt a spending limit of the type proposed requires a judgment that the benefits of exerting greater control over federal spending outweigh problems in estimating each of the three crucial elements in the equation. The difficulties in estimating total tax expenditures appear to differ neither in quantity nor in quality from those involved in estimating total outlays or GNP.

In estimating total tax expenditures, the issue also arises whether only the tax expenditures in the income tax should be taken into account or whether tax expenditures in other federal taxes should be included. For example, an unofficial tax expenditure list has been prepared for the federal estate, gift, and generation-skipping taxes.[53] If the approach of the Giaimo bill were adopted, CBO should be instructed to prepare an official list to add to the income tax expenditure total. The Social Security tax should also be examined to see if tax expenditures are present there.

Some tax expenditure programs are the functional equivalents of loans rather than of direct grants. Typically the tax loan programs take the form of accelerated deductions. If an accelerated depreciation deduction is permitted, for example, the loan is made in the form of reduced taxes in the earlier years and is repaid in the later years, when the taxpayer's deductions fall below those that would have been allowed under normal depreciation rules.

In effect, under the Giaimo bill total tax expenditures would include the gross tax expenditure loans made each year. As in the treatment of some direct federal loan programs, repayments of the loans would be included in revenues but would not affect the allowable spending limit. As we mentioned earlier, direct loan programs are actually treated in three different ways for budget purposes:

1. The gross funds lent in a year are included in outlays, and repayments are included in revenue receipts.

2. Funds lent and amounts repaid are netted and only the net expenditure figure (if any) is shown as an outlay.

3. Loans are completely off budget and have no effect on outlays.[54]

The Giaimo bill in effect adopted the first treatment for tax expenditure loan programs and would appear to be acceptable.

The business community has opposed inclusion of tax expenditures in spending limitation systems, although it has generally supported limiting direct spending. The objections raised are similar to those used by business in opposing inclusion of tax expenditures in proposals to "sunset" federal spending programs and are discussed in a later section.

EVALUATING, COORDINATING, AND CONTROLLING SPECIFIC TAX EXPENDITURES

The growth of federal spending and the proliferation of spending programs have caused many in Congress to seek procedures to ensure regular and systematic review, evaluation, and coordination of both tax and direct spending programs. The principal proposals have taken three forms: establishing an automatic termination date for each program, establishing a procedure for sunset review, and establishing a prescribed review schedule for both tax and direct spending programs. All differ in their ability to achieve the desired budget policy objectives.

AUTOMATIC TERMINATION DATES

One technique to ensure review of tax expenditure provisions is to establish termination dates within each program. Various special provisions in the Internal Revenue Code have used this technique.[55]

The individual termination date procedure does provide a scheduled review point for the particular tax expenditure. Moreover, in the abstract, there is something to be said for tailoring review and possible termination dates to the particular program under consideration. A priori, it is not evident that five years is the ideal point at which to review every type of spending program. Some programs may be ripe for review after two or three years; others may not be susceptible to thorough analysis until after they have been in operation for, say, seven years.

An automatic termination date ensures sanctioned termination of the program if review fails to take place. The use of a sanction has the desirable effect that beneficiaries and proponents must come forward to show that there is continued need for the program and, if there is, that the tax expenditure as structured is efficient, effective, equitable, and preferable to a similar direct program.

On the other hand, this approach has several problems. For one thing, it seems most appropriate for newly enacted tax expenditures. But if this approach is to be effective, Congress would also have to set individualized and automatic termination dates for all tax expenditure programs that currently contain none. In such a major task, the legislative battles over each termination date would likely be as controversial and time-consuming as actual proposals to terminate. The beneficiaries of each tax expenditure could be expected to marshal arguments that their tax expenditure is "unique" and hence should have no termination date, and that if a termination date is necessary, it must be fifteen, twenty-five, or fifty years away, again because of the "special nature" of the program.

Another problem with this approach is that Congress has shown itself reluctant or unwilling to impose the sanction of termination. Several tax expenditure provisions have reached their scheduled termination dates within the past several years. In a few instances the programs were allowed to expire; in most cases the program was extended, sometimes retroactively to the scheduled original termination date. But whether lapse or extension resulted, the tax-writing committees do not seem to have required or followed the studies and review procedures necessary to provide Congress and the public with adequate data to evaluate the continued (or expired) need for the program and its efficiency, effectiveness, and equity. This experience demonstrates that the review and evaluation procedures recommended in chapter 4 for each individual tax expenditure are crucial prerequisites to the proper functioning of any institutional procedure Congress may adopt.

Finally, the automatic termination date procedure does not provide any mechanism to coordinate a review and evaluation of a given tax expenditure program with direct outlay programs in the same area.

Thus, although the sanction of termination may be useful for reasons discussed below, it is neither a substitute for nor a guarantor of performance of the fundamental tasks of review and evaluation.

THE SUNSET PROCEDURE

In the 1970s the Senate expended considerable effort to enact sunset legislation. The basic purpose of the legislation was to ensure regular, periodic review of the need, effectiveness, and efficiency of each authorized program; the program was to be terminated if the requisite review did not occur.[56] Under a 1976 proposal, authorization of federal programs would terminate every five years on a staggered basis unless reenacted. The 1976 legislative proposal was reintroduced as S. 2 in January 1977. Like the 1976 bill, S. 2 included tax expenditures in the sunset process. Title IV of the 1977 bill established a procedure whereby five-year termination dates would be set for each tax expenditure within "any tax."[57] In the year before the termination date of the tax expenditures, the tax-writing committees would be required to conduct a sunset review of them.[58] Subsequent versions of S. 2, however, eliminated the tax expenditure title, primarily to avoid opposition from the Senate Finance Committee.

The 1979 House version of the sunset legislation, H.R. 2, not only provided a termination sanction but also stipulated that the review of tax expenditure provisions should occur at the same time as the review of their corresponding budget category outlay programs.[59] This approach thus sought to accomplish both review and coordination of tax expenditures and direct outlays. The termination sanction was designed to ensure that the efforts necessary to meet these objectives would in fact be made.

Although this sunset approach, in conjunction with the Budget Act, would provide greater coordination of tax and direct expenditures, it was recognized that additional congressional procedures would be required, addressing delicate questions of committee jurisdiction. These procedures would be necessary to ensure that related tax and direct expenditure programs favorably reported were in fact complementary and would have to deal with those that were not. With these additional procedures clearly set forth, a properly structured sunset mechanism could help achieve coordination between tax and direct spending programs.

Whether or not the sunset technique is the best solution, the fact remains that if Congress ever adopts a sunset procedure for direct outlays, it must adopt the same procedures for tax expenditures. Failure to do so would constitute an open invitation to wholesale avoidance of sunset review and evaluation procedures. Any program that the executive branch, a private interest group, or a member of Congress wished to exclude from sunset review would be drafted as a tax expenditure rather than as a direct outlay provision. For example, drafting all export incentives for U.S. business as tax expenditures rather than as direct outlays could exempt the entire program from sunset review. A national health insurance program using tax credits rather than direct physician payments could likewise be completely exempt from sunset. All or a major part of the nation's welfare programs could be exempt from sunset if direct payments were structured as tax credits. Existing programs for higher education could also be exempted by being redrafted as tax credits. Congress in the 1974 Budget Act recognized that a budget control process that did not include tax expenditures was a budget under no control at all. Likewise, a sunset mechanism to ensure review and evaluation of government spending programs that does not cover tax expenditures is no insurance at all against excessive spending.

The necessity to cover tax expenditures in a sunset procedure seems clear as a matter of past budgetary experience and logic. It is therefore useful to consider in some detail the arguments advanced against sunset of tax expenditures by some business leaders and members of Congress (notably in the Senate). Because nearly all opponents of sunset for tax expenditures professed strong support for sunset of direct outlays, it is important to see if the distinctions they relied on stand up to analysis.

Members of the business community advanced two major propositions for exclusion of tax expenditures from the sunset process (and for exclusion of tax expenditures from the spending limitation proposals discussed earlier). The propositions and their supporting arguments can be summarized as follows:

1. Sunset review and possible termination of a tax expenditure are undesirable or impossible for the following reasons:
    a. Scheduled review and termination dates would create uncertainty in the business community that would impede investment.
    b. Business tax expenditures would be at greater risk of termination than would tax expenditures for personal purposes.
    c. Termination of a tax expenditure would represent an automatic tax increase for the beneficiaries of the program, without an affirmative vote of Congress.
    d. Tax expenditures cannot be defined.
    e. The tax expenditure concept rests on the philosophical premise that all income belongs to the government; because that premise is unacceptable, no procedure based on it can be approved.
    f. Review of tax expenditures would increase congressional staff and government bureaucracy.
2. Even if review of tax expenditures is desirable, sunset is unnecessary because tax expenditures are already reviewed with some frequency by the tax-writing committees.[60]

Neither proposition withstands careful analysis. The arguments advanced in support of the first proposition are defective for several reasons.

The argument that scheduled review of tax expenditures would create uncertainty in the business community is an argument that, if true, would apply equally to sunset of direct outlays for business. Yet business asserted that it supported sunset procedures for direct spending programs. Thus the argument is either an argument against the sunset procedure in its entirety or it is no argument at all. The following list presents some tax expenditure and direct outlay programs that benefit business and are in the same budget category.

International Affairs
Tax expenditures	DISC
Direct outlays	Export-Import Bank; Commodity Credit Corporation programs

Energy
Tax expenditures	Percentage depletion, intangible drilling costs deduction, energy tax credits
Direct outlays	Financing research and development projects to find new sources of energy

Pollution Control
Tax expenditures	Five-year amortization, investment credit, industrial development bonds
Direct outlays	Research, development, and demonstration projects to improve pollution control techniques

Agriculture
Tax expenditures	Cash method of accounting, expensing of certain capital outlays, capital gains treatment for certain income, special farm cooperative rules
Direct outlays	Commodity price support programs; deficiency payments programs; payment in kind (PIK), crop insurance and disaster relief, research and service programs; soil and water conservation programs

Housing
Tax expenditures	Interest and property tax deductions and deferral or exemption of gains for homeowners, accelerated depreciation methods

Direct outlays	and capital gains for rental housing Sections 235, 236, and 8 programs; Federal Housing Administration programs; Veterans Administration programs; section 312 rehabilitation loans
Maritime Transportation	
Tax expenditures	Deferral of tax on income set aside for construction
Direct outlays	Operating and construction differential subsidies

This partial list makes it clear that if the business community were sincere, it would also have to oppose sunset for direct outlays that benefit business. The fact that business supported the latter makes its opposition to sunset of tax expenditures highly suspect, presumably based on a lack of confidence in its ability to prove the need for or effects of the various tax expenditures for business. The same is true of the business position on spending limitation proposals.

It is difficult to discern the factual basis for the second business objection, that business tax expenditures would be put at greater risk than personal tax expenditures. A cursory review indicates that tax legislation since 1961 has affected individual tax expenditure items at least as much as business tax expenditures. Moreover, neither the sunset process nor the tax expenditure concept is based on the proposition that tax expenditures should not be used. The concept merely makes it clear that the same standards and procedures should apply to direct and tax spending programs. Since the business argument is supported neither by history nor by theory, presumably it is again based on concern that if business tax expenditures were examined under the criteria discussed in chapter 4, they would be found wanting. But in this respect, business tax expenditures would be on an exact par with individual tax expenditures and are therefore at no greater risk.

The argument that sunset termination of a tax expenditure would constitute an automatic tax increase without a vote of Congress is clever but misleading.[61] Although superficially the argument does seem to demonstrate a different effect between sunset of tax expenditures and sunset of direct outlays, deeper analysis reveals that in fact it does not.

First and quite broadly, repeal of a tax expenditure and repeal of a direct program produce the same result: more revenues are available to Congress, which it can then use either for tax reduction or for other tax or direct spending programs. Furthermore, Congress will decide what to do with the increased revenues resulting from any terminated program, whether it is a tax or a direct spending program. If it decides to reduce tax rates, the beneficiaries of the former tax spending programs may not suffer any net financial detriment from repeal—indeed, some could be better off.

Second, on a more subtle and conceptual level, repeal of a tax expenditure does not involve a real increase in the beneficiary's taxes. The tax expenditure concept posits both an imputed payment of the tax called for by the normative income tax structure *and* an imputed simultaneous payment of a government subsidy to the taxpayer. No checks are exchanged and extra paperwork is thereby avoided. But the economic effect is the same as if the taxpayer had in fact paid the higher normative tax due and then received a subsidy check. Repeal of a tax expenditure does not change the taxpayer's normative tax liability. From an economic standpoint, the beneficiary of a repealed tax expenditure pays the same normative tax as before but remits a larger check to the government because he is receiving a lower government subsidy. For example, suppose a taxpayer incurs $10,000 in tax, gets the benefit of no tax expenditures, but receives a $5,000 direct government subsidy. Repeal of the direct subsidy leaves the tax liability unchanged, and no one would argue that by repeal Congress has increased taxes without a vote. The same analysis is true if the taxpayer has a $10,000 normative tax liability and a $5,000 tax expenditure program is terminated.

Thus, the "backdoor tax increase" argument rests on a basic misconception about what government is doing when it utilizes—or terminates—a tax expenditure. In fact the results of terminating a tax expenditure program and of terminating a direct outlay program are identical in their economic effect on taxpayers and on congressional decision making regarding the resulting increased revenues.

The arguments that tax expenditures cannot be defined and that the concept rests on the view that all income belongs to the government represent a form of budgetary nihilism unacceptable to any government that desires to control its budget. The conceptual framework for defining tax expenditures, discussed in chapter 7, is now well established. The view that all income belongs to the government confuses the issues of what is to be included in the tax base and what is the

proper level of tax rates. A decision to impose a tax on all the net income of taxpayers does not imply that all income belongs to the government; it is simply the tax base that the government has chosen.
Only if a 100 percent rate of tax were imposed would the argument
have any force. But tax expenditure analysis does not posit any particular rate structure as normative and certainly does not start with the
proposition that a 100 percent rate of tax applied to the net income
base is appropriate. Thus, the business arguments reflect either a total
lack of understanding of what constitutes a normative tax on net income or a deliberate effort to divert attention from the real need to review and evaluate tax expenditures.

Finally, the argument that review of tax expenditures would increase congressional staff and government bureaucracy is merely an
argument that business does not want its tax subsidies examined. Review might or might not increase staff, depending on the procedures
adopted. But more fundamentally, the argument, if true, applies
equally to direct outlay programs. The question in either case is
whether the cost of review is worth the benefits of that review. If it is
not worth it for tax expenditures, it will not be worth it for direct outlays either.[62]

The second proposition advanced by some business leaders—that
review of tax expenditures already takes place if review is really necessary—also fails to provide any basis for treating tax and direct
spending differently under sunset. After all, direct outlay programs are
reviewed quite frequently, some as often as annually. Yet many in
Congress still felt that a sunset procedure was necessary for the direct
programs. Anyone satisfied with the current frequency of congressional review of tax expenditures must be satisfied with the much
more frequent review of direct spending programs. The argument
really cuts against the business community. If direct outlays, which
are reviewed annually with varying degrees of thoroughness, should
be subject to a sunset process, a fortiori, tax expenditures, many of
which are rarely or never reviewed, must be subject to sunset.[63]

In the Senate debates over subjecting tax expenditures to sunset
procedures, other objections were advanced. For example, in the 1977
hearings on S. 2 before the Subcommittee on Intergovernmental Relations of the Senate Committee on Government Operations, Secretary
of the Treasury Blumenthal stated that the Treasury was "not opposing" the use of termination dates for tax expenditures. He proceeded,
however, to dwell at some length on technical problems the Treasury

foresaw in implementing such a procedure. Terminating a tax expenditure, in the Treasury view, was more complicated than terminating a direct program. Because of the technical interrelationships between code provisions, termination of one provision frequently requires changes in others; therefore, extensive study would be required to determine the full economic effects of a given change. Furthermore, for tax expenditures created by regulation and rulings—such as the then total exclusion for Social Security benefits and the tax deferral for income earned by foreign subsidiaries of United States corporations—the Treasury contended that substantive legislation to terminate, not mere termination dates, would be required. Finally, the Treasury noted that because business and economic decisions are based on tax considerations, total termination without transition rules might prove unfair.[64]

These objections were correct as technical drafting points. As the Treasury subsequently came to understand, however, they were capable of satisfactory resolution and did not serve as a basis for excluding tax expenditures from any sunset process that might be adopted.[65] It would be appropriate, for example, to instruct the congressional tax staffs, the Congressional Budget Office staff, and the Treasury to submit six months to one year in advance of scheduled termination the statutory language that would be required if Congress decided to terminate the tax expenditure upon its expiration date. This procedure would appear to solve the problems raised and would permit Congress and taxpayers alike to examine well in advance the technical issues involved in any termination.

It is also true that the termination of tax expenditures would create transition problems. This fact, however, applies equally to direct outlay programs. The solution is to restructure the tax expenditure programs scheduled for review into corresponding direct outlay programs, so that the same transition approaches could be used for both. If a tax expenditure loan program is scheduled to terminate, for example, the same transition criteria should be applied as when direct loan programs are terminated. The same is true of tax expenditure grant programs and direct outlay programs. Matters such as the treatment of contracts entered into, or programs in midstream, prior to termination should be treated alike. Again, once the similarity of the transition problems is recognized, congressional and CBO staff, working with the Treasury, should be required to submit suggested drafts of transition rules some six months to one year in advance of the scheduled termination date of each tax expenditure.

During floor consideration of the Revenue Act of 1978, Senator Muskie offered the Senate version of the sunset legislation as an amendment, covering only direct outlays. Senator Glenn then submitted another amendment to apply the sunset process to tax expenditures. Under a rather complex parliamentary situation, both amendments were ruled out of order and the Senate never cast a decisive vote on sunset for either tax or direct outlays. During the debate, Chairman Long and other Finance Committee members vigorously opposed the Glenn amendment.[66] Most of their arguments were similar to those advanced by the business community. The most fundamental objection advanced by the committee, however, was that it did not want to have to assume the burden of proof to reauthorize a tax expenditure. Under existing legislative procedures, the burden of challenging a tax expenditure rests with those seeking repeal. Under sunset, proponents of a tax expenditure would have to persuade Congress and the President that it should be reenacted. Under this process a particular tax expenditure would terminate, for example, if thirty-four Senators filibustered the proposed reauthorization and prevented cloture or if the President vetoed a congressionally approved reauthorization and there were not enough votes to override the veto.[67] Again, the answer to this objection is that precisely the same procedure applies to direct spending programs. The Finance Committee presented no reasons to justify a different procedure for tax expenditures.

SCHEDULED REVIEW OF TAX EXPENDITURES

Another technique suggested to ensure more effective congressional oversight was to establish a prescribed review schedule for all tax and direct programs. The most detailed proposal of this type was introduced by Congressman Gillis Long, chairman of the House Rules Subcommittee on the Legislative Process. The procedure outlined in his Sunset Review Act of 1980 (H.R. 5858)[68] differed sharply from previous sunset proposals in that it did not use the sanction of termination to ensure review of individual programs. Congressman Long had earlier articulated the need for a comprehensive approach:

> Letting the sun set on only one form of Federal spending has an effect beyond just the failure to review those vast segments of the budget. The effect is what I have coined as "Long's First Law of Program Review": Being, new programs will rise where there is no sunset. If we exempt one form of spending from review, sure as the crocuses bloom in the spring, new programs will rise in

those spending categories that escape the review. Clamping
down on direct spending programs only, will lead to the instant
growth in demand for new loan guarantees and tax expenditures.[69]

The sunset review process of H.R. 5858 would have required the
tax-writing committees to prepare in the first session of each Congress
an agenda of the tax expenditures it intended to review during that
Congress and a projected review scheduled for the succeeding four
Congresses (a total ten-year span). The review agenda would be approved or modified by Congress, and the tax-writing committees
would have until May 15 of the second session to report legislation that
would modify, continue, or terminate the tax expenditures under review in that Congress.

The process proposed in H.R. 5858 was designed to answer several
of the objections to sunset discussed above. Because there would be no
automatic termination, there could be no "backdoor tax increase"
without a vote of Congress. Congress would have the opportunity to
act on the tax-writing committees' recommendations; thus only an af-
firmative majority vote of Congress would terminate any spending
program. The alleged uncertainty engendered by review arguably
would be further mitigated, since a tax expenditure could not be terminated by congressional filibuster efforts.

H.R. 5858 was correct in applying the same review procedures to tax
and direct spending. Whether the techniques provided in the bill
would effectively ensure review, however, is questionable. Some sunset advocates would view the absence of the termination sanction as a
fatal defect. But at least the procedures would be equally effective or
ineffective for direct and tax expenditure programs. The bill also contained a precatory provision that the task of coordinating review of tax
and direct expenditures would be a part of the overall process. In preparing their revised agendas, the legislative committees would be required "to the extent practicable" to provide for the review of related
programs and tax expenditures, or of related regulatory programs, in
the same budget subcategories during the same Congress. Moreover, to
assure review of related tax and direct programs during the same Congress "to the extent that the legislative schedules of the committee involved permit," in preparing their review agendas the tax-writing
committees would be instructed to "consult" with the legislative committees having jurisdiction over related direct programs. Thus H.R.

5858 gave considerable weight to the jurisdictional sensitivities inherent in the congressional committee structure.[70]

REVISION OF THE 1974 BUDGET ACT

Notwithstanding the objectives and procedures established in the 1974 Budget Act, many in Congress continue to seek and advocate additional mechanisms for improved control, evaluation, and coordination of tax and direct spending.[71] In their view, either the procedures established in the act are inadequate or they have not been followed. If the former is the case, the congressional budget process itself should be revised so that additional procedures such as spending limits and sunset would be unnecessary.

Efforts in Congress between 1975 and 1983 to bring tax expenditures within the discipline of the Budget Act have had mixed success. But the conclusion seems inescapable that the current Budget Act procedures do not enable Congress to control tax expenditures effectively or to coordinate them with direct expenditures. (By 1984 there was mounting evidence that the Congress could not use this process effectively with respect to direct spending either.) In the instances marked by some success, other legislative techniques have been employed to reinforce the budget process. The past and projected growth of tax expenditures is simply too great to permit continued reliance on ad hoc measures. Amendments to the Budget Act are needed to bring tax expenditures and the tax-writing committees under greater control. More formal power must be given to the budget committees to coordinate the two forms of spending and thus to eliminate irrational and wasteful overlaps.

Existing procedures to control aggregate tax spending are clearly inadequate. The Budget Act treats tax expenditures not as outlays but as revenue reductions. Accordingly, although the tax-writing committees are subject to the overall revenue figure, they are free to increase or decrease tax spending at will within that figure. The legislative experience has demonstrated that if tax expenditures are to be brought under control, the budget committees should include in the budget resolution itself, and not just in the accompanying committee report, directions to reduce existing tax expenditures by a specified amount. Or they could specify in the budget resolution the amounts to be permitted for both tax expenditures and direct outlays in each functional category.[72] Section 301(a)(6) of the Budget Act appears to grant authority for such action. It directs that the First Concurrent Resolution shall include not only the recommended levels of revenues and the aggregate level of revenue increases or decreases but also "such other matters relating to the Budget as may be appropriate to carry out the purposes of [the Budget] Act." The First Concurrent Resolution would only set targets. But the second, if it contained comparable limits, would establish binding ceilings—either an overall figure for tax expenditures or individual totals by budget category. If this statutory language does not empower the budget committees to set limits on tax expenditures in the budget resolution itself, an amendment along the lines suggested is essential to achieve the requisite control.

As was mentioned earlier, section 303(a) of the Budget Act prohibits consideration of any measure that would provide for an increase or decrease in revenues effective in a fiscal year for which the First Concurrent Resolution has not yet been adopted. Section 303(b), however, specifies an exception for measures that would take effect in the second succeeding fiscal year—the so-called "leapfrog" provision. This provision produces the absurd result that unlimited out-year tax reductions are permitted, say, in the 1985 budget for fiscal 1987 and following, but not for fiscal 1986. The leapfrog exception is obviously an aberration in a rational budget process. More fundamentally, the existing Budget Act fails to control out-year tax expenditure increases generally. Repeal of section 303(b) would alleviate but not solve this basic problem.

The congressional committee system increases the problems of controlling tax expenditures. Committee jurisdiction is of critical importance. With respect to tax expenditures, the result is that many legislative issues can easily become "tax matters" through a simple restructuring of the suggested solution. Thereafter the issues are within the jurisdiction of the tax committees rather than that of the legislative committees. Although the House and Senate must ultimately vote on any bill reported by a committee, it is of great importance which committee, committee chairman, and committee staff—and, often as concomitant, which executive agency—develop the bill. Put another way, the tax committees have the jurisdictional ability to take over much of the legislative field by providing a "tax answer" to the issue.

Thus, if the objective is to increase energy conservation by encouraging homeowners to insulate their homes or by encouraging businesses to use solar energy, the legislative committees with jurisdiction over energy can produce a program of direct assistance for these activities. But the tax committees can obtain jurisdiction—and the Treasury can enter the act—by providing a tax incentive for these activities, such as a special tax deduction or credit for money spent on home insulation or solar energy equipment. If the goal is to encourage the purchase of new homes, the banking committees can offer direct assistance, but the tax committees can obtain jurisdiction by providing a tax credit for such purchases. These automatic shifts in jurisdiction apply to almost any issue involving government financial assistance. They can also apply to issues involving government control. Thus, if policymakers deem it desirable to discourage cooperation by U.S. companies in the Arab boycott of Israel, the legislative committees can produce a program of direct controls specifying standards and direct sanctions. But the tax committees, using the same standards, can obtain jurisdiction by denying a foreign tax credit for participation in the boycott. The same technique can be used for pollution control or any other field in which a monetary sanction can be devised. The use of tax sanctions to control conduct is akin to the use of expenditures to encourage conduct. Both control and encouragement are essentially governmental nontax policies engrafted onto a normative tax system and channeled through it instead of being implemented through direct nontax programs.

The problems created by the committee system in Congress are similar to those experienced in the executive branch. If Congress is to assert rational control over tax expenditures and to coordinate them with direct spending, it must take one of two steps. Both entail recognition that under existing procedures the tax-writing committees serve as both authorizing and appropriations committees; that is, a vote for a tax expenditure program simultaneously authorizes it and appropriates the funds for it. With the normal two-step authorization-appropriation process thus circumvented, there is no possibility of coordinating tax expenditures with direct programs being authorized by the substantive legislative committees. One solution would be to require that the appropriate nontax legislative committees authorize tax expenditures, with the tax-writing committees then serving in effect as appropriations committees to vote the funds.[73]

An alternative approach, similar to the one recommended for use by the executive branch, would require the budget committees to allocate both tax and direct spending by functional categories to the appropriations committees (and then to their appropriate subcommittees). A total including both tax and direct expenditures would be assigned to each budget function. The appropriations committees would be required, in each budget category, to stay within the expenditure total by considering both tax and direct expenditures. If tax expenditures were to be increased in a particular category and the budget total was thereby exceeded, direct outlays would have to be correspondingly reduced, and vice versa. Conversely, if the tax-writing committees wished to initiate tax expenditure legislation, the appropriations committees would have to consider that legislation before it could proceed to a floor vote.

Both of these approaches represent radical departures from current congressional practice and would severely restrict the largely unchecked budgetary power of the tax-writing committees. Implementation of either would presumably encounter strong resistance from the tax committees. But without some such step, existing Budget Act procedures simply will not permit effective congressional coordination of tax and direct spending programs. As in the past, several tax expenditure programs will continue to overlap or directly conflict with the effects of comparable direct spending programs.[74]

The years since the 1974 Budget Act have revealed the rich potential of the tax expenditure concept for more open and effective management of the federal budget. It seems likely that its theoretical and practical implications for federal budget policy have only begun to be explored. It is essential, as the tax expenditure budget continues to represent an ever-increasing portion of total federal spending, that those concerned with and responsible for federal budget policy and processes vigorously pursue the search for even more effective techniques to control and to integrate tax and direct spending.

3

TAX POLICY
AND ADMINISTRATION

TAX POLICY spans a wide range of decisions made in the federal tax system. It covers *macroeconomic* decisions as to whether taxes should be increased or decreased for fiscal or social reasons, and the extent and method of the change. These policy decisions primarily involve determinations of which taxes are to be changed or added, the shape of the tax rate schedule, and the amount of any minimum exemption level for the particular taxes. Tax policy also covers *microeconomic* decisions relating to major structural components of a particular tax and their application to those people subject to the tax. Under an income tax, for example, these decisions involve the unit subject to the individual income tax—such as whether individuals are to be treated separately or the family treated as a single taxpaying unit. Tax policy also extends to a host of minor decisions regarding the *technical structure* of a tax. These issues should be resolved with reference to the normative concept of the tax; two such issues related to the income tax are the distinctions between consumption expenses and income-producing expenses and between taxable and nontaxable fringe benefits. Other tax policy decisions involve the *administration* of a tax. All these structural decisions apply regardless of the type of tax involved, be it an income tax, a consumption tax, a wealth transfer tax, or even a specific excise tax. These policy decisions and the complex legislative and executive processes through which they are reached lie outside the scope of tax expenditure analysis.

Other decisions, usually denominated as tax policy, involve provisions classified as tax expenditures, owing to the choice of the tax system as the vehicle for providing financial assistance. Accordingly, the legislative and executive processes that produce those decisions are similar to those involved in structural tax policy decisions. A government's decision to provide assistance through the tax system, however, is really a fiscal policy decision disguised as a tax policy decision. Accordingly the approach and analysis applied should be similar to those used in direct budget spending decisions.

Policy decisions involving tax expenditures do affect the normative structure. The amount of tax expenditures influences the rate structure required to produce the net revenue obtained under the tax. An increase in the amount spent through tax expenditures may require an increase in rates. The amount of the increase will depend on whether the same amount of spending would occur if direct programs were used instead of tax expenditures and, if the amount is not the same, whether some other spending programs would utilize the funds involved in the tax expenditures. The presence of tax expenditures also directly affects the complexity of the tax system as a whole. This complexity may make the normative tax system harder for taxpayers to comprehend and thus may affect compliance. Similarly, tax expenditures have a direct effect on the agency administering the tax sytem. If the Internal Revenue Service must allocate attention, budget, and personnel to both the normative structure and the various tax expenditure provisions, the administration of the normative structure must suffer. The administration of the tax expenditures may also be less efficient than it would be if the program were structured and administered as a direct program by a nontax agency.

Because tax policy decisions on tax expenditures involve spending decisions, they also necessarily involve the congressional committees and executive branch agencies that have jurisdiction over direct spending programs in the same substantive areas.

Many, perhaps most, of the recent tax controversies in the Congress have involved tax expenditure items.[1] This was certainly the case with regard to most of President Carter's 1978 tax proposals. Some of these controveries have involved tax reform in the traditional sense of eliminating or reducing existing tax preferences and thereby improving tax equity. In cases in which traditional tax reform is not involved, and instead the legislation relates to new or increased tax incentives, any controversy over those incentives is necessarily a tax expenditure controversy. Examples are the income tax credit provisions of the 1980 Crude Oil Windfall Profit Tax Act and the new and increased tax expenditures contained in the Economic Recovery Tax Act of 1981. On the other hand, with a turn of the legislative wheel, tax expenditures were reduced or eliminated in the Tax Equity and Fiscal Responsibility Act of 1982 and the Tax Reform Act of 1984. All in all, tax expenditures consume a significant part of the time and energy of those involved in tax policy decisions.

Implications for Tax Reform Efforts

EQUITY ISSUES

Treasury Department data continue to show that some very high-income individuals pay little or no direct tax; more accurately, they are the beneficiaries of very substantial amounts of tax expenditures.[2] In fiscal 1977 the top 1.4 percent of taxpayers, with expanded gross income of $50,000 or more,[3] received 31.3 percent of the assistance delivered through tax expenditures—over $26 billion out of a total of almost $84 billion. On the average, taxpaying units in this select group received federal subsidies of $71,429. The 49,000 taxpayers with incomes above $200,000, representing 0.05 percent of total returns, on the average received federal tax subsidies of $535,653. Most items in the tax expenditure budget reflect the upside-down character of tax expenditures. In fiscal 1977, for tax expenditures going to individuals, the top 1.4 percent of taxpayers received from 66.7 percent to 80 percent of tax expenditures for natural resources; 85.4 percent of tax expenditures resulting from exemption of the interest on state and local bonds; 87 percent of tax expenditures for industrial development bonds issued for pollution control; 86.3 percent of tax expenditures for industrial development bonds generally; 75.6 percent of tax expenditures for rental housing; 60 percent of benefits from the asset depreciation range (ADR) system; 73.3 percent of revenues involved in the charitable contributions deduction for education; 58.8 percent of revenues from the charitable contributions deduction for health; 43.2 percent of revenues for all other charitable contributions deductions; 67.7 percent of tax expenditures resulting from preferential treatment of capital gains; and 100 percent of the benefits of the maximum tax on earned income.[4]

In fiscal 1977 only fourteen of the sixty-nine tax expenditures reflected a progressive distribution pattern, that is, the greatest percentage of benefits went to lower-income groups, with the percentage declining as income increased. Moreover, these fourteen tax expenditures involved only $10.9 billion. In short, in fiscal 1977 less than 13 percent of all tax expenditures were distributed on a progressive basis.[5]

A Treasury study in 1982, covering only some tax expenditure items, showed a similar upside-down distribution. The 4.4 percent of taxpayers with adjusted gross income over $50,000 received 94.1 percent of the benefit from exclusion of interest on state and local bonds; 86.8 percent of the alternative, conservation, and new technology supply incentives; 75.1 percent of the exclusion of income earned abroad by U.S. citizens; 55.3 percent of the charitable contributions deductions; and so on. In only four items—tax credit for the elderly, exclusion of untaxed unemployment insurance benefits, exclusion of disability pay, and earned income credit—did the share of the top group fall below 4.4 percent, and in these cases limitations on the extent of the tax expenditures were the reason.[6]

Table 4 reflects the continuation of this upside-down pattern since the rate reductions in 1981. In 1984 taxpayers with expanded incomes above $50,000 received the following percentages of selected tax expenditures: 66.4 percent from the capital gains exclusion; 54.9 percent from the charitable contributions deduction; 50 percent from the state and local income tax deduction; and 37 percent from the real estate tax deduction. Yet the over-$50,000 income group contained only about 5 percent of all taxpayers. As another example, it has been estimated that 45.5 percent of the benefits from 1981 changes increasing the deductions for contributions to individual retirement accounts (IRAs) will go to the $50,000–$100,000 income group.[7]

Thus the overwhelming majority of tax expenditure programs disproportionately benefit the upper-income groups. Not only are the tax expenditure provisions the primary cause of perceived tax inequity, but it also seems safe to say that they fail to achieve what most Americans would perceive to be a fair distribution of funds, measured by criteria applied to direct spending programs.[8]

In addition to the upside-down effect, the use of deductions, exclusions, and exemptions to provide tax expenditure assistance automatically excludes nontaxpayers such as individuals below taxable levels, loss proprietorships and loss corporations, exempt organizations, and governmental units. The exclusion of nontaxpayers exists even in cases in which the upside-down effect is alleviated by the use of a credit against tax instead of an exemption or deduction.

A description of a few of the tax expenditure items, analyzed in

Table 4. Distribution of selected tax expenditures under individual income tax, by expanded income class (thousands of dollars)[a]

Tax item	Expanded income class[b]									Total
	Below $5,000	$5,000– 10,000	$10,000– 15,000	$15,000– 20,000	$20,000– 30,000	$30,000– 50,000	$50,000– 100,000	$100,000– 200,000	$200,000 and over	
Age exemption										
Amount	32,000	342,000	329,000	227,000	351,000	305,000	186,000	68,000	22,000	1,863,000
Returns	390	2,418	1,718	966	1,175	772	325	98	30	7,893
Blindness exemption										
Amount	—	6,000	3,000	3,000	4,000	8,000	1,000	c	c	26,000
Returns	—	49	22	16	21	31	3	1	c	143
Dividend exclusion										
Amount	3,000	14,000	22,000	22,000	60,000	119,000	91,000	28,000	7,000	365,000
Returns	243	919	1,157	939	1,914	2,736	1,485	380	95	9,868
Disability pay exclusion[d]										
Amount	29,000	40,000	10,000	1,000	c	—	—	—	—	80,000
Returns	63	63	27	1	3	—	—	—	—	166
Medical deduction										
Amount	3,000	76,000	143,000	195,000	434,000	576,000	346,000	99,000	84,000	1,956,000
Returns	249	1,212	1,937	2,561	5,864	6,700	1,988	346	82	20,938

Table 4. (Continued)

Tax item	Below $5,000	$5,000–10,000	$10,000–15,000	$15,000–20,000	$20,000–30,000	$30,000–50,000	$50,000–100,000	$100,000–200,000	$200,000 and over	Total
					Expanded income class[b]					
Real estate tax deduction										
Amount	7,000	71,000	169,000	262,000	1,034,000	2,394,000	1,593,000	527,000	206,000	6,263,000
Returns	385	1,519	2,267	2,861	8,132	9,438	2,757	457	93	27,907
State and local income tax deduction										
Amount	3,000	31,000	120,000	301,000	1,467,000	3,812,000	3,102,000	1,491,000	1,185,000	11,512,000
Returns	524	1,682	2,383	3,390	8,630	9,597	2,748	465	106	29,526
State and local sales and other tax deductions										
Amount	12,000	58,000	121,000	226,000	871,000	1,741,000	963,000	299,000	134,000	4,425,000
Returns	713	2,077	2,919	3,806	9,758	10,542	3,073	522	120	33,530
Home mortgage interest deduction										
Amount	33,000	171,000	375,000	822,000	3,599,000	7,203,000	3,854,000	927,000	217,000	17,201,000
Returns	751	2,131	2,490	2,875	7,687	8,643	2,292	328	57	27,254

Deductibility of nonmortgage interest in excess of investment income										
Amount	4,000	43,000	123,000	320,000	1,440,000	2,403,000	1,064,000	375,000	128,000	5,900,000
Returns	402	1,216	1,888	2,994	7,923	8,275	1,950	264	44	24,957
Charitable contributions deduction[d]										
Amount	3,000	38,000	121,000	231,000	856,000	1,951,000	1,525,000	881,000	1,488,000	7,095,000
Returns	411	1,826	2,847	3,797	9,346	10,467	3,123	585	148	32,551
Casualty loss deduction										
Amount	3,000	2,000	7,000	27,000	53,000	72,000	74,000	29,000	16,000	283,000
Returns	3	12	34	44	46	39	22	4	1	205
Elderly credit[d]										
Amount	—	37,000	28,000	23,000	22,000	12,000	6,000	1,000	—	129,000
Returns	—	204	125	61	60	32	16	1	—	499
Child care credit[d]										
Amount	[c]	75,000	182,000	188,000	368,000	395,000	83,000	7,000	1,000	1,300,000
Returns	31	296	550	628	1,374	1,448	253	19	2	4,601

Table 4. (continued)

| | | | | | Expanded income class[b] | | | | | |
Tax item	Below $5,000	$5,000–10,000	$10,000–15,000	$15,000–20,000	$20,000–30,000	$30,000–50,000	$50,000–100,000	$100,000–200,000	$200,000 and over	Total
Earned income credit[e]										
Amount	561,000	1,132,000	—	—	—	—	—	—	—	1,694,000
Returns	1,844	3,866	—	—	—	—	—	—	—	5,710
Political contribution credit										
Amount	c	8,000	13,000	19,000	39,000	57,000	30,000	9,000	3,000	179,000
Returns	10	195	339	452	743	1,078	501	136	40	3,494
Capital gains exclusion										
Amount	144,000	172,000	278,000	338,000	1,018,000	2,144,000	2,674,000	2,034,000	3,394,000	12,196,000
Returns	173	411	573	477	968	1,349	833	241	64	5,090

Source: Staff of the Joint Committee on Taxation, Tax Expenditures: Current Issues and Five-Year Budget Projections for Fiscal Years 1984–1988 (1983), 19–24.

a. Estimated for the present law at 1984 rates and at 1981 income levels.
b. Expanded income equals adjusted gross income plus minimum tax preferences (mostly excluded capital gains) less investment interest expense to the extent of investment income.
c. Less than $500,000 or 500 returns.
d. This distribution is subject to substantially higher sampling variability than most of the others.
e. Includes the refundable portion of the earned income credit.

spending program terms, demonstrates their upside-down character. One of the special deductions granted by the Internal Revenue Code is the deduction for interest on home mortgages. This is not a cost of producing income since it does not relate to any income that is included in an individual's income tax return. The deduction is included in the Internal Revenue Code to encourage the purchase of homes by families.[9] In effect it is a form of cost sharing by the federal government for interest incurred by homeowners on their mortgages. Because it is an itemized personal deduction, the amount of the federal share is determined by an individual's income tax bracket. The interest deduction as a housing program may thus be restated as a promise to a homeowner that the government will bear a portion of each $100 of interest incurred on a home mortgage. A married homeowner with $3,400 of taxable income writes a check to the mortgage company for $100; the government will pay nothing. The homeowner who has $4,000 income—and is thus in the 11 percent bracket—in effect writes a check to the mortgage company for $89; the federal government will pay the other $11. A homeowner with $15,000 income—and thus in the 16 percent bracket—writes a check to the mortgage company for only $84; the government will pay the $16 balance. The homeowner who is making $50,000 a year writes a check for only $62; the government will pay the $38 balance. And the homeowner making more than $162,400 a year—and thus in the 50 percent bracket—writes a check for only $50; the government will pay the $50 balance. In short, the interest deduction as a spending program rests on the assumption that the higher an individual's income is, the greater the portion of home mortgage interest costs the government should bear.

Only those who itemize their personal deductions are eligible for this tax expenditure housing subsidy program. Since 70 percent of the taxpayers in the country use only the standard deduction (zero bracket amount) and do not itemize personal deductions, and since 70 percent of that group have incomes of less than $15,000 per year, an overwhelming majority (85 percent) of homeowners in the group below $15,000 receive no benefit from the deduction.[10] Thus the housing program effected through the interest deduction is very largely a program for upper-income families—roughly only the top quarter. A poverty-level individual need not apply for the program at all, since a deduction is of no benefit unless the individual incurs tax liability. Data from a 1981 study, presented in table 5, show the disproportionate advantage enjoyed by upper-income taxpayers among the 50.5 million who

Table 5. Distribution of taxpayers owning homes who itemized home mortgage deduction in 1981, by income group

Income group	Number of homeowners	Number who itemized	Average tax saving
Under $5,000	5 million	100,000	$ 60
$5,000–10,000	7.6 million	900,000	145
$10,000–15,000	8.8 million	3.6 million	259
$15,000–20,000	7.9 million	3.6 million	431
$20,000–30,000	12.2 million	7.5 million	691
Above $30,000	8.6 million	5.7 million	1,221–4,487

Source: Congressional Budget Office, 97th Cong., 1st sess., *The Tax Treatment of Homeownership: Issues and Options* (1981).

owned homes.[11] The average tax savings rose from $60 per homeowner for those with incomes under $5,000 to almost $4,500 per homeowner for those with the highest incomes.

Table 5 also reveals that 85 percent of homeowners with incomes under $15,000 received no benefit from the interest deduction. It is safe to say that Congress would never approve a direct program to encourage home ownership that specifically stated that it would provide no benefits to the 85 percent of homeowners who make less than $15,000 a year, and that the benefits would increase as a homeowner's income grew, so that the richest people reaped the maximum benefits. Yet this is precisely the program that exists in the Internal Revenue Code in the form of the interest deduction for home mortages.[12]

Since the encouragement of home ownership is presumably a priority in the United States, there are several direct programs to promote this policy (although the tax expenditure programs are much larger), such as mortgage interest assistance. These programs are not upside-down and restrict their use to persons with more modest incomes. Thus, under the HUD section 235 homeowner assistance program, which provides a subsidized lower mortgage interest rate, 80 percent of the benefits go to households in the $10,000–$20,000 income range and 19 percent to households under $10,000. But, given the open-ended character of the tax expenditure deduction for mortgage interest (and also for property tax payments)—making it into an unrestricted entitlement program—the tax expenditure assistance for home ownership far exceeds that provided under direct programs, roughly an estimated $16 billion compared to $112 million in 1979.[13]

Another example of upside-down assistance is the medical expense deduction. Despite much debate about a national health insurance program, few people recognize that such a program already exists, run through the Internal Revenue Code. It has many of the features of a normal health insurance program. There is a *deductible:* only medical expenses in excess of 5 percent of adjusted gross income qualify for the tax deduction. There is a *coinsurance* element requiring the insured to pay a portion of the medical expenses above the deductible level; the coinsurance element is a function of the individual's marginal income tax rate. If an individual in the 11 percent bracket incurs $100 of medical expenses above the deductible level (5 percent of adjusted gross income), under the coinsurance element he or she must pay $89 of those medical expenses and the government will pay $11. In contrast, an individual who makes $50,000 a year and incurs the same $100 of medical expenses above the deductible level will pay $62, and the government will bear the remaining $38. Finally, for the wealthiest taxpayers, those with more than $200,000 per year adjusted gross income, the government will pick up $50 of each $100 of medical expenses above the deductible level. Again, poverty-level taxpayers and those claiming the standard deduction are automatically excluded. Indeed, since home ownership with its accompanying deductions for interest and property taxes is almost essential to the itemization of personal deductions,[14] it is fair to say that the medical expense deduction constitutes a national health insurance program for well-to-do homeowners.[15]

Again, it is impossible to conceive of Congress's approving a national health insurance program structured like the tax expenditure program. None of the national health insurance proposals—from the most conservative to the most liberal—reflects the features present in the medical expenditure deduction scheme. All proposals aim at providing maximum government assistance to poverty-level taxpayers— the group that the tax expenditure program excludes. The direct government assistance would gradually decline as income increases—the exact reverse of the tax expenditure program.

These two tax expenditures illustrate the equity issues—viewed from the perspective of spending programs—present in tax expenditure assistance. There are of course many other examples, including the deductions for property taxes, charitable contributions, contributions to IRAs, and the capital gain and dividend exclusions. Analysis in each case reveals the same up-side down aspect and the same lack of correspondence to the format generally adopted for a national spending program.

Those who try to justify the upside-down effect of nearly all the tax expenditures assert that it is appropriate to provide a tax incentive that increases with income. But few attempt to explain just why this approach is appropriate.[16] Of course, if a deduction is part of the normative tax structure then it is proper that the value of the deduction be affected by the marginal rate of the taxpayer. Since the item reflected in the deduction is a cost of producing income and hence a proper normative deduction, the allowance of the deduction is necessary to produce the net income or net profit that is the measure of the tax base.[17] Indeed, denial of the deduction would be an upside-down tax penalty. But in the case of a tax expenditure there is no such a priori reason to justify its greater value to those with high marginal rates. Although an individual's tax burden under a progressive income tax will rise with income, it does not follow that government assistance should also rise with income; such a view is contrary to generally accepted notions of the terms on which government assistance should be granted.

If the assertion that a tax incentive should rise in value along with one's marginal tax rate means that a relatively greater financial incentive is required to get upper-income people to respond, then the statement should be equally true for government direct spending programs. Although this view may be empirically correct—that is, a small monetary incentive may not induce wealthy taxpayers to react in the manner desired—still it is very doubtful that direct spending programs would be so constructed. Presumably the view demonstrates that the program would be an unwise one to begin with. A similar conclusion emerges from the assertion that sometimes accompanies the one above, that the tax system is not a useful means of influencing the behavior of the growing number of people who pay little or no income tax.[18] Expressed in its converse form, this assertion simply says that if the government program does not offer an individual any funds, the program will not work. This claim is true, but why resort to the tax system as the vehicle for implementing the program? The assertion simply affirms the conclusion that most tax expenditures involve poorly designed programs, but that view should lead to the use of sensible direct programs or better constructed tax expenditure programs, and not to the use of tax incentives that benefit primarily upper-income groups.

Others appear to defend the upside-down character of tax expenditures by arguing that the elimination of a tax expenditure would increase the "disposable income" of the rich far more than it would that of the poor, and that therefore the tax expenditure should be retained. This argument has been made with regard to the deduction for charitable contributions. Thus, it is said that if the contributions deduction were converted to an equal revenue cost tax credit, with no accompanying changes in tax rates, the total effect (since the price elasticity of contributions is, under the calculations of some, greater than one) would be to increase for the rich their amount of "disposable-income-for-personal-purposes" while decreasing the amount of that income for the poor. The rich would save in lower contributions more than the amount by which their taxes were increased, and the poor would give up in higher contributions more than the amount by which their taxes were reduced.[19] But this seems indeed an upside-down argument. The resort to an increase in "disposable-income-for-personal-purposes" simply makes no sense as a test. The fact that a tax expenditure incentive in the tax system has induced upper-income taxpayers to channel more of their consumption in certain ways (in this case, in charitable contributions), so that elimination of the incentive would leave them additional funds to use for consumption in other ways (or for saving), does not mean that modification or elimination of the tax expenditure is undesirable. In fact, to make the argument proponents must assume that charitable contributions are a more desirable form of consumption than any other, although where this assumption comes from is never stated. It is doubtful that the same argument would be advanced to justify retention of a tax incentive for, say, travel abroad, even if its elimination had the same result. The final problem with the argument is that it assumes that the charitable deduction would not be replaced with a more efficient and equitable direct program to encourage donations to charity.[20]

A tax expenditure is a spending program and must therefore be analyzed in spending terms. To attempt to discuss the program as if it were a normative tax provision is to disregard this fact. Yet some writers persist in long analyses of the wisdom and structure of tax expenditures without observing that these provisions do not make much sense when considered as spending programs. They argue that the tax expenditures remain in the tax system because they embody desirable objectives favored by the public at large, such as care for the children of spouses who work, provision of low-income housing, pollution control, or economic growth.[21] What they do not state is whether the methods of accomplishing the desirable objectives meet the criteria of fairness applied to spending programs. Nor do they consider whether the public would prefer the tax provisions and their manner of delivering assistance rather than direct programs that did not hand out upside-down assistance. Yet the real choice lies between the upside-down assistance and more rational tax or direct spending programs.[22]

EFFICIENCY ISSUES

Another way to consider tax expenditures is to evaluate their efficiency as spending programs—to consider whether they achieve their actual objectives and whether their benefits outweigh their costs. There are few government studies of the efficiency of tax expenditures, perhaps because such evaluations are more complex than those involving equity, perhaps also because government agencies fail to realize that spending programs are involved. Few of the special budget analyses on various sectors of government mention tax expenditures, and even fewer discuss them, although much is said about direct programs. Analyses of direct programs came almost naturally once cost-benefit analysis was accepted. But most government agencies view tax expenditures as provisions in the tax law and thus as matters properly belonging to the "tax guys." But only recently have some government and other economists begun to apply cost-benefit analysis to tax expenditures.

The inefficiencies present in many—maybe most—tax expenditures arise from several different causes. Some tax expenditures simply pay individuals for continuing to engage in their activities.[23] For example, in 1981 Congress provided a $200/$400 interest and dividend exclusion. Ninety-five percent of the tax benefit went to savings and investments already being made. In other tax expenditure areas, such as charitable contributions, home ownership, two-earner families, student assistance, and home insulation, the dividing line between being paid for an activity that would in any event be pursued and being induced to enter into that activity varies, with a resulting variance in cost-benefit ratio. It is clear, however, that in each case there is a dividing line and that a part of the tax expenditure is thus a wastage of funds. A similar inefficiency exists for corporate tax expenditures. The tax deferral in the DISC provisions, for example, has been generally found not to produce significantly increased exports.[24] Other provisions that require the establishment of a dividing line between the windfall and incentive elements of a tax expenditure include the energy conservation credits, the research and development tax expenditures, and the natural resources tax expenditures (for example, percentage depletion and expensing of intangible drilling costs).

Other tax expenditures are inefficient because the tax savings (subsidies) greatly exceed the value of the activity induced. In these cases the government subsidy is provided on the assumption that the activity would not be undertaken if free market conditions prevailed. An example in the corporate area is the exemption (through the crediting of a hypothetical tax) for companies operating in Puerto Rico. The purpose of this exemption was to produce jobs for Puerto Ricans, but the tax savings obtained by the companies—and thus the cost to the Treasury—have far outweighed the value of the jobs created.[25]

Other tax expenditures are inefficient because they provide tax savings to middlemen who deliver the government assistance to the targeted beneficiaries. All such middlemen obtain a commission for their role. The commission in turn produces a gap between the revenue loss to the government and the amount of assistance obtained by the beneficiaries. A direct grant or properly structured tax expenditure would not require these middlemen and would not produce this gap.

The tax expenditure for the excluded interest on tax-exempt state and local bonds is an example of the commission phenomenon. A number of analyses have indicated that only 70 percent of the revenue loss to the Treasury from tax-exempt bonds is reflected in lower interest rates to the local government. The remaining 30 percent of the revenue loss is in effect the commission paid to taxpayers in the upper tax brackets who purchased tax-exempt bonds. To clear the market for the ever-increasing volume of tax-exempt bonds issued, it was necessary to make the interest rates appeal to investors in about the 30 percent taxable bracket. Thus all taxpayers above that bracket in effect received a windfall reflecting their commission and the wastage to the Treasury. In 1978 the Carter administration recommended that the federal government directly subsidize 40 percent of the interest payments if a state or local government elected to issue a taxable rather than a tax-exempt bond.[26] This proposal would have eliminated the middlemen and their commissions in tax-exempt bond financing. Several changes have occurred since 1978: individual income tax rates have been reduced, interest rates on tax-exempt bonds have risen to around 85 to 90 percent of the taxable bond rates, and commercial banks and casualty insurance companies have ceased to be significant purchasers of tax-exempt bonds, so that individuals have been required to absorb them. These changes do not appear to have affected significantly the 30 percent wastage. The need to eliminate the middle-man commission remains as acute as ever.

Tax shelters provide another example of the inefficiency resulting from the use of middlemen as delivery agents, though the method of delivery is somewhat different from that for tax-exempt bonds. It is often overlooked that the tax shelter activity that has nearly overwhelmed our tax system is built upon tax expenditures. The tax expenditures involved are so generous that in many cases the targeted beneficiaries do not have sufficient income tax liability to utilize them. They are thus in a position to sell the tax savings to others, who, through their purchase of the tax savings, become the middlemen delivering the assistance—the purchase price—to the intended beneficiaries. Like all other middlemen, these buyers of the tax savings obtain a commission, which again creates a gap between revenue loss to the government and the assistance obtained by the targeted beneficiaries.

The real estate tax shelter illustrates this form of inefficiency. The main tax expenditure for the real estate tax shelter is a combination of rapid tax depreciation (or a 25 percent credit in the case of the historic preservation tax shelter) and the leverage of nonrecourse debt plus the use of partnership syndicates to market the tax benefits to the middlemen individual investors.[27] Analyses have indicated that as a method of providing assistance to the developers of rental housing, either subsidized or nonsubsidized, the tax expenditures are highly inefficient.

One real estate syndication involved a low-income rental housing project with a direct federal subsidy provided through a low-interest mortgage. The developer, the person to be assisted by the tax expenditures, received only about 60 percent of the $2 million revenue loss involved in the tax expenditures because he had insufficient income to absorb the tax expenditure benefits and thus had to sell—syndicate—those benefits to individual investors. About 10 percent, or $200,000, went to the various professionals (underwriters, salespeople, lawyers, and accountants) who "marketed" the tax expenditures—that is, found the individual investors. The remaining 30 percent, $600,000, went to the middlemen investors in the project—the doctors, dentists, investment bankers, and lawyers who were in essence the conduits to deliver the government assistance to the developer. Clearly this $600,000 commission and the $200,000 to the marketers were wasted under the program. The government spent $2 million to deliver $1.2 billion of assistance to the developer.[28]

Analyses of other tax shelter programs reveal similar wastage, the amount varying with the type of tax shelter. Thus one study of the oil drilling tax shelter showed that one third of the Treasury revenue loss went to those who marketed the syndication (the underwriting group and their advisers and salespeople) and to the individual investors participating in the syndicate.[29]

The generous new method of accelerated depreciation—the accelerated cost recovery system (ACRS)—adopted in 1981 opened new tax shelter possibilities.[30] The combination of ACRS and the investment credit produced tax benefits so great that many corporate taxpayers could not use all of them. The 1981 act introduced a statutorily approved tax shelter scheme that carried the use of tax expenditures in tax shelters to its logical but ultimately unacceptable extreme, the "safe harbor leasing" provision. Safe harbor leasing provided a fictitious "tax lease" whereby tax benefits that could not be used because of inadequate taxable income or tax liability could be sold to profitable companies.[31] The resulting windfalls obtained by the profitable companies, the public's perception of the absurdity of the device and of a tax system that produced such a device, and a prevailing sense in Congress that the provision had been "slipped" past led to repeal of safe harbor leasing in 1982. But the entire issue of tax expenditure leasing remains in a state of flux. Although it eliminated safe harbor leasing, the 1982 act added a provision for a "finance lease" whereby loss companies will be able in effect to transfer their unusable tax benefits to profitable companies in exchange for reduced lease rentals.[32] Moreover, it must be recognized that the technique involved in safe harbor leasing persists in hiddden form in tax shelter partnerships.

Some writers argue that the ultimate benefits of these tax expenditures will justify their inefficiency. They assert that the tax reductions make the favored activities—tax-exempt bonds or tax shelters—so attractive that investors switch their investments to those areas, and that this inflow of funds reduces the net return so that the benefits are ultimately lost. The trouble with these assertions is that events in the real world do not necessarily correspond to pure economic theory.[33] Before 1981, tax-exempt bonds were sold not just to investors in the 70 percent bracket; instead, because the investor market had to be large enough to absorb all the bonds, they had to be attractive to those in the 40 percent bracket or even lower. Obviously, the 70 percent bracket investors obtained windfalls that continued as long as the interest rates on the bonds were geared to attract 40 percent bracket investors. The same situation applies under the 50 percent top bracket rate applicable after 1981, so that now advertisements for tax-exempt bonds solicit the 30 percent bracket investor. As for tax shelters, most were priced to attract 50 percent bracket investors, with the result that investors in higher brackets obtained a price windfall. With the 50 percent top bracket rate, the price target has fallen to around the 40 to 45 percent rate. Thus the need to expand the market of potential investors drives local government and tax shelter syndicators continually to reprice their investments to attract lower and lower tax bracket investors, providing a continuing windfall for higher-bracket investors who use these tax expenditures.

Although it is an interesting theoretical issue whether a given tax expenditure has been "capitalized" in the value of subsidized investments, it is essential always to keep in mind that tax expenditures are *spending* programs. From the standpoint of the total budget, it is irrelevant whether the subsidy has been capitalized or not; in either case the government must know the amount it is spending on the subsidy. For example, if the government provided a direct interest subsidy for tax-exempt bonds, the direct spending budget would reflect the cost of the subsidy even if it were capitalized in the value of the bonds. The same must be true of tax expenditure subsidies—even if the subsidy is capitalized, there is still a cost to the government that must be shown. Thus, although the capitalization issue is of interest for some purposes, it cannot be permitted to obscure the real point of tax expenditure analysis—the identification and quantification of government spending through the tax system.

Tax-exempt bonds and tax shelters represent situations in which the tax expenditure, to be useful, requires that the revenue loss go initially to a third party rather than to the intended beneficiary. In cases in which the tax incentive can be used directly, as when the taxpayer has a tax liability large enough to utilize an investment credit or income large enough to absorb accelerated depreciation, then the wastage of roundabout delivery does not occur. The issue in these cases is the effectiveness of the tax expenditure assistance without the middlemen. Here economic studies yield no certain answers. The studies on the investment credit, for example, reach conflicting conclusions, and the cautious conclusion reached is that the revenue loss involved produces overall additional investment equal to or perhaps slightly greater than that loss.[34] The tax expenditure does influence the direction of overall investment in the sector favored by the credit, here machinery and equipment. Many economists find this distortion in the allocation of capital investment itself to be highly undesirable. Presumably accelerated depreciation would show the same uncertainty and also the directional consequences for favored investment.[35] Studies of tax incentives for individual saving, which increase the aftertax return on the saving, are equally uncertain in their findings. The general conclusion appears to be that it cannot yet be shown with any degree of reliability that savings are any greater than they would be in the absence of the tax benefits.[36] In other words, unlike the investment credit, this tax subsidy is completely wasted. These tax expenditures used directly by the intended beneficiary involve uncertainties and ineffectiveness similar to those likely to characterize direct assistance programs.

The conclusion to be drawn from all this evidence is that many tax expenditure incentives or corresponding direct programs may have little justification. Certainly most existing studies on the efficiency of tax expenditure incentives indicate a low response in relation to the funds involved.[37]

INCIDENCE OF TAX EXPENDITURES

An issue closely related to the effectiveness of tax expenditures is the identification of the beneficiaries of particular tax expenditures—that is, the incidence of the tax expenditures. At the first level there is the overall initial target category, such as the aged, homeowners, consumers, certain kinds of employees, and certain kinds of investors. The next level is that of the income groups within this overall category, that is, the groups that actually obtain a monetary benefit from the tax expenditure and the extent of their benefit. As a result of the upside-down effect of most tax expenditures, the actual distribution of benefits will usually accrue disproportionately to only a small portion of the intended beneficiaries—to those who are already better off and who have the least need for assistance.

A third level represents the ultimate beneficiaries as the consequences of the tax expenditure make themselves felt throughout the economy. Tax expenditures for home ownership will aid the construction industry; tax expenditures for investors in residential real estate will aid the construction industry and perhaps tenants; tax expenditures for the interest on state and local bonds will aid those governments and may also aid local property owners through a reduction of property taxes; tax expenditures for students will aid schools; and so on. The removal of the tax expenditure will have its own set of effects: the construction industry may suffer; tenants may have their rents raised; state and local governments may resort to higher taxes on some groups; schools may lose students; and so on. Obviously an analysis of ultimate economic beneficiaries involves making revenue estimates beyond first-order estimates of revenue loss[38] and involves the difficult, almost endless, task of tracing the effects of the tax expenditure through the economy. Essentially, this task becomes an analysis of the desirability of the tax expenditure itself—what the expenditure really accomplishes and whether the achievement is worth the cost in terms of revenue, equity, and spending inefficiency.[39]

There is an inherent difficulty in pursuing analysis through the third level. Data on and understanding of real-world effects may be lacking or too indirect to be traced. Moreover, there is an inherent temptation to pursue the analysis so far that the imponderables of the various choices available begin to defeat an understanding of the effects of the tax expenditure or its removal. Thus, it has been pointed out that a wealthy investor in a state tax-exempt bond may not gain as much as one might expect from the exclusion of the interest on the bond, because, if the exclusion were eliminated, the state, to meet its added interest costs, might have to create new taxes or increase existing ones, either of which may affect the investor. But this conjecture is almost impossible to quantify and distracts attention from the very real benefits now being obtained by that investor because of the tax expenditure.[40] It also distracts attention from the fact, discussed earlier, that under some tax expenditure items first-order recipients may extract a high commission for delivering the benefits to those whom Congress intended to assist.

In summary, there are always basic issues of efficiency and rationality in government spending. Cost-benefit and other forms of analysis are now customarily applied to direct government spending programs to determine the efficiency and rationality of those programs. They can and should be applied equally to tax expenditure programs. If experience so far is any guide, many tax expenditure programs would be found to lack any priority spending status. Moreover, those that do represent appropriate goals would be found to lack fairness and efficiency. Appropriate priorities and economy and efficiency in government spending would be well served by a careful reexamination of items in the tax expenditure list. This recommendation does not, as some assert, constitute an "idealization of the appropriations process."[41] The appropriations process is indeed far from ideal—but the tax expenditure process is even further from that ideal.[42]

TAX EXPENDITURES AND TAX REFORM

The basic spending or government assistance nature of tax expenditures has an influence on tax reform efforts that many tax reformers fail to appreciate. It is obvious that when viewed just as tax provisions nearly all tax expenditures offend traditional notions of horizontal and vertical tax equity and thus are targets for tax reform. The tax reformers have generally sought to eliminate these targets completely. But since the tax expenditures are spending assistance that the legislators really do want to provide, these efforts must often fail. Viewed as a tax provision, the tax-exempt bond exclusion is inequitable, but it is also a means of delivering fiscal aid to states and localities. Because legislators appear to be committed to this objective, elimination of the tax exemption leaves an unacceptable vacuum. Tax reform seems likely to succeed only if it is accompanied by a substitute direct spending program or a properly structured tax assistance program. Accordingly, recent tax reform efforts directed at the bond tax exemption have been linked to a subsidy for taxable bonds issued by state and local governments or to a tax credit to bondholders that is itself includable in income.[43] So far these efforts have failed, in part because of lobbying by investment banking houses specializing in tax-exempt bonds, but also in part because some state and local officials have convinced themselves and legislators that once the tax exemption is withdrawn the states and localities will be at the mercy of federal government largesse and that the direct subsidy will later also be dropped. This view appears unrealistic; it is not clear why a tax exemption can be preserved but a direct subsidy cannot. Moreover, given the influence of states and localities upon Congress, it is unclear why they should reject a proposal that offers *more* assistance. On the other hand, events in the early 1980s seemed to justify these fears: the Reagan administration's budget cuts affected many direct outlays but very few tax expenditures.

Congressional organization and procedures make it difficult simultaneously to eliminate a tax expenditure and to substitute an acceptable direct program: tax provisions are handled by one set of committees and in one set of bills, direct programs in another set of bills and under the jurisdiction of other committees. An effort by the House Ways and Means Committee involving tax-exempt bonds failed even when this tax committee concluded that it also had jurisdiction over the direct spending program.[44] Congress must also have confidence in the efficiency and expertise of the agency that would administer the direct program. Thus the belief of many legislators, correct or incorrect, that HUD is not an efficient agency appears to have hindered progress in cutting back the real estate tax shelter. Together, these factors may constitute the strongest case for substituting better-designed tax expenditures, such as taxable tax credits, for existing poorly designed ones. This approach, however, raises still other issues, discussed in a later section.

Of course many existing tax expenditures represent unneeded government assistance and should yield to tax reform efforts with no substitution of another program. Examples in this category include domestic international sales corporations (DISCs) and the deferral of tax on the profits of foreign-controlled subsidiaries.[45] But logic does not always prevail over the lobbying efforts of those who now receive tax expenditure assistance and who realize that they would never succeed in obtaining direct programs. In situations in which the need for a direct substitute program is recognized, tax reformers must seek out and join forces with lobbyists willing to work to obtain the substitute. But finding such allies is a difficult and often lonely task.[46]

Tax expenditure analysis reveals that the proponents and opponents of tax reform are really talking about different issues. The proponents are stressing traditional tax equity. The opponents are stressing the necessity of government assistance to accomplish asserted national goals or priorities. Because that assistance is provided through the tax system, the jargon and debate are phrased in tax reform terms. But the real issues relate to the desirability of the tax expenditures as spending programs, both as to whether the funds should be spent at all and, if so, whether the program design embodied in the tax expenditure is sensibly constructed and should remain a tax spending program rather than be converted to a direct program. Tax reform thus really becomes spending reform and requires the analytical tools used in evaluating spending programs.

Implications for Tax Simplification Efforts

Tax simplification continues to surface periodically as an important tax policy issue. The causes of tax complexity, though well known for a long time, not only have gone unremedied but have intensified. For decades, those addressing tax simplification have recognized that tax preferences are a major source of complexity.[47] The tax expenditure budget now lists and quantifies those tax preferences. This very process provides guidelines as to the scope of the tax simplification issue, a more realistic perception of the obstacles to simplification, and a more refined strategy for achieving simplification.

As was discussed earlier, certain sections in the Internal Revenue Code provide the structure necessary to implement a normative tax on net income. These provisions must be applied to complex situations such as corporate-shareholder relationships, transactions across international borders (especially by a related group of corporations), and intricate financial transactions involving the capital structures of large corporations and partnerships. In these situations, the underlying transactions to which the tax laws must be applied are extraordinarily complex, and effective application of the income tax inevitably requires complex but logically and structurally coherent statutory formulations.[48]

In a second category are the tax expenditure provisions that so dominate the Internal Revenue Code. These provisions are not necessary to implementing a tax on net income; thus they add unrelated complexity to the code. However, if tax expenditures are used to provide financial incentives or relief, further complexity in the code is unavoidable.

Tax simplification of structural provisions and of tax expenditure provisions involves distinct and generally not interchangeable criteria and objectives. A normative tax on net income—computed annually by varying taxable units, with progressive rates applied to an infinite variety of economic activities—inherently contains a significant and unavoidable degree of complexity. Tax simplification of normative provisions involves ensuring that such rules are clear, consistent, and logically coherent. The normative income tax should respond to simple or complex transactions with appropriately simple or complex tax rules. The simplification issues related to tax expenditures are quite different. In this case the complexities of spending programs become complexities of the tax system. When a spending program is to be implemented through the Internal Revenue Code, tax language must be employed to describe the program, and the tax return must be complicated with a further series of lines and instructions. The inevitable result is further complexity in the tax system.

Some examples will illustrate this point. Over time the maximum allowable investment credit has been set at varying levels of tax liability; currently it is set at 85 percent of tax liability. Varying the maximum allowable credit is a technique commonly used to prevent tax provisions from producing zero tax liability or to control the revenue costs of such provisions. But such a limitation makes no sense at all in a spending program. No Secretary of Commerce would ever suggest, or even think of, limiting a direct subsidy for machinery and equipment to a percentage of the recipient's tax liability to the Treasury Department. Yet the framers of tax legislation in the Treasury have almost always assumed that an individual must have some tax liability in order to qualify for the credit. Public concern over high-income individuals who pay little or no tax reinforces this view. But the existence or lack of tax liability to the Treasury is utterly irrelevant to direct subsidy programs developed in other departments.

From a spending standpoint, the limitation on the investment credit is illogical. Accordingly, advisers of loss companies and of companies whose credits exceed the limit developed the complex equipment-leasing tax shelter transactions to avoid it. In response tax reformers introduced provisions such as the minimum tax, the general prohibition on the use of the credit by individual investor-lessors, and the at-risk rules. Then, as discussed earlier, in 1981 the device of a safe harbor lease was added to the tax law to allow marketing of excess credits along with the excess depreciation allowance (ACRS). In 1982 safe harbor leasing was repealed, but there emerged in its place the finance lease, a statutory modification of the pre-1981 leverage equipment-lease transaction used in equipment-leasing tax shelters, which had been governed by IRS guidelines and court decisions. And so additional layers of complexity are added to the tax system.

Another example of mushrooming complexity is the use of the tax system to provide interest-free loans to selected industries or activities. When such a decision is made, tax technicians normally think in terms of provisions to accelerate deductions. The interest-free aspect flows automatically because the loan program is phrased as part of the tax computation of current income. Interest-free loans, however, are not normally employed in direct loan programs. It would be possible to introduce an interest charge into the tax loan programs, perhaps by requiring the taxpayer to pay a specified interest rate to the Treasury each year on the tax saving produced by the acccelerated deductions claimed. But most tax experts find such an interest charge a somewhat strange concept, although experts in direct government programs would be surprised by a loan program that is interest free, unsecured, and increasing in amount as a function of the tax rate.

As in the case of the investment credit, tax advisers responded to the introduction of accelerated deductions by devising transactions that enabled otherwise ineligible businesses (those without sufficient taxable income) to take advantage of the tax loans. Tax officials then grew concerned over the impact on tax equity and introduced countermeasures that make sense from a tax standpoint but usually rendered the expenditure programs even more irrational as spending programs, such as limitations on investment interest, minimum taxes, at-risk rules, and a 20 percent reduction in certain corporate tax expenditures.

Thus the use of tax expenditures has added a double level of complexity to the tax laws—the first when the tax expenditure provision is introduced and the second as tax reformers seek to limit the adverse effects of the tax expenditure on tax equity. The net result is a tax system of ever-increasing complexity and financial assistance programs that are often irrational and sometimes counterproductive.

Accordingly, the question is whether overall governmental simplification would be achieved if most of the tax expenditures were eliminated. If the tax expenditures were not replaced by direct programs, the answer is clearly yes. If they were replaced with direct programs, the answer depends in part on whether the direct programs in themselves would be more complex, perhaps with regard to qualification requirements and other details. Generally, direct programs are constructed, wisely or unwisely, with much more detail than the counterpart tax expenditure programs.[49] Notwithstanding this difference, converting a tax expenditure to a direct program would achieve the following results: the tax laws and their administration would be less complex; administration of the tax expenditure programs would be dispersed among a number of agencies; tax lawyers would have less work and their nontax colleagues more; taxpayers would find it much easier to complete their tax returns, since they would no longer have to read numerous items having no application to them;[50] and beneficiaries of the direct programs would have to fill out more forms, the number of forms depending on the particular programs, and send them to other agencies. Although the dispersal of programs and resulting forms would increase complexity elsewhere, the reduced complexity in the income tax system could still produce a net gain in cost-benefit ratios.

In 1982 many legislators and others began to call for a "flat rate" individual income tax. Proponents stressed the desirability of reducing marginal tax rates and eliminating progressivity. Many in Congress, however, saw merit in some progressivity, accompanied by lowered rates. Flat rate proponents also stressed tax simplification, to be accomplished through a broadened tax base marked by no exclusions or deductions (other than those incurred in earning income). This broadened, simplified income tax base can be obtained only through elimination of the individual tax expenditures. This aspect of the flat-rate approach received considerable support from tax experts and many legislators—though not from the groups that benefit from the existing tax expenditures. Most of these groups kept their silence, awaiting debate on actual proposals. Moreover, in the rush of support for simplification, no real thought was given to whether some of the government assistance involved in the abandoned tax expenditures would have to be provided through direct programs.

The clamor for a flat tax is unlikely to produce a single-rate income tax. It remains to be seen whether it will even achieve a broadened, simplified tax base with fewer brackets and a much lower top rate. Discussion of the flat rate and of its possible consequences at least has the merit of focusing more attention on the tax expenditure list and its contribution to tax complexity.[51] Whether tax reform and simplification—that is, the elimination of tax expenditures—will come all at once under the impetus of variations on the flat-rate concept remains to be seen.

Implications for Tax Administration

The existence of tax expenditures enormously complicates the task of tax administration. In the United States the basic task of the Commissioner of Internal Revenue is to administer the federal tax system.

Given the population of the United States and the fact that the income tax has a broad coverage—over 85 percent of adult citizens file tax returns—this is a tremendously difficult task. The inclusion of numerous tax expenditures in the tax system imposes an added burden. The Commissioner performs the roles of a Secretary of Energy to administer energy tax expenditure programs, of a Secretary of Agriculture to administer agricultural tax expenditures, and of every other cabinet officer some of whose department's spending programs are embedded in the tax code. No other official or agency is saddled with this burden. Such an arrangement impairs the efficiency of basic tax collection and also the administration of the various tax expenditure programs. Decisions of interpretation and application are made by tax-trained personnel instead of by the experts in the agencies with programs comparable to those contained in the tax expenditures. In 1977 Commissioner of Internal Revenue Jerome Kurtz described the effects on himself, on his agency, and on taxpayers:

> Each of [the tax expenditure] provisions is, in effect, a non-revenue related expenditure program written into the tax law. Each entails its own special set of issues, definitions and imitations . . . Because of these provisions I find myself, a Commissioner of Internal Revenue, administering programs of many other agencies. If these programs were parceled out to those agencies, the concentration of programs would be diffused and the tax law and administration would be vastly simpler . . . the administrative problems which result . . . are formidable. To help taxpayers and officials alike, we must provide an inventory of 368 different forms for public use, along with instructions for each . . . When a provision is placed into the tax law which applies only to a relatively small segment of the taxpaying population, it nevertheless requires additional instructions and lines on the tax return which is distributed to all taxpayers. Thus, each narrowly applicable provision increases the filing burden for everyone, both for those to whom the provision does not apply as well as for those to whom it does.[52]

Clearly, even if only ideally structured tax expenditures were included—tax expenditures that are appropriately treated under the tax system and are refundable to nontaxpayers, so that the IRS is only the agency delivering the funds and no tax unfairness or inequity is involved—the administration of the normative income tax system would remain hopelessly burdened. As long as the Internal Revenue Service must implement, regulate, audit, and litigate over 100 programs that have nothing to do with the collection of taxes, the performance of its primary task of administering the normative structural rules necessary to implement an income tax system will suffer. In addition, it is questionable whether IRS tax lawyers, accountants, agents, engineers, and administrators represent the most competent group to implement and oversee specific spending programs. Obviously some agency of the federal bureaucracy must administer the financial assistance programs. But it is less than obvious why the Internal Revenue Service is better equipped, for example, to handle a national program to encourage and support the arts, through the deduction for charitable contributions for the arts, than is the National Endowment for the Arts.[53] Clearly, every revenue agent cannot be an expert both in the intricacies of the normative income tax and in the details of over 100 spending programs encompassing every area in which government operates.

A related concern is the considerable impact and costs of the paperwork generated by federal programs. The tax forms have borne a good deal of the blame for the perception that the government requires excessive paperwork from the private sector.[54] Whether or not the paperwork burden is indeed excessive,[55] it seems clear that the task of completing tax forms will remain onerous as long as Congress and the executive branch continue to channel 25 percent of total federal spending through the tax system.

The use of tax expenditures has increased the burden on tax administration in still another way. Because the Internal Revenue Service must administer spending programs, it is occasionally drawn into disputes about the way in which it is performing its responsibilities. An example is the controversy over the agency's development of court-required procedures to prevent federal funds from flowing to private racially segregated schools.[56] The IRS was involved in this emotion-laden controversy only because of the use of a tax expenditure mechanism—the charitable contributions deduction—to encourage charitable giving. Those who are angered by the actions in these cases may not differentiate between the agency's responsibilities for collecting revenue and its responsibilities for administering tax expenditure programs. Residual resentment from a tax expenditure controversy may well make some taxpayers less willing to cooperate in our self-assessment tax system, even in situations involving no tax expenditure. The operation of our self-assessment system is a source of legitimate pride, but it rests on a very fragile foundation of public confidence, trust, and respect. Those positive public attitudes are unlikely to survive intensive hammerings by controversies in emotional areas in which tax expenditures embroil the Internal Revenue Service.

From what we already know, it seems clear that tax expenditures have greatly complicated and overburdened the tax administrators. But improvement of the situation depends on amassing detailed information to convince those who remain skeptical. The first step is to determine how much time the Internal Revenue Service spends administering the normative income tax system and administering the tax expenditure programs. The second step is to ascertain the costs of implementing spending programs through the tax system in terms of planning, forms, regulations development, rulings issuance, collection, audit, litigation, and public attitudes. The final step is to calculate the gains or losses associated with converting tax expenditures to direct programs—dealing with only potential program beneficiaries instead of with more than 94 million individuals filing tax returns annually. Detailed information of this kind should help Congress and the executive branch decide whether to implement spending programs directly or through the tax system.

Strategies for Achieving Tax Reform and Tax Simplification

It is clear from the discussions above that increased tax equity, simplification, and efficiency in administration could be achieved by repeal of all the tax expenditures in the income tax. But the tax expenditure budget itself reveals how futile it is to expect any such action in the near future. No more than a few of even the most ardent congressional tax reformers or tax simplifiers would support wholesale repeal of over 25 percent of the federal budget. In a number of instances, the purposes for which funds are provided through tax expenditure programs are objectives that virtually everyone would agree should be supported by federal financial aid. In some cases the tax expenditure program is the only or the largest federal program currently in force. Even the promise of using the revenues from repealed tax expenditures for general rate reductions seems unlikely to assuage tax expenditure program beneficiaries—who suspect that increased funds in taxpayers' pockets will not find their way back into the particular activity supported by the tax subsidy.

Although wholesale repeal of tax expenditures presumably is not realistic—or even desirable—tax reform and tax simplification can be achieved through a step-by-step analysis of tax expenditures if realistic strategies are used. Objective and comprehensive studies of existing and proposed tax expenditures suggest four different strategies:

For tax expenditures for which no equivalent direct federal program is needed, outright repeal, perhaps coupled with use of the revenue involved for general rate reduction, is the appropriate strategy. The preferential treatment of capital gains would be a candidate for such treatment.[57]

For tax expenditures for which a federal program is needed but which overlap with or closely resemble existing direct programs, repeal should be coupled with a corresponding transfer of all or part of the revenues to the direct program, modified as necessary to encompass the scope of the tax expenditure program. The special tax preferences for farm operations, pollution control, and state and local taxes are potential candidates for such treatment.

For tax expenditures for which a federal program is needed but for which no adequate direct program exists, a new direct program must be developed. Examples of such tax expenditures would probably include the medical expense deduction and the charitable contributions deduction.

For tax expenditures for which a federal program is needed and for which a tax expenditure is preferable to a direct program, the tax expenditures must be revised to make them more equitable and efficient.

Given that more than 100 tax expenditure programs are involved, implementation of substantive tax reform and tax simplification will obviously be a lengthy process. Moreover, the approach we suggest requires the development of more sophisticated, coordinated techniques for considering tax expenditures both within the executive branch and the Congress.[58]

4

CHOOSING BETWEEN TAX EXPENDITURES AND DIRECT PROGRAMS

TAX EXPENDITURES are now seen as a form of government spending available to meet objectives that the government considers to require financial assistance. The direct budgetary tools used to provide that assistance, such as grants, loans, guarantees, and interest subsidies, are thus amplified by various forms of tax expenditures—exclusion from gross income, deduction from gross income, credit against tax, deferral of tax, special rate of tax. Each general form of government assistance—direct programs and tax expenditure programs—contains its own subset of devices available for selection. Once a government has decided to provide financial assistance to achieve a particular objective, it must decide which of the two principal routes to use—the direct program or the tax expenditure. Thereafter the terms of the objective itself will determine which subset to use. This chapter examines the factors that should be considered in making the fundamental choice between the tax and direct spending routes.

Any financial aid or incentive program may be written either as a tax expenditure or as a direct program. Legislative draftsmen are able to formulate either form of assistance at the direction of policymakers. Thus existing tax expenditures can be translated into direct programs, and direct programs can be rewritten as tax expenditures. A similar alternative is available for new programs. The choice rests with the policymakers.

The fact that policymakers are free to make a choice does not mean that the choice is an easy one. Very little is known about just what factors impel such a choice or indeed whether governments consciously recognize that a choice is possible. More likely, governments without considered thought pick one approach or the other and the drafters take over the details. But with increasing recognition of the spending significance of tax expenditures should come increased awareness of the need for making a deliberate choice. It is therefore important to consider the factors that should and should not affect a decision.

Several claims are sometimes mistakenly used to justify or explain the choice of a tax expenditure over a direct program.

Tax expenditures do not involve the use of government funds. Although the costs of direct programs show as line items in the regular budget, whereas costs of tax expenditures are absorbed in the overall revenue figures, both involve the use of government funds. To ignore this fact is simply to ignore realities.

Tax expenditures encourage the private sector and private decision making. According to one prominent economist, "The choice between tax incentives and federal expenditures turns out to involve more than the selection among technical financing mechanisms. The choice involves altering the balance between public and private power in one society."[1] Another has noted that for Republicans, "Tax expenditures have proved consistent with the ideology of free enterprise and individual initiative."[2] In 1976, for example, Senator Domenici proposed a tax credit of seventy-five dollars to elderly and poor heads of households. The Senate approved the proposal by a vote of eighty-eight to two. In a subsequent interview, "Domenici explained . . . that his proposal, unlike a federal grant program, would give the elderly the responsibility to take care of themselves. 'My natural inclination,' he said, 'is to let people do the problem-solving rather than the government.' "[3]

These views are sheer illusion. Whether government places funds in private hands through a direct program or through a tax expenditure, the fact remains that the funds come from government. There is no more or less encouragement of private initiative or private decision making under one course or the other. The government, however, may decide to use a tax expenditure to foster the illusion that the private sector is making the spending decisions.

Tax expenditures are simpler programs than direct programs. Several Republicans in Congress have stressed the program simplicities of tax expenditures:

If the money to finance a program does not flow through Washington, Domenici said, the federal government does not have to spend a lot of money to administer it. Nor does it have an opportunity to smother the program in red tape, he added. The absence of red tape is one of the reasons why Sen. Bob Packwood, R-Ore., is one of the Finance Committee's leading advocates of tax expenditures.

"With any federal grant program," Packwood said in an interview, "there's a tendency for us in Washington to be convinced that we know best what the recipients should do with their money." Packwood said he is a firm believer in the opposite principle: that individuals know best what they need.

When the federal government assigns to itself the job of administering a program or writing the regulations that govern what recipients can do, Packwood said, almost invariably it makes a mess of things. "We can set goals pretty well," he said, "but we can't manage very well."

Packwood added a related point: that federal management or regulation often forces uniformity on the recipients of federal aid. If the federal government established a grant program for the families of college students, he said, it might load the program down with so many regulations that students attending only certain kinds of colleges would qualify. On the other hand, he said, a tax expenditure would promote a diverse system of higher education . . .

Rep. Barber B. Conable, Jr., of New York, the ranking Republican member of the Ways and Means Committee, said it was appropriate for Congress to tie fewer strings to money that it leaves in private hands through tax expenditures than to money that it collects in taxes and redistributes in spending programs. "And we Republicans tend to resist the devices for financing social purposes that carry with them tighter controls," Conable said in an interview.[4]

None of the congressmen quoted explained why, if they strongly desire simplicity and initial private choice, they do not so structure direct programs. Either a tax expenditure or a direct spending program can have as few or as many controls as are desired. Indeed, given the complexities of regulations for tax expenditures such as pension plans, charitable deductions, and the investment credit, it is simply untrue that tax expenditures inevitably are not as tightly controlled as direct programs. Many recipients of tax expenditure assistance share the congressmen's illusion and simply do not want to recognize the government's participation.

Other claims attribute to tax expenditures negative characteristics that also affect direct programs.

Tax expenditures pay recipients to engage in activities that they would engage in anyway. Critics assert that tax expenditures frequently are sheer windfalls because they pay taxpayers for doing what they would do anyway. This assertion, which may well be true in some situations, also holds for direct programs. It may be possible to reduce, though not to eliminate, the windfall risk by making the programs incremental in structure; thus direct funds would be paid or a tax expenditure allowed to the extent that the desired taxpayer activity in the current year exceeds the activity of previous years. But this is a matter of program design that affects both kinds of assistance.

Tax expenditures distort the choices of the marketplace and the allocation of resources. This statement is as true of direct programs as it is of tax expenditures. Indeed if it were not true, both types of programs would involve only a windfall effect, as discussed above. Both are based on policies directed at achieving a change in the recipients' activities. The government assistance provided by the program is the lever to produce the change. Whether the direction of change is wise or unwise, whether the cost-benefit ratio involved in the effort is too high and the program thus inefficient, are matters of program objectives and design, not of differences between the two types of spending.

Tax expenditures keep tax rates high. This statement is equally true of direct grants and of tax expenditures. In both cases government spending must be paid for, and the increased cost produces higher tax rates.

Tax expenditures are open-ended. Tax expenditures, phrased as exclusions, deductions, and the like, are available to any taxpayer who meets the eligibility requirements. Whether the tax expenditure is widely or narrowly used, and thus whether the revenue cost and government spending are high or low, cannot be determined until the taxable year is over. The decisions rest with the taxpayers. Direct entitlement programs, such as Social Security, are also open-ended. In addition, it may be possible to limit the use and revenue cost of a tax expenditure by requiring a taxpayer claiming eligibility to obtain a certificate from a government agency and by limiting the number of certificates and the amounts that can be issued.

Tax expenditures allow taxpayers to decide on their own eligibility. Most tax expenditures involve private decision making, allowing taxpayers to declare themselves eligible for an exclusion or deduction. The Internal Revenue Service may later examine that conclusion during an audit. This self-declaration of eligibility may have an important psychological effect in that the individual does not have to apply for government funds directly. It may also make administration simpler than would securing agency approval beforehand. But some tax expenditure programs require taxpayers to obtain certification from a government agency prior to claiming the benefit on their tax returns. Conversely, some direct spending programs are run on a payment-first, audit-later basis.[5]

Several aspects of tax expenditures, discussed in preceding chapters, are either not present or not significant in direct programs.[6] These aspects need not preclude the choice of a tax expenditure, but they must be considered in an intelligent decision-making process.

Upside-down effect. Tax expenditures structured as exclusions or deductions from income (either permanent or operating as a deferral of tax) work to the greatest benefit of people with the highest marginal tax rates. They have the same effect even if a special tax rate lower than the top marginal rate is used. It seems very unlikely that a direct program would be so structured. There are ways to eliminate or mitigate this upside-down effect: to use a method such as a taxable credit against tax (discussed later) or to use a tax expenditure that vanishes at a certain income level and thus benefits only taxpayers below that level.

Exclusion of nontaxpayers. Tax expenditures—exclusions, deductions, deferrals of tax, credits against tax, special rates—usually take forms that are useful only if the recipient has a large enough income or tax liability to absorb the benefit. The groups likely to fall outside the scope of the tax expenditure are low-income individuals, loss corporations, and tax-exempt private or government organizations. The objectives of the program must determine whether this effect is desirable. A refundable credit, discussed later, may counteract this effect.

Dependence on the regular rate structure. Tax expenditures are hostage to the regular rate structure. In 1981, for example, Congress reduced the top 70 percent rate under the individual income tax to 50 percent and scheduled the other rates for reduction over three years.

These macroeconomic rate changes automatically reduced the value of any tax expenditure phrased as an exemption or deduction. Direct spending programs experienced no such effect; Congress debated cuts in these on an individual basis. Although the legislators were probably unaware that the tax expenditure programs were being cut, the beneficiaries of these programs—such as the organizations dependent on charitable contributions—understood the effects clearly.[7] Nevertheless, they could scarcely argue for higher tax rates. Similarly, an increase in the zero bracket amount or in the personal exemptions level automatically reduces the scope and cost of tax expenditures implemented by itemized personal deductions and most credits.

It is extremely unlikely that any rational direct program would be operated with the same uncertainties and sudden changes as occur with tax expenditures because of tax-rate and similar decisions. Although the availability of sufficient overall revenues to support the direct budget is always an issue, direct programs slated for cuts or elimination are considered on their individual merits, within the context of the size of the overall deficit. In contrast, tax rate reductions involve an across-the-board reduction of tax expenditures, without regard to the merits of individual programs.

Lower visibility. Woven as they are into the myriad provisions of the Internal Revenue Code, tax expenditures are largely invisible. Only the tax expenditure budget acknowledges their existence, and the documents containing that budget are not widely circulated. This mingling of tax expenditure provisions with other tax provisions in turn affects congressional and public perceptions of tax spending; legislators or presidents who do not want to appear to be "big spenders" can comfortably approve tax expenditures without damaging their image of fiscal conservatism.[8] Also, focusing on the tax aspect of a tax expenditure permits debate to shift away from the real issues. Consider the attacks on President Carter's 1978 proposals to reduce or eliminate certain expense account entertainment deductions. Opponents asserted that the proposals would curtail spending in luxury restaurants, creating unemployment for the workers there, and would also seriously affect theater and sports activities because of their dependence on entertainment ticket purchases.[9] Essentially, these challenges did not debate the merits of the proposals as aspects of a proper tax structure but instead sought to maintain existing tax rules by claiming that they provided necessary financial assistance to the activities benefited.[10] It is unlikely, however, that any of the legislators making these arguments would sponsor either a bill giving a direct government grant to a luxury restaurant, with the grant increasing in proportion to the luxury of the restaurant, or a bill giving a direct grant to high-level advertising or other business executives if they promised to continue to eat in luxury restaurants. It is obvious that a resourceful mind could devise a large number of direct programs to protect luxury restaurants—and it is just as obvious that no legislator would choose to defend those programs. The very use of these arguments to attack a tax proposal illustrates how the political rules change when a tax program is the focal point of a debate. Furthermore, because major tax bills run to considerable length, a tax expenditure amendment with complex structural provisions can often easily find its way into a bill.

The relative invisibility of tax expenditures inevitably causes many congressmen to think almost immediately of a tax response to a particular social, business, or other problem of concern to them. The immediate leap to this tax response forecloses consideration of an equivalent direct program, and a new tax expenditure thus gets its start.

Difficulty of predicting uses of tax expenditures. The tax shelters that have dominated the tax scene for a decade or more are by-products of tax expenditure provisions. Most of these provisions initially had a narrow focus—to assist an oil developer (intangible drilling deduction) or farmer (cash accounting method instead of inventory), to help a manufacturer obtain machinery (investment credit, accelerated depreciation), to promote construction of rental housing (accelerated depreciation). But investment professionals soon learned to package these tax benefits and to syndicate them in partnership form so that they benefited any reasonably well-off person who had money (his or her own or borrowed) to invest and who desired immediate deductions to reduce the direct tax on income from professional or other sources unrelated to the activity. These unforeseen spin-offs became so widespread that the continuance of the tax shelters, rather than the initial intent, came to be seen as the rationale for many tax expenditures. Dissipation of much of the assistance over a wide range of middlemen—investors, brokers, lawyers, and accountants—resulted in larger revenue losses from the tax expenditure. Direct grants, on the other hand, generally do not appear to involve the costs of supporting these middlemen.

Complexity and tax administration. Much of the complexity of our tax law derives from the tax expenditure provisions. This complexity—both in the tax statutes themselves and in the regulations and rulings spawned by them—causes problems for both taxpayers and tax administrators. Each tax expenditure requires a place on the tax return, a supporting schedule and explanatory information, and taxpayer documentation. Each tax expenditure is an additional item to be audited, involving both additional training of agents and loss of time from other audit activities. Thus the Internal Revenue Service must expend time and effort to administer programs unrelated to the determination of a taxpayer's liability under the normative income tax. Given limitations on personnel and funds, the administration of that tax inevitably suffers.

Confusion over responsibility for programs. If a tax expenditure were rewritten as a direct spending program, it would fall under the operative jurisdiction of the appropriate agency in the executive branch; the Treasury would not be involved at all. But if a program is written as a tax expenditure, its administration becomes the responsibility of the Treasury Department. Usually both the Treasury, which undertakes legislative development of the program, and the IRS, which is responsible for administration of the program, lack expertise on the subject matter and must divert their energies to obtain that expertise. Furthermore, in keeping with their general desire to keep a tight rein on deductions or exclusions, the Treasury and the IRS tend to develop strict eligibility requirements. Finally, both may lack interest in the effectiveness of the program and in changes that could improve it. In contrast, government assistance cast as a direct program presumably receives informed attention by the agency involved, and its relationship to other direct programs is kept in mind. Close coordination between the Treasury and the executive agency responsible for the area involved could eliminate many of these problems. But efforts at coordination between government agencies often produce delay and confusion rather than cooperative activity.[11]

Similar confusion exists in Congress. Tax expenditures come under the jurisdiction of the tax committees, the House Ways and Means Committee and the Senate Finance Committee, whereas most direct programs in equivalent areas are under the jurisdiction of the other congressional committees.[12] Like the Treasury and the IRS, in considering a tax expenditure the tax committees often lack the expertise, background, and staff resources of the other committees. As a result, the tax committees and their staffs tend to approach many tax expenditures as new matters. A new program often seems attractive at first glance, especially if its flaws and relationships to other programs are not recognized or understood. Furthermore, the tax committees presumably welcome expansion of their jurisdiction (power). Here also coordination between committees might serve as a counterbalance, but, as in the executive branch, such coordination is usually incomplete and cumbersome.

Perceived unfairness of the tax sytem. Because tax expenditures are implemented by reductions in income tax liabilities, they create a perception that the tax system is unfair. Many people view them as escape routes for the favored individuals or corporations. Especially when many people do not understand that spending is involved, tax expenditures can undermine the self-assessment system on which we rely so heavily.

Other special aspects of tax expenditures are regarded by some as positive.

Acceptability as subsidies in a capitalist economy. Business generally dislikes the idea of government subsidies, with its implication that the private sector is incapable of performing on its own. Tax expenditures, which business does not view as subsidies, carry no such negative psychological effect. The beneficiaries of a tax expenditure can, and do, regard it as just one more tax provision applicable to them. So seen, it becomes merely a step in the determination of tax liabilities and does not threaten the independence of the private sector.[13]

It is difficult to assess the importance or even the reality of this psychological effect. Certainly many businesses take advantage of subsidies from direct programs. The business perception of the benefits of tax expenditures may be only a rationalization to cloak the realization that tax expenditures are more securely embedded than direct programs and thus will remain in effect considerably longer. In any event it is clear that the government cannot accept the arguments made by private interests as to why business prefers tax expenditures. For example:

> *Argument:* Tax expenditures do not involve government funds (handouts?).
>
> *Reply:* It is obvious that money is involved—that is why the tax expenditure is being sought—and that the money reduces revenues and increases the deficit.

Argument: Tax expenditures do not involve bureaucrats and red tape.

Reply: A revenue agent is a bureaucrat, and the tax law has its own red tape. Which bureaucrat should administer the program and how much red tape must be present are matters of program design, and the design of corresponding tax and direct spending programs should not differ in essential details.

Utilization of an established framework of administration. Proponents of tax expenditures regard the Internal Revenue Service as an effective administrative mechanism already in place to be utilized. Unlike the alternative case involving a direct program, there is thus no need to establish a new process of administration, perhaps a new agency. This outlook, of course, is at the opposite extreme from that of tax administrators. Some legislators may view the decision as one that must depend on the needs, objectives, and appropriate structuring of each new spending program as it is being considered. But this approach overlooks the harm done to tax administration by the cumulative burden of tax expenditure programs it must handle.[14]

Solutions to Some Negative Aspects of Tax Expenditures

There are several ways to ameliorate the negative aspects of tax expenditures.

USE OF REFUNDABLE AND TAXABLE CREDITS AGAINST TAX

An exclusion from gross income or a deduction reducing gross income, since each operates at the marginal rate of tax, necessarily has an upside-down effect: the better off the taxpayer, the greater the financial benefit. One way to mitigate this effect is to structure a tax expenditure as a credit against tax. The determination of the amount of the credit, like the determination of an exclusion or deduction, is a function of the program design. The amount so determined is applied against the tax liability, reducing it dollar for dollar. Thus, whether the taxpayer is in a high bracket or a lower bracket, the dollar benefit of a given amount of assistance is the same.

This is not to say that the amount of the assistance would be the same. Whether the benefit of the tax expenditure will go mainly to high-bracket or to low-bracket taxpayers or be distributed in some other fashion is a function of the tax expenditure program. For example, it appears that the dollar amounts of the residential energy credits, such as for home insulation, are concentrated in the middle- to upper-income groups. A study of these credits stated:

> The concentration of the energy tax credits in the middle to upper income groups is directly related to the concentration of expenditures for residential energy conservation property. This concentration of dollar expenditures is, in turn, attributable to two factors: (1) middle- to upper-income households displayed a greater probability of undertaking energy conservation investments; and (2) middle- to upper-income households were predisposed to spend more, on average, for energy conserving and renewable energy source property than lower income groups.[15]

A distinction must therefore be made between the amount of the credit, which depends on the program design, and the tax effect of using the credit so determined. Only the latter is generally the same for all tax brackets. A tax credit may, however, have a cutoff point that restricts the use of the credit to lower brackets, such as the tax credit for the elderly.

A credit against tax, however, is beneficial only if the taxpayer has sufficient tax liability to utilize the credit. If the tax liability is less than the credit, then some of the credit, and thus part of the financial assistance, is lost. This loss can occur, for example, if an individual is in a low-income bracket or is not a taxpayer at all; if a corporation has a loss and hence no tax liability; if the entity is a tax-exempt organization or a state or local government and therefore not a taxpayer. In these situations the matter becomes one of program design: is it desirable that financial assistance not be provided to these groups, or should they be brought within the coverage? It would seem odd under most direct spending programs to exclude nontaxpayers. Why, for example, should a jobs tax credit not extend to hiring by a tax-exempt organization, or a home insulation credit to a low-income taxpayer, or an investment credit to a loss corporation?

If the unavailability of the tax credit to nontaxpayers is regarded as an undesirable feature of program design, structuring the credit as a refundable credit can eliminate the problem. Then the IRS would pay the excess of allowable credit over tax liability directly to the individual or entity involved. In effect, a refundable credit becomes the equivalent of a direct grant to the taxpayer. However, although the Senate has viewed refundability as a logical way to structure tax expenditures, the House and the Treasury have opposed it. As a result, there is only one refundable tax expenditure credit, the earned income credit for low-income individuals. The refundability of the earned income credit was necessary to effect its purpose: to provide low-income individuals with an exemption from the Social Security tax.

The House and Treasury objections to refundable credits are twofold: refundability is costly in dollar terms and presents administrative problems. The increased cost merely reflects the fact that the financial assistance is provided to more people. The administrative problems for the IRS arise from the need to reach individuals not covered by the income tax. Because poverty-level families are not generally required to file tax returns, they constitute a group that lies outside the agency's experience; it is a group more likely to be found under direct welfare programs. Also, refundability would require the IRS to increase the scope of its contacts with tax-exempt organizations and loss corporations. Both objections have obvious substance. But if accepted, they place a limitation on the use of credits against tax and result in tax expenditure programs that are either upside down or incomplete.

Another problem related to the use of credits against tax involves the proper way to reflect the grant in the computation of income tax liability. If a direct grant is excluded from income under normative income tax rules, the result is a tax expenditure. In the case of some subsidies to business that are regarded as contributions to capital, the normative rule requires a reduction in the cost basis of the asset obtained through the use of the subsidy. Without this basis reduction, the subsidy is treated as a tax expenditure. Given that a credit against tax is similar to a direct grant, proper treatment requires that the credit itself be included in the recipient's taxable income (or be treated in appropriate situations as a basis reduction). If this inclusion of the credit in income is not required under the program design for the tax expenditure credit, then an additional tax expenditure arises, which is in effect an increase in the amount of the basic tax expenditure, the credit itself. In other words, the credit itself must be taxable. If it is not taxable, the credit will have the same upside-down effect as a deduction or exclusion.

Congress has been slow to recognize the need to include a tax credit in income. The only direct treatment for existing credits is the credit for alcohol fuel. The code specifically requires that the amount of the credit be included in income. In addition, the mathematical equivalent of taxability is provided in the technical structuring of the targeted jobs tax credit. Under the jobs tax credit program, the deduction for wages paid must be reduced by the amount of the credit allowed. The initial purpose of the reduction was to prevent the combination of the wage deduction and credit from producing tax write-offs in excess of 100 percent of wages actually paid. Another way to avoid such a result would have been to make the jobs tax credit taxable. The net effect is thus precisely the same as if Congress had provided that the amount of the jobs tax credit constituted taxable income to the taxpayer claiming the credit.[16]

If a program of government assistance is designed as a refundable, taxable credit against tax, it is equivalent to a direct spending program properly treated under normative rules. The refundable, taxable credit is classified as a tax expenditure only because it is a subsidy program adminstered by the IRS without any normative connection to the tax system. The refundable, taxable credit thus presents the straightforward decision as to which government unit should handle the program, the IRS or the agency whose objectives the credit implements.

COORDINATION BETWEEN THE IRS AND OTHER ADMINISTRATIVE AGENCIES

The decision to implement an assistance program through a tax expenditure means that the IRS administers the program. But there are ways to structure the program to make use of the expertise of the administrative agency normally responsible for the program area. One is to condition the allowance of the tax benefit un a certification of eligibility by the appropriate agency. The tax expenditure credit for the rehabilitation of historic buildings is an example; unless the building is listed in the National Register the taxpayer must obtain certification from the Secretary of the Interior before the IRS can allow the credit. Another method, involving a looser connection with the responsible administrative agency, is to require the Treasury and the responsible agency jointly to approve the Treasury Regulations governing the tax expenditure. For example, Treasury Regulations on some of the energy credits can be prescribed only after consultation with the Secretary of

Energy, the Secretary of HUD, and other appropriate federal officials. The effectiveness of these arrangements depends on the rapport established between the two government units and on the method of coordination.

Congress could use a similar approach to incorporate the expertise of the congressional committee normally responsible for the substantive area involved. Again, the effectiveness of the linkage would depend on committee and staff relationships. The resulting division of responsibility and the issue of which committee should have jurisdiction over the operation of the program would tend to militate against successful coordination. Currently no tax expenditure program involves such a linkage.

Preliminary Questions: Need and Design

Before policymakers choose between a direct outlay program or a tax expenditure program, they must decide whether in fact there is sufficient need for a program of government assistance to achieve the proposed objective. The objective may not have a high enough budgetary priority to justify any expenditure of government funds. If the objective is to induce a change in business behavior, for example, the change sought could perhaps better be left to the marketplace without an injection of government funds. If the objective is relief from a situation considered to involve hardship, the degree of hardship must be weighed in relation to other needs. These issues—the initial assignment of priorities and the estimated effectiveness of a given program—are present in any decision on budgetary practices. Similar questions must affect a decision to replace an existing tax expenditure program with a direct one.[17]

Any evaluation of a proposed program of government assistance should also include the following questions:

How much will the program cost? Is the cost consistent with overall budget objectives and priorities? Are mechanisms built into the program to control the costs? Many existing and proposed tax expenditures are structured so that their revenue costs are largely uncontrollable. Thus there is no rational cap on the cost of the percentage depletion subsidy. If oil prices go up, the federal subsidy automatically increases too. The same is true of the tax expenditure for medical costs; rather than placing a limit on rising medical costs, the program is structured to pay a larger subsidy as hospital costs, doctors' fees, and the prices of medication rise.

Is the program structured to produce a favorable cost-benefit ratio? Only with detailed information can policymakers determine whether a dollar of federal revenue is producing enough benefits to meet the needs targeted by the program.

Is the program designed to produce an effective response to the identified problem? The medical expense deduction, for example, is intended to provide relief from the hardship of extraordinary medical costs. But the data show that if the medical expense deduction were the sole itemized personal deduction, only about 2 percent of taxpayers would qualify; the qualifying expenses of the other 98 percent do not exceed the zero bracket amount. Thus for most taxpayers, qualification for the federal health program inherent in the medical expense deduction is not triggered solely by extraordinary medical costs but by the action of buying a home (and thus obtaining deductions for home mortgage interest and property taxes) or paying high state income taxes.

What are the techniques for review and evaluation? In most direct federal spending programs, the enabling legislation mandates review and evaluation of the efficiency and effectiveness of the program. Some recent tax expenditure legislation has included similar requirements; examples are the Treasury studies required for DISC, the targeted jobs tax credit, and the possessions tax credit in section 936. The review and evaluation mechanisms for individual programs may vary, but the Treasury and Congress should see that such provisions are written into all tax expenditure programs adopted.

Another evaluation technique that has been used in direct spending programs is the pilot program approach. Similarly, Congress might try out a new tax expenditure program on a limited basis before implementing it nationwide. If a pilot approach is desirable and feasible in a direct spending program, it is equally desirable and feasible in a corresponding tax expenditure program.[18]

The literature on the budgetary process provides a full discussion of the methods of evaluating proposed programs of government assistance, together with the issues involved. No evaluation or other decisions should be made, however, unless the proposed objective has a high enough budgetary priority to warrant the spending of government funds.

Methodology for Choosing between a Tax Expenditure and a Direct Program

Establishing the need for federal financial assistance and the design of a program to meet that need does not tell policymakers whether to use the tax or the direct spending technique. As the discussion in this chapter has made clear, most perceived differences between tax and direct expenditure programs are not inherent in the two approaches. Instead, they generally reflect differences in program design. Accordingly, it is critical for policymakers to be sure that they are choosing between two different spending approaches for the same program rather than between two different programs.

Suppose an agency in the executive branch or a member of Congress suggests the desirability of encouraging job training and proposes a tax expenditure program to achieve the objective. The Office of Management and Budget determines that the objective has a high enough priority to warrant the spending of government funds. The suggested tax expenditure program would give tax credits to employers who train unemployed workers. The estimated revenue loss of x billion dollars is acceptable in terms of the objective's budgetary priority. The next step is to ask why the tax expenditure program would be more appropriate than a direct spending program. OMB could phrase the question this way: "The Treasury is opposing any new tax expenditures. Suppose we say that we have closed the Internal Revenue Code. Now what program do you suggest?"

The Department of Labor returns with a program under which it will directly reimburse employers who undertake the requisite training. OMB examines this program and concludes that it is structured to reach only large employers and only certain classes of the unemployed.

At this point OMB is not in a position to decide between a tax expenditure and a direct program. It must first determine whether the difference in program design stems necessarily from the difference in the two assistance routes, or whether for whatever reason the structures of the programs indicate a difference in viewpoint on the objective, such as which employers are to be encouraged to do the training, which persons are to be trained, the length of time the employer is to be assisted, and the amount of the assistance. If no essential difference in objective is desired, OMB should ask the agency to narrow the differences in design so that either type of program will reach the same employers, potential trainees, and so on. Only when the program designs are similar is a clear-cut choice possible. Once OMB is satisfied it is choosing between two types of assistance and not between different programs, it can choose the appropriate route.[19]

As another example, suppose an agency suggests an employment program phrased as a tax expenditure that would give private employers financial assistance to hire unemployed persons. Another agency suggests that a government-funded public works program structured as a direct budget program would be a better way to provide jobs. In this situation, the basic choice facing OMB is whether to use assistance to the private sector or a public works program to reduce unemployment. That fundamental choice must be made before it can be determined whether a tax expenditure is preferable to a direct program. If OMB decides to assist private employers, then it must choose between comparably designed tax and direct programs.[20]

Finally, whether the tax or the direct spending route is chosen, the treatment of the subsidy under normative income tax principles must be resolved. If the government decides to render financial assistance through direct spending, as it has in the case of unemployment benefits, Social Security payments, and veterans' benefits, the issue is how the assistance should be treated under the income tax. A decision to make the assistance nontaxable results in a tax expenditure, which will increase the overall government assistance provided for the program. If the assistance is to be taxable, policymakers must consider the effect of taxation on the level of assistance provided. Because taxation of the assistance reduces the after-tax benefit, the decision may be to increase the level of assistance. If financial assistance is provided through a tax expenditure, such as an investment tax credit, the same issues must be addressed.

Actual Cases Involving an Explicit Choice

There appear to be only a few cases in which policymakers or legislators have made an explicit choice between a tax expenditure and direct spending. Although many of the tax expenditures enacted have presented an opportunity for choice, rarely has a nontax alternative been offered and a choice compelled.

One exception involved legislation to provide tuition tax credits. As far back as 1962, proponents of such a credit succeeded with little debate in having a credit approved as an amendment to the tax bill then before the Senate. The Treasury reacted adversely and urged the floor leader of the bill, Senator Kerr, to take steps to drop the amendment. The senator did so the next day, with a promise that the Treasury would study the matter. Recognizing that there was considerable support for aid through a tuition credit and that only a direct aid program could defeat the proposal, the Treasury then asked the Department of Health, Education and Welfare to develop a direct program to aid college and graduate students. Joint discussions among the Treasury, HEW, and the White House resulted in enactment of the student guaranteed-loan program.

During its consideration of tuition tax credits in 1978, however, Congress saw that a real choice existed between a tax expenditure and a direct spending program.[21] The tax committees on their own developed tax credit proposals that eventually passed both houses in modified form. Meanwhile, HEW fought the adoption of a tuition tax credit by recommending an enlargement of existing student grant and loan programs. The education committees, which opposed the tuition tax credit, approved the HEW program. The budget committees, which had jurisdiction to make a choice and to discuss the factors affecting the choice, did neither. They simply left room in the budget resolutions for an amount that would permit either course. Congress finally enacted the HEW measures, which the President supported. A last-minute conference committee on the tuition tax credit could not resolve differences between the House and Senate, and the legislation was defeated. The President had said he would veto the credit if it had passed. As in 1962, vigorous opposition to a tax expenditure, combined with forceful presentation of a nontax option, forced a choice between the tax and direct spending routes.

These two occasions underscore how seldom a choice really emerges for public scrutiny. We know very little about the extent to which the executive branch and Congress recognize that a choice exists in a particular situation.[22] Nor do we know whether the issues involved in the choice are clearly understood and the decisive factors clearly expressed.[23] If both branches adopted the methodology suggested in the preceding discussion for choosing between tax and direct spending tax programs, the public could evaluate that choice more effectively than it can now.

In the final analysis, there appear to be no inherent differences between tax expenditures and direct expenditures, in terms of either tax policy or budget policy. A refundable, taxable credit and a direct grant program can produce identical results in terms of beneficiaries, distribution of benefits, and desired objectives. The same is true of direct loans and repayable, interest-bearing tax credits. The principal factors that remain to affect the choice between tax expenditures and direct spending programs are the agency that will run the program and the congressional committee that will exercise jurisdiction over the program.

If a tax expenditure is chosen, the IRS will run the program, with the consequences for tax administration and tax simplification discussed earlier, and the tax committees will have jurisdiction. In addition, two competing psychological effects appear to be involved in the choice. On the one hand, many taxpayers may view the tax expenditure as a means of creating unjustifiable tax loopholes, with a corresponding adverse effect on the self-assessment tax system. On the other hand, beneficiaries of a tax expenditure may respond more favorably because they do not perceive themselves as beneficiaries of government subsidies. The other problems affecting tax expenditures, such as lack of visibility, regular review, and control, are not inherent. They are simply defects in the current budget processes that can and should be corrected by the methods discussed previously.

5

THE TAX EXPENDITURE
CONCEPT IN THE COURTS

THE U.S. CONSTITUTION and some statutory legislation impose restraints on the spending of government funds. Thus, under constitutional doctrines, the government may in general not engage in activities that are discriminatory in terms of race or sex, for example, or act without due regard for fair procedures and process. Direct government spending programs that involve such practices can be challenged in the courts.[1] Private entities that receive significant support from government funds and engage in such practices are likewise subject to challenge.[2] The question discussed in this chapter is whether these constitutional doctrines also apply to tax expenditure benefits and to private entities receiving them. Given that tax expenditures are government assistance programs, it would seem almost axiomatic that they should.

The issues described below are among those that may involve an interaction between constitutional rights and tax expenditures.

1. The grant of direct government aid to a private school or other entity that practices race discrimination is unconstitutional.[3] Is the grant of a charitable deduction to individuals who contribute to the school or entity similarly subject to challenge?

2. A grant of funds to parents who send their children to parochial schools is unconstitutional as state aid to religion.[4] Does the grant of an income tax credit to those parents also violate the Constitution?

3. It is arguable that an owner of an apartment building constructed in part with federal funds cannot evict tenants without allowing them a fair hearing.[5] Is the owner of an apartment building who utilizes an

investment tax credit, accelerated depreciation, and the rapid amortization of certain construction costs subject to the same constraints?

The underlying issue in all these situations is whether tax assistance is equivalent to direct assistance. If the answer is yes—and we contend that under rational governmental and judicial decisions it must be—a court need not search through the entire income tax system to determine which tax provisions involve government assistance. The tax expenditure list contained in Special Analysis G of the federal budget is a ready index to provisions that should be subject to the same constitutional restrictions as parallel programs financed by direct government spending. The federal budget itself now describes tax expenditures as "alternatives to budget outlays, credit assistance, or other policy instruments."[6] According to the Senate Budget Committee, "These [tax expenditure] provisions may, in effect, be viewed as the equivalent of a simultaneous collection of revenue and a direct budget outlay of an equal amount to a beneficiary taxpayer."[7] The provisions "are comparable to entitlement programs under which benefits are paid to all eligible persons."[8] Given this congressional view of tax expenditure assistance, it would seem difficult—and wrong—for courts to apply different rules to direct programs and to tax expenditures. Yet litigation concerning tax expenditures has not yet focused on the tax expenditure list, and few lawyers arguing for constitutional restrictions have seen the connection between tax spending and the restraints imposed on direct government spending.

Constitutional Cases

GENERAL

Any person or organization against whom the government is *asserting a tax liability* can challenge a tax provision on constitutional grounds. Thus the 1894 income tax fell under attack as a violation of the Article I prohibition against unapportioned direct taxes, thereby necessitating the Sixteenth Amendment.[9] The 1913 income tax and subsequent acts have been challenged at various times on grounds that the progressive rates, the shape of deductions, or other provisions discriminated against the taxpayer in violation of the Fifth Amendment,[10] denied the taxpayer equal protection under the law,[11] denied free speech in a discriminatory fashion,[12] or violated the Article I requirement of geographic uniformity.[13] Most of these constitutional challenges to the income tax have failed, for the courts have been loath to use these grounds to interfere with the congressional responsibility for the tax laws.[14] These cases, most of them arising decades ago, usually involved the normative provisions of the tax law.[15]

Several recent cases have involved constitutional challenges under the First Amendment, not against the government's assertion of a tax' liability but against the government's refusal to allow a tax benefit in the form of tax-exempt status. In these declaratory judgment suits against the Commissioner of Internal Revenue the issues are the same as those in an assertion of liability, for the Commissioner is attempting to remove a tax-exempt status previously granted or to deny that status to a taxpayer claiming it for the first time. The cases indicate that, like normative provisions, tax expenditure provisions are subject to attack on constitutional grounds. Our concern here, however, is whether the tax law is more or less vulnerable to attack than a benefit provided by a direct grant would be.

In *Regan v. Taxation With Representation of Washington*,[16] TWR claimed that it was entitled to tax-exempt status as an educational organization under section 501(c)(3). The IRS had denied that status because the organization engaged in substantial activities to influence legislation by lobbying in the public finance field, which is a disqualification under section 501(c)(3). TWR was interested primarily in receiving tax-deductible contributions. Its ability to qualify as a recipient for those contributions required a tax-exempt status under section 501(c)(3). The organization sought judicial relief, basing its case on two principal arguments. The first was that Congress could not, under the First Amendment, condition section 501(c)(3) status on an organization's refraining from lobbying. The second argument asserted that an unconstitutional discrimination under the Fifth Amendment resulted from the congressional grant to veterans' organizations of both tax-exempt status (section 501(c)(19)) and permission to receive deductible contributions while remaining free to engage in lobbying (section 170(c)(3)).[17]

The Supreme Court, on cross-appeals, held against TWR. On the First Amendment point the Court set the background by stating that the benefits received by tax-exempt organizations constitute a form of subsidy:

> In this case, TWR is attacking the prohibition against substantial lobbying in §501(c)(3) because it wants to use tax-deductible contributions to support substantial lobbying activities. To evalu-

ate TWR's claims, it is necesssary to understand the effect of the
tax exemption system enacted by Congress.

Both tax exemptions and tax-deductibility are a form of subsidy that is administered through the tax system. A tax exemption has much the same effect as a cash grant to the organization
of the amount of tax it would have to pay on its income. Deductible contributions are similar to cash grants of the amount of a
portion of the individual's contributions . . .

TWR contends that Congress' decision not to subsidize its lobbying violates the First Amendment. It claims, relying on *Speiser
v. Randall,* 357 U.S. 513 (1958), that the prohibition against
substantial lobbying by §501(c)(3) organizations imposes an "unconstitutional condition" on the receipt of tax-deductible contributions. In *Speiser,* California established a rule requiring
anyone who sought to take advantage of a property tax exemption to sign a declaration stating that he did not advocate the
forcible overthrow of the Government of the United States. This
Court stated that "to deny an exemption to claimants who engage
in speech is in effect to penalize them for the same speech." *Id.,* at
518.

TWR is certainly correct when it states that we have held that
the government may not deny a benefit to a person because he
exercises a constitutional right. See *Perry v. Sindermann,* 408
U.S. 593, 597 (1972). But TWR is just as certainly incorrect when
it claims that this case fits the *Speiser-Perry* model. The Code
does not deny TWR the right to receive deductible contributions
to support its non-lobbying activity, nor does it deny TWR any
independent benefit on account of its intention to lobby. Congress has merely refused to pay for the lobbying out of public
monies. This Court has never held that the Court must grant a
benefit such as TWR claims here to a person who wishes to exercise a constitutional right.[18]

Having established this point, the Court stated that this aspect of the
case was controlled by *Cammarano v. United States,* which upheld
against a First Amendment contention a Treasury Regulation denying
business expense deductions for lobbying activities.[19] Indeed, in an aspect not discussed by the Court, the *TWR* case represented an a fortiori situation, since *Cammarano* imposed a tax penalty by denying a
normative tax deduction.[20]

The Court then held against the equal protection argument of TWR, on the ground that the distinction between veterans' organizations and other charitable organizations is not at all like distinctions based on race or national origin and does not require strict scrutiny by the courts. "It is also not irrational for Congress to decide that even though it will not subsidize substantial lobbying by charities generally, it will subsidize lobbying by veterans' organizations . . . Our country has a long standing policy of compensating veterans for their past contributions by providing them with numerous advantages."[21]

While recognizing that tax expenditures are subject to constitutional challenge, the Court went far to establish that such cases are to be decided in a fashion similar to the one applied to direct grants. Though it did not directly use tax expenditure language, this opinion is clear on the proposition that a tax benefit—tax subsidy—is a government program similar to a direct cash grant, and the Court approached its decision on that basis.[22] The Court's recognition in TWR of the similarity between tax benefits and direct grants should serve as a basis for argument in future cases. It also may cast doubt on earlier decisions.[23]

In cases in which a person or organization is attacking the exclusion from a tax expenditure benefit as the imposition of an excessive tax liability, a constitutional inquiry is clearly recognized, and the tax provision has no more immunity than any legislation, although a court may find the tax underbrush too thick to penetrate. As for challenges to normative tax provisions, once people became accustomed or reconciled to the existence of the income tax, constitutional challenges against tax liabilities asserted by the IRS ceased except for arguments, say, that the tax need not be paid because revenues were used in the conduct of the Vietnam War or defense activities.[24] Instead, the constitutional cases concern tax expenditure provisions, and most involve persons or organizations attacking as invalid the tax expenditures received by others, on the ground that the beneficiaries are in some way injuring the plaintiffs. The contention in these cases is that the benefit should be withdrawn from a particular recipient because of the latter's actions. The cases involve issues of racial discrimination, establishment and free exercise of religion, free speech and political activity, sex discrimination, and state action.

RACIAL DISCRIMINATION

The racial discrimination tax cases present an interesting judicial history. The first case involving tax assistance and racial discrimination was *Green v. Kennedy,* in 1970.[25] A group of black federal taxpayers and their minor children attending a public school in Mississippi brought a class action to enjoin the Secretary of the Treasury and the Commissioner of Internal Revenue from according tax-exempt status and allowing deductible contributions to private segregated schools in Mississippi. Intervenors in this case were representatives of the parents and children who supported or attended private, nonprofit segregated schools in Mississippi. The racial issue aside, the schools qualified as tax-exempt organizations entitled to receive deductible charitable contributions. A three-judge federal court in the District of Columbia granted a preliminary injunction. The court found no constitutional difference between outright tuition grants to students of racially segregated schools and the grant of tax benefits via a tax exemption. It concluded "that the tax benefits under the Internal Revenue Code mean a substantial and significant support by the Government to the segregated private school pattern." In the court's view, "the support which is significant in the context of this controversy is not the exemption of the school from taxes laid on their income, but rather the deductions from income tax available to the individual, and corporations, making contributions supporting the school."[26]

In the late 1960s and in *Green v. Kennedy* the IRS had taken the position that it could deny exempt status only if there was state involvement in the segregated school in some form other than the tax exemption.[27] Subsequent to the preliminary injunction, the Internal Revenue Service announced that it would no longer grant tax-exempt status and would deny charitable deductions to private segregated schools.[28] The IRS gave no reason for the decision, but the Commissioner, testifying in hearings before a Senate select committee, stated: "An organization seeking exemption as being organized and operated exclusively for educational purposes, within the meaning of section 501(c)(3) and section 170, must meet the tests of being 'charitable' in the common-law sense."[29] The IRS obviously felt that the decision in *Green v. Kennedy* removed the barrier to an earlier issuance of such a ruling. Indeed, the temporary injunction, though applying only to Mississippi since the plaintiffs had asked only for that relief, made the new position almost inevitable. It is also likely that the Solicitor General's Office, anticipating a possible appeal, did not desire in effect to defend racial discrimination.

On final hearing, the court granted the permanent injunction requested by the plaintiffs.[30] It rested its decision on an interpretation of section 501(c)(3) derived from the federal policy against racial segregation in schools: "The Internal Revenue Code provisions on charitable exemptions and deductions must be construed to avoid frustrations of Federal policy. Under the conditions of today they can no longer be construed so as to provide to private schools operating on a racially discriminatory premise the support of the exemptions and deductions which Federal tax law affords to charitable organizations and their sponsors."[31] By basing its decision on an interpretation of the code, the court avoided the need to determine the constitutional propriety of tax benefits for segregated schools:

> We are fortified in our view of the correctness of [this] construction by the consideration that a contrary interpretation of the tax laws would raise serious constitutional questions, such as those we ventilated in our January, 1970, opinion. Clearly the Federal Government could not under the Constitution give direct financial aid to schools practicing racial discrimination. But tax exemptions and deductions certainly constitute a Federal Government benefit and support. While that support is indirect, and is in the nature of a matching grant rather than an unconditional grant, it would be difficult indeed to establish that such support can be provided consistently with the Constitution. The propriety of the interpretation approved by this court is underscored by the fact that it obviates the need to determine such serious constitutional claims . . .
>
> The case at bar involves a deduction given to reduce the tax burden of donors, a meaningful, though passive, matching grant, that would support a segregated school pattern if made available to racially segregated private schools. We think the Government has declined to provide support for, and in all likelihood would be constitutionally prohibited from providing tax-exemption-and-deduction support for educational institutions promoting racial segregation.[32]

This is the language of the tax expenditure concept and clearly establishes the equivalence the court saw between direct government assistance and tax assistance.

Another District of Columbia decision soon explicitly decided the constitutional issue. In *McGlotten v. Connally*,[33] a black American denied membership in a local lodge of the Benevolent and Protective Order of Elks, a fraternal organization, on the basis of race brought a class action to enjoin the Secretary of the Treasury and the Commissioner of Internal Revenue from granting tax-exempt status and allowing deductions for contributions to segregated nonprofit clubs and fraternal orders. The plaintiff had challenged the constitutionality of tax laws that authorized such tax benefits. The court responded as follows:

> To demonstrate the unconstitutionality of the challenged deductions plaintiff must, of course, show that they in fact aid, perpetuate, or encourage racial discrimination. He alleges, subject to proof at trial, both the substantiality of the benefits provided and a causal relation to the discrimination practiced by the segregated organizations. But more is required to find a violation of the Constitution. Every deduction in the tax laws provides a benefit to the class who may take advantage of it. And the withdrawal of that benefit would often act as a substantial incentive to eliminate the behavior which caused the change in status. Yet the provision of an income tax deduction for mortgage interest paid has not been held sufficient to make the Federal Government a "joint participant" in the bigotry practiced by a homeowner. An additional line of inquiry is essential, one considering the nature of the Government activity in providing the challenged benefit and necessarily involving the sifting and weighing prescribed in Burton [v. Wilmington Parking Authority].[34]

The court concluded that the charitable exemption mechanism did involve the government in the activities of exempt organizations:

> [Here] the Government does more than simply authorize deduction of contributions to any cause which the individual taxpayer deems charitable. The statute, regulations, and administrative rulings thereunder, define in extensive detail not only the purposes which will satisfy the statute, but the *vehicles* through which those purposes may be achieved as well. A contribution, even for an approved purpose, is deductible *only* if made to an organization of the type specified in §170 and which has obtained a ruling or letter of determination from the Internal Revenue Service. Thus the government has marked certain organ-

izations as *"Government Approved"* with the result that such organizations may solicit funds from the general public on the basis of that approval.[35]

In the court's view, this degree of government involvement distinguished the charitable contributions deduction from other deductions allowed in the code:

> The public nature of the activity delegated to the organization in question, the degree of control the Government has retained as to the purposes and organizations which may benefit, and the aura of Government approval inherent in an exempt ruling by the Internal Revenue Service, all serve to distinguish the benefits at issue from the general run of deductions available under the Internal Revenue Code. Certain deductions provided by the Code do not act as matching grants, but are merely attempts to provide for an equitable measure of net income. Others are simply part of the structure of an income tax based on ability to pay. We recognize that an additional class of deductions—such as accelerated depreciation for rehabilitated low income rental property, or deductions for mortgage interest—do act as "incentives" favoring certain types of activities. But unlike the charitable deductions before us, these provisions go no further than simply indicating the activities hoped to be encouraged; they do not expressly choose fraternal organizations as a vehicle for that activity and do not allow such organizations to represent themselves as having the imprimatur of the Government. This seems to us a significant difference of degree in an area where no bright-line rule is possible.[36]

Here again the language is that of the tax expenditure concept, and although the opinion does not mention that concept specifically, its language and references indicate that the court must have been fully aware of the concept. Of critical importance was the court's recognition of the difference between deductions that form part of the normal structure of the tax system and special deductions such as that for charitable contributions, with the constitutional tests being applied to the latter.

With these two cases the rule apparently was established,[37] both on statutory and constitutional interpretation grounds, that the tax law could not grant racially discriminatory organizations tax-exempt status and the right to receive deductible contributions. But the decisions placed a heavy burden on the Interal Revenue Service, requiring it to determine whether a school (or other organization otherwise eligible) was practicing racial discrimination. In 1975 the IRS published guidelines to inform taxpayers and its agents of the tests to be used.[38] Later the agency became aware that its tests were considerably less stringent than those being applied by the Civil Rights Division of the Department of Justice and by the courts in deciding cases involving direct aid.[39] Accordingly, on August 21, 1978, the IRS published revised guidelines involving stricter tests for eligibility, which it considered to parallel the tests in the civil rights cases.[40] This action brought a storm of protest from parties who defended the position of the private schools. The protesters ranged from groups that clearly were not practicing racial discrimination to groups that obviously were. A special line of protest came from schools associated with religious organizations. The IRS received more mail on this proposed procedure than on any other issue. After holding hearings on the procedure, the agency revised the tests to meet some of the objections to the original wording, but the tests remained more stringent than those promulgated in 1970.[41] The revision, however, did not stop the protests, particularly from southern and religious schools. The controversy then shifted to Congress. The tax committees held hearings,[42] statements attacking the commissioner for intruding into the area and for using the tax laws to attack discrimination appeared in the *Congressional Record*, and a number of bills were introduced to reverse the new position.[43] Significantly, however, Congress did not take action to invalidate the 1971 ruling.

The attack on the Commissioner for injecting the Internal Revenue Service and the tax system into the matter of racial discrimination was both ironic and misguided. Congress itself had chosen the tax route to supply assistance to charitable organizations, including schools. The courts had held that the tax assistance was not within the statute if the recipient practiced racial discrimination. They had also indicated that any different interpretation would render the statute unconstitutional, just as it would any direct grant voted by Congress.[44] These views inevitably drew the Commissioner directly into the sensitive and complex area of social policy involved in racial questions. Many who attacked the Commissioner either did not understand these forces or refused to acknowledge that Congress, through its choice of the tax route, had caused the Commissioner's involvement. It would, of course, be within the oversight responsibility of Congress to consider whether the tests applied were appropriate, from both legal and administrative perspectives. But it was nonsensical to say that the tax administration should refrain from determining what constitutes racial discrimination. A more sensible question would have been whether it is proper to use the tax laws as the vehicle to grant assistance to any charitable organization and thereby cause the Internal Revenue Service to become involved in civil rights issues. But the congressional discussions concerning the IRS and racial discrimination never addressed that question.

In 1979 Congress took the extreme step, in the act appropriating funds for the Internal Revenue Service for the fiscal year ending October 1980, of including a provision stating that the IRS could spend no funds to carry out its revised procedures for testing eligibility of recipients on grounds of racial discrimination.[45] This step raised serious constitutional and separation of powers issues.[46] The plaintiffs in Green v. Connally had, at about the time the IRS was proposing revisions in its procedures, brought suit alleging noncompliance with the injunction granted in that case, on the ground that the existing IRS tests were inadequate under that injunction. In 1980, in Green v. Miller, the court responded by supplementing the injunction to tighten its enforcement.[47] The restriction imposed by the 1980 appropriations act was renewed by legislation in the 1981 act. This time, however, IRS action within Mississippi was in effect excepted from the restriction, in recognition of the injunctions issued in Green v. Connally and Green v. Miller, which had applied to Mississippi, the state involved in the original suit.[48]

The courts will have to decide what tests are required under the injunction, what role Congress can play in that inquiry, and whether restrictions such as those in the appropriations acts are unconstitutional.[49] In this regard it seems almost inconceivable that Congress would enact a direct assistance program both prohibiting recipients from practicing racial discrimination and denying the administrative agency any funds to determine whether there has been compliance with the requirement. Yet in effect that is the action Congress took in 1979 and 1980 in its handling of school discrimination. Congress did not, however, enact legislation to overrule Green v. Connally, and indeed the appropriations acts, by focusing only on the proposed revised procedures, indicated congressional acquiescence both in that decision and in the initial IRS action under it.

Events involving racial discrimination issues then took a bizarre turn that eventually brought a Supreme Court decision. In 1970 the IRS had informed Bob Jones University, a religious school in South Carolina, that its tax-exempt status would be ended because it practiced racial discrimination in the form of racial exclusion. The university sued to enjoin the IRS, but in *Bob Jones University v. Simon*[50] the Supreme Court held that the injunction route was not open for the university. The university then paid $21 in unemployment tax and immediately sued for refund, tax-exempt organizations not being liable for that tax. By this time the university did admit blacks but discriminated against them through a prohibition on interracial marriage or dating. The IRS counterclaimed for $489,675.59 in back unpaid unemployment taxes. The university won in the district court,[51] but a divided Fourth Circuit court overruled the decision.[52] The court followed the interpretative path developed in the *Green* cases by the District of Columbia Circuit. It also held that the revocation of tax-exempt status did not violate the free exercise and establishment clauses of the First Amendment, a matter not decided until then.

During this period a second school was involved in litigation. Goldsboro Christian Schools, a religious secondary school, had been informed on audit in 1972 that because it excluded blacks it was not tax exempt. The school paid back unemployment taxes and sued for refund. The district court, though assuming that the racial discrimination was based on a sincerely held religious belief, denied exempt status.[53] The Fourth Circuit court affirmed *per curiam* on the basis of the *Bob Jones University* decision.[54]

Both schools then sought certiorari in the Supreme Court. The Department of Justice argued that the Fourth Circuit decisions were correct but urged the grant of certiorari to "dispel the uncertainty surrounding the propriety of the Service's ruling position and foster greater compliance on the part of the affected institutions."[55] The petitions were granted. The Tax Division of the Justice Department then prepared a brief on the merits, once more supporting the Fourth Circuit decisions. Just before its brief was due, however, the department suddenly reversed its position. The Acting Solicitor General filed a memorandum in January 1982 informing the Court that the Treasury intended to initiate the steps necessary to revoke its basic 1971 ruling and to recognize the tax-exempt status of the schools. The memorandum suggested that therefore the cases were moot.

This action by the government caused an immediate political and legal uproar. Political critics claimed that the government was turning its back on a significant civil rights position followed by the Nixon, Ford, and Carter administrations. In the face of these denunciations the government retreated, saying that it favored the denial of tax-exempt status to racially discriminatory schools but that Congress and not the IRS had to establish that denial. It therefore sent to Congress proposed legislation to that end.

On the legal side, various organizations and lawyers countered the Justice Department's reversal of position by denying that the cases were moot and seeking to act as *amici curiae*. Congress held a hearing on the matter but chose not to enact legislation.[56] Various legislators pointed out that Congress had already acted, as was evidenced by the IRS ruling.

The Court of Appeals for the District of Columbia then acted decisively. In *Wright v. Regan*,[57] in which black plaintiffs were seeking a broad injunction that would in effect sustain the IRS's proposed revised procedures, the court had held in a divided decision that the plaintiffs had standing to litigate the issue. In February 1982 the court issued an order in the case enjoining the government from granting tax-exempt status to any school that practiced racial discrimination.[58] The *Bob Jones University* and *Goldsboro* cases were thus decidedly no longer moot, and the Supreme Court appointed William T. Coleman, Jr., a distinguished black attorney, as *amicus curiae*. Congress underscored its adverse reaction to the government's change of position by denying approval of a rider similar to those in the 1980 and 1981 appropriations acts. In November 1982, when Congressman Dornan moved the same rider, his position was strongly attacked and his amendment defeated.[59]

In 1983, in *Bob Jones University v. United States*,[60] the Supreme Court sustained the Fourth Circuit in a strong opinion by Chief Justice Burger. The decision essentially followed the interpretative positions of *Green* and the 1971 IRS ruling. It stressed that the term "charitable" colors the language throughout section 501(c)(3), including the specific reference to "educational purposes"; that the term embraces the common-law concept of "charity"; and that this concept requires that the organization be a benefit to society and that its purpose not be illegal or violate established public policy. The opinion stated that racial discrimination in education violates deeply and widely accepted views of elementary justice. The Court fortified its position by references to congressional legislation, executive branch actions, and judicial decisions. The Court then said that the IRS interpretation of the requirements of section 501(c)(3) regarding racial discrimination was both correct and within the agency's authority to interpret the tax laws. The opinion stressed that decided nonaction by Congress to reverse the IRS ruling, of which Congress was fully aware, made out an unusually strong case of legislative acquiescence in and implicit ratification of the ruling. The Court here gave weight both to the enactment of section 501(i) and to the restricted scope of the appropriation acts riders. Finally, the Court upheld the application of the IRS ruling to schools that engage in racial discrimination on the basis of sincerely held religious beliefs, a point discussed later.[61]

The Court expressly noted that the ground of its decision made it unnecessary to reach the constitutional issue of equal protection: "Many of the amici curiae, including Amicus William T. Coleman, Jr., (appointed by the Court), argue that denial of tax-exempt status to racially discriminatory schools is independently required by the equal protection component of the Fifth Amendment. In light of our resolution of this case, we do not reach that issue. See, e.g., *United States v. Clark,* 445 U.S. 23, 27 (1980); *NLRB v. Catholic Bishop of Chicago,* 440 U.S. 490, 504 (1979)."[62] But the Court's findings on public policy do rest on its decision in *Norwood v. Harrison,*[63] invalidating a direct grant on equal protection grounds.

Bob Jones University reflected the Supreme Court's increasing sophistication concerning tax expenditure provisions in the Internal Revenue Code. In describing the effects of tax exemptions and the deduction for charitable contributions, it stated: "When Government grants exemptions or allows deductions all taxpayers are affected; the very fact of the exemption or deduction for the donor means that other taxpayers can be said to be indirect and vicarious 'donors.' "[64] The same language would also precisely describe the effects of a direct federal matching grant program for gifts to charitable organizations. Examined from this perspective, the decisions reached by the courts in the racial discrimination cases were almost inevitable. It is difficult to believe that Congress would intentionally enact legislation providing direct financial benefits to schools or other organizations that practice racial discrimination or that, if it did, the courts would uphold the legislation. The tax exemption cases established the necessary corollary that the same conclusions apply when the mechanism for federal aid is the Internal Revenue Code.

ESTABLISHMENT AND FREE EXERCISE OF RELIGION

The courts have had to decide whether the provision of tax assistance to religious organizations violates the First Amendment prohibition against establishment of religion.

In *Walz v. Tax Commission of the City of New York*,[65] a real estate owner sought an injunction to prevent the New York City Tax Commissioner from granting property tax exemptions to religious organizations; the plaintiff contended that the financial aid thus provided violated the First Amendment prohibition against establishment of religion. In holding that there was no First Amendment violation, the Supreme Court rather naively analyzed the nature of the property tax exemption as follows:

> Granting tax exemptions to churches necessarily operates to afford an indirect economic benefit and also gives rise to some, but yet a lesser, involvement than taxing them. In analyzing either alternative the questions are whether the involvement is excessive, and whether it is a continuing one calling for official and continuing surveillance leading to an impermissible degree of entanglement. Obviously a direct money subsidy would be a relationship pregnant with involvement and, as with most governmental grant programs, could encompass sustained and detailed administrative relationships for enforcement of statutory or administrative standards, but that is not this case. The hazards of churches supporting government are hardly less in their potential than the hazards of government supporting churches; each relationship carries some involvement rather than the desired insulation and separation. We cannot ignore the instances in history when church support of government led to the kind of involvement we seek to avoid.
>
> The grant of a tax exemption is not sponsorship since the government does not transfer part of its revenue to churches but simply abstains from demanding that the church support the state. No one has ever suggested that tax exemption has converted libraries, art galleries, or hospitals into arms of the state or

put employees "on the public payroll." There is no genuine nexus between tax exemption and establishment of religions. As Mr. Justice Holmes commented in a related context "a page of history is worth a volume of logic." *New York Trust Co. v. Eisner,* 256 U.S. 345, 349 (1921). The exemption creates only a minimal and remote involvement between church and state and far less than taxation of churches. It restricts the fiscal relationship between church and state, and tends to complement and reinforce the desired separation insulating each from the other.[66]

Whether or not one agrees with the *Walz* decision, the court's discussion of the nature of the tax exemption will not withstand economic analysis. More to the point was Justice Douglas's question in dissent: "A tax exemption is a subsidy. Is my Brother Brennan correct in saying that we would hold that state or federal grants to churches, say, to construct the edifice itself would be unconstitutional? What is the difference between that kind of subsidy and the present subsidy?"[67]

It soon became clear that the Supreme Court's analysis in *Walz* was inadequate. In *Committee for Public Education and Religious Liberty v. Nyquist,*[68] the Court ruled on the constitutionality of two New York statutes that granted financial aid to parents of children at private elementary and secondary schools: one provided direct tuition reimbursement; the other effected reimbursement through tax deductions from adjusted gross income. Under the direct grant program, parents with taxable incomes of less than $5,000 per year whose children attended private schools were entitled to a tuition reimbursement of $50 for each child in elementary school and $100 for each child in secondary school, subject to an overall limit of 50 percent of total tuition paid. The tax program was for parents whose annual income exceeded $5,000. Its benefits were designed to pick up where the direct tuition reimbursement system left off and to phase out gradually as income increased. Thus the tax deductions gave the same dollar amount of assistance to parents with incomes just above $5,000 as the direct grants gave to parents below that level. The tax assistance ended at the $25,000 income level. Benefits under both programs were available to parents whose children attended sectarian, nonpublic schools. Since about 85 percent of the children in private elementary and secondary schools attended church-affiliated schools (practically all Roman Catholic), the Court considered the grants and tax deduction in the context of the First Amendment. A three-judge district court had held that the direct grant provisions were unconstitutional but had sustained the validity of the tax benefits.[69] The Supreme Court affirmed the decision on the direct grant program but reversed the one on the tax allowances. The direct grant program was held to be unconstitutional because its "principal or primary effect" was to advance religion. The tax provisions were held unconstitutional on the same grounds:

> In practical terms there would appear to be little difference, for purposes of determining whether such aid has the effect of advancing religion, between the tax benefit allowed here and the tuition grant allowed under §2. The qualifying parent under either program receives the same form of encouragement and reward for sending his children to nonpublic schools. The only difference is that one parent receives an actual cash payment while the other is allowed to reduce by an arbitrary amount the sum he would otherwise be obliged to pay over to the State. We see no answer to Judge Hays' dissenting statement below that "[i]n both instances the money involved represents a charge made upon the state for the purpose of religious education." 350 F. Supp. at 675.
>
> Appellees defend the tax portion of New York's legislative package on two grounds. First, they contend that it is of controlling significance that the grants or credits are directed to the parents rather than to the schools. This is the same argument made in support of the tuition reimbursements and rests on the same reading of the same precedents of this Court, primarily *Everson* and *Allen*. *Our treatment of this issue in [the Court's consideration of the direct tuition grant program] is applicable here and requires rejection of this claim.*[70]

Clearly, this description of the economic effects of tax benefits was at odds with the one in *Walz* concerning property tax exemptions. Justice Powell distinguished *Nyquist* from *Walz* on two grounds: (1) property tax exemptions for church property date back to colonial times and thus have an aura of historical approval; and (2) unlike the New York tax benefits, which primarily aided religious institutions, the property tax exemption provided financial assistance to charitable institutions generally and had neither the primary purpose nor the primary effect of aiding religious institutions.[71]

Like the majority in *Nyquist,* the three dissenting justices drew no distinction between the direct tuition grant assistance and the tax assistance. They would have held both forms of assistance constitutional. Their dissenting views underscore the Court's unwillingness to develop in First Amendment cases a different constitutional test for government aid cast in the form of a direct grant and government aid cast in the form of tax assistance.[72]

In *Mueller v. Allen*[73] the Supreme Court revisited the issue of tax benefits provided by states to assist in educational costs. Minnesota permits taxpayers to deduct from gross income the tuition, textbook, and transportation expenses of each dependent attending an elementary or secondary school. Justice Rehnquist, writing for the majority, sustained the constitutionality of the Minnesota statute against a claim that it violated the establishment clause of the First Amer.dment.[74] In this case Justice Rehnquist's opinion was considerably less clear about the nature of tax deductions than was his earlier opinion in *Regan v. Taxation With Representation.* He recognized that "financial assistance provided to parents [through the tax deductions] ultimately has an economic effect comparable to that of aid given directly to the schools attended by their children."[75] But he failed to sustain his earlier view that there was a difference between special (tax expenditure) deductions and deductions necessary to define net income: "Under our prior decisions, the Minnesota legislature's judgment that a deduction for educational expenses fairly equalizes the tax burden of its citizens and encourages desirable expenditures for educational purposes is entitled to substantial deference."[76] The notions of equalizing tax burdens and encouraging desirable expenditures are inconsistent. The former involves normative provisions necessary to define net income; the latter involves tax expenditures.

Justice Rehnquist added unnecessarily to the confusion about the Court's treatment of special tax provisions by focusing on a footnote in the *Nyquist* opinion, which stated: "Since the program here does not have the elements of a genuine tax deduction, such as for charitable contributions, we do not have before us, and do not decide, whether that form of tax benefit is constitutionally acceptable under the 'neutrality' test in *Walz.*"[77] Though acknowledging that "the economic consequences of the program in *Nyquist* and [of the program] in this case may be difficult to distinguish," Justice Rehnquist nonetheless felt that the Minnesota plan embodied a "genuine tax deduction," and that this factor was of "some relevance" in upholding its validity.[78] Justice

Marshall correctly pointed out that Justice Rehnquist had made a false distinction: any program of financial aid can be cast as a deduction, a credit, or a direct grant.[79] Although the value of a deduction varies with the taxpayer's tax bracket whereas a credit usually does not, it is possible to construct a credit that does vary with income or a deduction that does not (in effect a credit). In attempting to make such a distinction, Justice Rehnquist and the majority obscured issues that they had done much to clarify in their earlier decisions in *Taxation With Representation* and *Bob Jones University.*

The question may be raised whether the existing charitable deduction as applied to contributions to religious organizations is constitutional. It would seem that if the income tax provided a deduction *only* for contributions to religious organizations the deduction should be unconstitutional under *Nyquist.* However, the current deduction for contributions to religious organizations is a part of the general statutory charitable contribution deduction that provides government assistance to all eligible nonprofit organizations. The statutory structure would thus allow the Court to find a purpose for the assistance other than the support of religion. Given the majority approach in *Mueller v. Allen* and *Walz,* it appears that this deduction would be upheld even though contributions to religious organizations represent about 60 percent of the deductions taken for charitable contributions.[80] The critical question remains, however, whether Congress constitutionally could provide *any* direct aid (for example, through direct matching grants) to religious organizations, even as part of a program covering charitable organizations generally. The constitutionality of the charitable contribution deduction must depend on the answer to this question.

The free exercise clause of the First Amendment was also involved in *Bob Jones University v. United States.*[81] Since the schools before the Court were religious schools teaching specific religious doctrines, and since the racial discrimination they practiced was assertedly based on sincerely held religious beliefs, the schools contended that the denial of tax exemption violated their right to the free exercise of religion under the First Amendment. The Court spent few words rejecting the claim:

> On occasion this Court has found certain governmental interests so compelling as to allow even regulations prohibiting religiously based conduct. In *Prince v. Massachusetts,* 321 U.S. 158 (1944), for example, the Court held that neutrally cast child labor

laws prohibiting sale of printed materials on public streets could be applied to prohibit children from dispensing religious literature. The Court found no constitutional infirmity in "excluding [Jehovah's Witness children] from doing there what no other children may do." Id., at 170 . . . Denial of tax benefits will inevitably have a substantial impact on the operation of private religious schools, but will not prevent those schools from observing their religious tenets.

The governmental interest at stake here is compelling . . . The Government has a fundamental, overriding interest in eradicating racial discrimination in education—discrimination that prevailed, with official approval, for the first 165 years of this Nation's history. That governmental interest substantially outweighs whatever burden denial of tax benefits places on petitioners' exercise of their religious beliefs. The interests asserted by petitioners cannot be accommodated with that compelling governmental interest, see United States v. Lee, supra, 455 U.S., at 259-260; and no "less restrictive means," see Thomas v. Review Board, supra, 450 U.S., at 718, are available to achieve the governmental interest.[82]

Is the decision in accord with or contrary to Walz? It is interesting that the case was not cited. As interpreted by Nyquist and Mueller v. Allen, the Court in Walz decided that the neutral grant of tax exemption to all charitable organizations, including churches, was not assistance contrary to the First Amendment and therefore did not violate the establishment of religion clause. Bob Jones University decided that the neutral denial of exemption to all racially discriminatory schools, including religious schools, was not a violation of the free exercise of religion clause. On the basis of this stress on "neutrality," the cases appear consistent.

FREE SPEECH AND POLITICAL ACTIVITY

In Marker v. Schultz[83] the plaintiffs, members of a labor union, asserted that the grant of income tax exemption to their labor union was unconstitutional. They alleged that the union engaged in substantial political activity with which the plaintiffs disagreed. They then asserted that the tax exemption accorded to labor unions constituted a federal subsidy and that, because Congress had prohibited labor unions from using union dues for political purposes, the tax exemption should be removed. The court of appeals rejected the plaintiffs' constitutional arguments:

> Plaintiffs misapprehended the basis and reach of *Green* and *McGlotten,* involving charitable organizations engaged in racially restrictive policies. There the courts were confronted with a combination of (a) a provision inserted in the law to give positive Government support—including benefits (tax deductibility) to donors making supporting contributions—to organizations substituting for the government in performing beneficial functions and (b) constitutional rights rooted in the Civil War and the Amendments passed in the wake of the Civil War, which operate to eradicate any government involvement whatever, however "minimal and remote," that might in any way foster racial discrimination in the schools. This distinction was noted in *Green,* . . . 330 F. Supp. at 1168–69, and following cases. See, e.g., Pitts v. Wisconsin Department of Revenue, 333 F. Supp. 662, 668 (E.D. Wis. 1971). Even under the *Green-McGlotten* approach state support consisting only of furnishing services equivalent to the necessities of life, such as police and fire protection provided to all without any connotation of approval vel non, does not constitute fostering or encouragement of racial discrimination that is constitutionally objectionable. Moose Lodge No. 107 v. Irvis, 407 U.S. 163, 173 (1972). There is no constitutional wrong when a state involvement in an institution is devoid of any nexus with the activity causing injury.
>
> These precedents are dispositive. The tax exemption granted to receipt of dues by labor unions was not based on support of each aspect of their activities, but rather on the concept that what was involved was essentially a pooling of the individual resources of the members, as contrasted with enterpreneurial profit of corporations. This appears from the history of the exemption, which first appeared in 1909. Plaintiffs are not protected by the Constitution from a Governmental decision that union dues, or other cooperative contributions, as to an agricultural or fraternal organization, are not proper objects of taxation.[84]

Section 501(c)(5) exempts labor organizations from income tax. Aside from the question whether union dues are income to the organization, the exemption applies to any business income related to the organization's exempt function and to any income the organization may have from the investment of its funds, assuming that its deductions do not offset that investment income. The exemption thus goes beyond the "pooling of the individual resources of the members." Union dues are deductible to the members, but as trade or business expenses and not as charitable contributions, so that a deduction for those expenses is part of a normative structure.[85] The only tax benefit thus present is the tax-exempt status. In this regard *Marker* appears to be inconsistent with the later Supreme Court view in *Taxation With Representation*,[86] which correctly analyzed the "subsidy" present in tax exemption. Technically, however, the issue raised in *Marker* was not before the Court in *Taxation With Representation*. In *TWR*, the issue was not whether Congress could validly grant exemptions to veterans' organizations that lobbied but whether, because of that exemption, nonveterans' organizations were entitled to lobby without losing their exemptions. Thus if a veteran challenged the validity of allowing tax exemptions to a veterans' organization that lobbied for political ends contrary to those supported by the complaining veteran, the Supreme Court might well reach the same conclusion it did in *Marker*, even though it found a subsidy present in the exemption. That is, even though the tax exemption for veterans' organizations provides a federal subsidy, the Court might conclude that there is not a sufficient relationship between the subsidy and the objectionable activity to constitute prohibited "state action."

SEX DISCRIMINATION

In *McCoy v. Schultz*,[87] the plaintiffs had been denied admission to the Portland City Club because they were females. The club controlled the activities of the Portland City Club Foundation. The plaintiffs sought to revoke the tax-exempt status of the foundation under section 501(c)(3). They relied on *McGlotten v. Connally*,[88] in which the court had developed the distinction between organizations exempt under section 501(c)(7) (social clubs), for which no tax subsidies were held to be involved, and section 501(c)(8) (fraternal organizations), which did provide tax subsidies. The court in *McCoy* dismissed the constitutional claims of the plaintiffs, stating that section 501(c)(3) organizations "are more closely aligned with those diverse organizations exempted under section 501(c)(7) than the distinctive fraternal orders which enjoy a special tax exemption status under section 501(c)(8)."[89] The court concluded:

> [Tax exemptions] constitute *some* action by the state . . . [but] the critical question is whether there is *significant* state involvement in the challenged activity so that otherwise private conduct may be reasonably considered the action of the state . . . It seems clear that the acts of the defendant in administering the Internal Revenue Laws is so far removed from the alleged discrimination of the (tax-exempt organization) as to negate any possibility of their complicity in the discrimination. As part of its general duty of administering the tax laws, the federal government does not in any way associate itself with or influence the internal decisions, composition, or membership practices of private clubs or institutions. The mere fact that the government generally grants favorable tax treatment to eligible organizations does not suddenly make the acts of these organizations in denying membership applications the acts of the state . . . The tax classification of private entities no more transforms that entity into an arm of the government than the grant by the state of tax exemption to a religious body constitutes state establishment of religion . . . Since the defendants' impartial administration of the tax laws cannot be said to in any way "foster or encourage" sexual discrimination, this Court concludes the government has not "significantly involved itself with invidious discriminations" . . . so as to bring the discriminatory action "within the ambit of constitutional prohibition."[90]

The *McCoy* opinion is thus in the same category as the *Marker* case—tax-exempt status does not constitute significant state involvement with the organization. But its analysis of the effects of the exemption was inadequate. Contributions to the Portland City Club Foundation were deductible by the donors as charitable contributions. The court should have considered whether, given that additional form of tax assistance, as decided in *Green v. Connally* and *McGlotten v. Connally,* a constitutional issue was involved because of the sex discrimination. In addition, *Taxation With Representation* made it clear that the exemption itself is a form of federal subsidy. The court in *McCoy* therefore should have considered whether a direct grant of assistance to the foundation would have been constitutional, given the sex discrimination practiced by its controlling organization, the Portland City Club. The result might have been the same, but the court's inadequate analysis of a tax-exempt status leaves the possible outcome unclear.

The decisions in the sex discrimination tax cases may be explained by the fact that the sex discrimination cases in the Supreme Court in nontax matters are not as decisive as the racial discrimination cases. Nor has the Internal Revenue Service issued a ruling on sex discrimination comparable to its ruling on racial discrimination. Code section 501(i) denies tax-exempt status to social clubs discriminating against "any person on the basis of race, color, or religion" (the religious aspect has been modified by a later amendment) but does not mention sex. The tax exemption issue where sex discrimination is involved seems to remain an open one.

THE CONCEPT OF STATE ACTION

Numerous court decisions and legal commentaries discuss the concept of state action in connection with suits against private parties in which the plaintiffs claim to have been deprived of a constitutional right because of the conduct of those parties. The decisions turn on whether there is a sufficient nexus between some form of government assistance, regulation, approval, or action and the conduct of the private parties. If the requisite relationship exists, then the involvement of the state makes the action of the private parties unconstitutional if similar action by the state itself would be unconstitutional. Our concern here is the relationship of the tax expenditure list and tax expenditure analysis to the state action concept.[91]

Because a tax expenditure is the equivalent of a direct government grant, the first issue to consider is whether a similar direct government grant would involve state action. If it does, the question turns to whether the relationship between government and private activity is significant. To address this issue, the courts have developed various tests: the proportion of the government assistance to the activities of the private party; whether the assistance constitutes "approval" of those activities; whether any regulatory characteristics of the assistance involve government control over those activities; and the "joint participant," or "entanglement," test.[92] Whichever test a court applies in a given case, it should use the same test for tax expenditure and for similar direct assistance. Likewise, the courts should use the same criteria for a tax expenditure as for similar direct government assistance when deciding whether the constitutional right alleged to be affected—free exercise of religion, freedom of speech, freedom of assembly, equal protection, due process safeguards—requires a particular form of application of the state action tests.

If the suit is brought against the government itself, as in *Nyquist,* *Green v. Connally,* and *McGlotten v. Connally,* the decision should be the same for a tax expenditure as it would for direct assistance.[93] The suits against the government have recognized the equivalence between tax expenditure and direct government subsidy. Even *Marker v. Connally* and *McCoy v. Schultz* can be said to be consistent with this approach if those decisions can be read as holding that although tax-exempt status does provide financial assistance, there is not the requisite "nexus" (*Marker*) or "significant involvement" (*McCoy*) to support state action, though the decisions are none too clear on the comparison of tax with direct assistance.

The decisions of and literature on the state action cases involving the conduct of private parties are in a confused condition. As in some of the suits against the government, the confusion largely results from the problem of how to view the tax-exempt status of the defendant private party. In the past the *Walz* decision was likely to weigh against the presence of state action.[94] Now, however, after *Taxation With Representation, Walz* may decline in importance so that the assistance in the tax-exempt status cases would become state action.

Courts unable to distinguish one type of tax provision from another can go astray in these state action cases. They are tempted to treat every deduction alike or, if they recognize the distinction between tax expenditure and normative deductions, to fail to assign a given deduction to its proper category. Thus, as discussed earlier, in *McGlotten v. Connally* a black American challenged the tax-exempt status of a segregated fraternal organization. The court, in analyzing the nature of the deduction for charitable contributions, attempted to distinguish it from normative deductions as follows:

> Certain deductions provided by the Code do not act as matching grants but are merely attempts to provide for an equitable measure of net income. Others are simply part of the structure of an income tax based on ability to pay. We recognize that an additional class of deductions—such as accelerated depreciation for rehabilitated low income rental property, or deductions for

mortgage interest—do act as "incentives" favoring certain types of activities. But unlike the charitable deductions before us, these provisions go no further than simply indicating the activities hoped to be encouraged.[95]

Clearly the court was wrong in classifying accelerated depreciation and mortgage interest (if the reference is to a home mortgage and not to a business loan) as "an additional class of deductions."[96] Both are tax expenditures and, by government description itself, are not designed as a measurement of ability to pay but as financial assistance for the activity involved.[97] As a result of this error, in order to distinguish the charitable deduction from the other tax provisions mentioned in its opinion, the *McGlotten* court was forced to find both "state approval" of the private-party defendant and "state involvement" in the latter's activities. But the resort to these factors was unnecessary as a ground of distinction. The distinction likewise is not supportable under the terms of the tax provisions; thus there may be more "regulation" under the accelerated deduction for rehabilitated rental housing than under the charitable deduction for fraternal organizations.[98]

Given the equivalence between tax and direct expenditures, the view that the Internal Revenue Code is immune from the restrictions of the Constitution is fundamentally wrong. Thus Professors Bittker and Kaufman have expressed strong reservations about the *McGlotten* decision. Their arguments may be correct regarding some of the tests applied in *McGlotten*—such as approval and regulatory involvement—to determine whether state action was present.[99] But that criticism does not address the main issue, which is whether the Internal Revenue Code is immune from constitutional examination concerning civil rights. Bittker and Kaufman did not appear to object to applying state action tests to direct federal grants, yet they rejected the tax expenditure concept of financial assistance. They thereby rejected the federal government's own characterization of tax expenditures in Special Analysis G as "alternatives to budget outlays, credit assistance or other policy instruments." Bittker and Kaufman used an argument frequently quoted in briefs asserting that the IRS is wrong to refuse to grant tax-exempt status where racial discrimination is involved: "If full sway is given to the *McGlotten* theory that tax allowances are equivalent to direct grants of public funds and hence impose constitutional obligations on the recipient, no one will be immune . . . The Internal Revenue Code is a pudding with plums for everyone."[100] It is true that the more than 100 tax expenditures in the Internal Revenue Code constitute a lot of plums. But to exempt almost $270 billion of tax expenditure assistance from the constitutional scrutiny that is applied to other forms of government assistance would be a most peculiar result. Merely placing government assistance in the Internal Revenue Code as tax credits, deductions, or special exclusions rather than providing assistance through comparable direct spending programs would permit restrictions imposed on constitutional rights by private parties receiving government assistance to be protected from scrutiny.[101]

An interesting question not raised in the literature on state action is whether a litigant can successfully argue that an item in the budget's tax expenditure list is not federal spending. Suppose a private party's discriminatory conduct is alleged to be unconstitutional because he or she receives federal assistance under an item in that list. Could the defendant successfully urge that the item has been wrongly included in the list and that the item therefore does not involve government assistance but instead is part of the normative tax system? Although the court would probably have to address the contention, it is difficult to see how it could agree with the defendant. Acceptance of the argument would involve rejection of the government's own characterization of its spending and financial assistance programs. On the other hand, suppose a litigant contesting private conduct contends that government financial assistance does exist even though the item being litigated is not on the tax expenditure list. This would seem a supportable position: Special Analysis G does declare that the list is not comprehensive.[102] Furthermore, the *McGlotten* court did find that the granting of tax-exempt status to fraternal organizations resulted in financial assistance—or state action—even though this item was not in the Treasury tax expenditure list.[103] Finally, suppose the alleged financial assistance—the tax expenditure characterization—relates to the estate tax, for which the government has not as yet published a list. It is recognized that the tax expenditure concept does extend to other global taxes, which would include the estate tax.[104] The absence of an official list should not therefore be a barrier to the contention that a particular estate tax provision does involve government assistance. A court would have to decide the issue by applying the tax expenditure concept to the estate tax.

Tax Benefits as Financial Assistance under Other Federal Statutes

In some situations the federal government has specifically legislated that private parties receiving direct financial assistance from the government cannot engage in certain conduct, such as racial discrimination. In these instances an interpretative issue exists as to whether tax expenditure assistance constitutes financial assistance within the terms of the legislation. Thus the court in *McGlotten v. Connally* had to decide whether the allowance of a charitable deduction for contributions to a fraternal organization and the granting of tax-exempt status to the organization constituted financial assistance under the 1964 Civil Rights Act. That act prohibits racial discrimination by a private party receiving such assistance. The court decided that the tax benefits were a form of financial assistance.

> Section 602, 42 U.S.C. §2000d-1 defines "federal financial assistance" as "assistance to any program or activity by way of *grant, loan, or contract other than a contract of insurance or guaranty*" [emphasis added]. The apparently standard regulation issued by federal agencies pursuant to §2000d-1 reads:
>> The term "federal financial assistance" includes (1) grants and loans of Federal funds, (2) the grant or donation of Federal property and interests in property, (3) the detail of Federal personnel, (4) the sale and lease of, and the permission to use (on other than a casual or transient basis), Federal property or any interest in such property without consideration or at a nominal consideration, or at a consideration which is reduced for the purpose of assisting the recipient, or in recognition of the public interest to be served by such sale or lease to the recipient, and (5) any Federal agreement, arrangement, or other contract which has as one of its purposes the provision of assistance.
>
> Plaintiff contends that since "federal financial assistance" has been construed to cover such indirect forms of aid as the detail of federal personnel, or the sale of property at a reduced consideration, it must necessarily cover the provision of similar aid through the income, estate, and gift taxes which, if direct, would certainly be covered by the statute. Nothing in the massive legis-

lative history of the 1964 Civil Rights Act sheds any light on whether assistance provided through the tax system was intended to be treated differently than assistance provided directly.

In the absence of strong legislative history to the contrary the plain purpose of the statute is controlling. Here that purpose is clearly to eliminate discrimination in programs or activities benefitting from federal financial assistance. Distinctions as to the method of distribution of federal funds or their equivalent seem beside the point, as the regulations issued by the various agencies make apparent.

Defendant's only argument as to why the Act should be construed to exclude from its coverage assistance plainly within its purpose, is that otherwise any deduction provided under the Internal Revenue Code becomes a potential vehicle for a suit against the Internal Revenue Service under Title VI. We have already indicated, however, that the deductions provided in the Code are not all cut from the same cloth. Most relate primarily to the operation of the tax itself, and thus would not constitute a grant of federal financial assistance. And where a Code provision does operate to provide such assistance, it is within the purpose of the statute and the possibility of litigation follows naturally . . .

We think there is little question that the provision of a tax deduction for charitable contributions is a grant of federal financial assistance within the scope of the 1964 Civil Rights Act. "The charitable contribution deduction is a special tax provision not required by, and contrary to, widely accepted definitions of income applicable to the determination of the structure of an income tax." It operates in effect as a Government matching grant and is available only for the particular purposes and to the particular organizations outlined in the Code. We see no difference between the provision of Federal property "at a consideration which is reduced . . . in recognition of the public interest to be served by such sale or lease to the recipient," and a tax deduction in the form of a matching grant provided for contributions to causes deemed worthy by the Internal Revenue Code.[105]

The defendant in *McGlotten* was the Treasury Department. Under the tax expenditure concept, the argument that the charitable contributions deduction was not a form of financial assistance was a weak one, made weaker still by the budget's later inclusion of the deduction in the tax expenditure list. Certainly the argument that "any deduction" is a possible vehicle for suit would no longer be appropriate. The Internal Revenue Service has since taken the position that a charitable deduction is financial assistance under the 1964 Civil Rights Act.[106]

Although there appear to be no other cases dealing with this subject, the *McGlotten* opinion seems correct. Only if the statutory language or legislative history specifically excludes tax assistance could a contrary result properly be reached. But in that case the legislation itself would be irrational.[107]

Standing to Sue

The tax expenditure cases involving a litigant's "standing to sue" illustrate the prevailing confusion on this topic.[108] "Standing" is a legal doctrine that determines whether a litigant has the right to have a court decide his or her case at all.

A person contesting an IRS assertion of a tax liability may challenge the action either as not in conformity with the tax law or as unconstitutional.[109] The litigation may be pursued in the Tax Court without payment of the deficiency, in the district courts by way of a suit for a refund, or in the United States Claims Court after the deficiency has been paid. Sometimes, to prevent the IRS from asserting a deficiency, taxpayers seek to enjoin the action or obtain a declaratory judgment denying the action. Two statutes, however, generally bar such steps. Section 7421(a) of the Internal Revenue Code (the Anti-Injunction Statute) states that no suit may be maintained to restrain the assessment or collection of any tax. Although the courts in extreme situations have permitted the suit to be maintained—when the taxpayer can establish that "it is clear that under no circumstances could the Government ultimately prevail" and that the plaintiff will "suffer irreparable injury if collection were effected"[110]—this statute almost always precludes the injunction route. Similarly, the Declaratory Judgment Act, 28 USC §2201, prohibits a declaratory judgment action "with respect to Federal taxes."[111]

In cases in which litigants sue to protest the allowance of a direct government expenditure, standing is generally denied on the basis of the long-established rule that federal taxpayers do not have standing to contest the uses to which their taxes are put.[112] Thus, standing was denied in two suits in which taxpayers who objected to U.S. involvement in Vietnam sought to challenge the use of tax revenues for the war;[113] in a suit in which a taxpayer argued that he was entitled to a "war crimes deduction" because to require him to pay taxes would make him an accomplice in alleged war crimes committed by the United States in Vietnam;[114] and in a suit in which a taxpayer challenged the constitutionality of sections 6096 and 9001–13, which provide for the designation of a portion of income tax payments to a presidential election campaign fund.[115]

Since 1968, however, the standing issue in the tax area has been in a state of flux. In *Flast v. Cohen,* the Supreme Court upheld the standing of taxpayers to enjoin federal expenditures under the Elementary and Secondary Education Act of 1965 to finance instruction in parochial schools: "[A] taxpayer will have standing consistent with Article III to invoke federal judicial power when he alleges that congressional action under the taxing and spending clause is in derogation of those constitutional provisions which operate to restrict the exercise of the taxing and spending power. The taxpayer's allegation in such cases would be that his tax money is being extracted and spent in violation of specific constitutional protections against such abuses of legislative power."[116]

Against this background our concern is whether the tax statutes or administrative actions that provide tax benefits may be challenged on the ground that the action is not authorized by the statute or, if the action is authorized, that it is unconstitutional. The decisions in these cases rest on the proposition that federal financial benefits effected through the tax system are to be tested under the same principles as expenditures resulting from direct appropriations by Congress.

In the early cases the courts had little trouble holding that litigants challenging tax expenditures (though the term was not used) had standing to present their suits. Thus in *Green v. Kennedy,* involving racial discrimination practiced by schools that obtained the benefit of the charitable deduction and maintained a tax-exempt status, the court devoted few words to sustaining the plaintiff's standing to sue:

> We take note of defendants' contention that plaintiffs have no standing to bring this action in their capacity as taxpayers. We need not consider that issue at this juncture. This case is properly maintained as a class action, pursuant to Rule 23 of the Federal Rules of Civil Procedure, by Negro school children in Mississippi and the parents of those children on behalf of themselves and all persons similarly situated. They have standing to attack the con-

stitutionality of statutory provisions which they claim provides
an unconstitutional system of benefits and matching grants that
fosters and supports a system of segregated private schools as an
alternative available to white students seeking to avoid desegregated public schools.[117]

In a similar racial discrimination case, *McGlotten v. Connally*, involving a tax-exempt fraternal organization, the court found little difficulty in holding that standing existed and that neither the
Anti-Injunction nor the Declaratory Judgment statutes barred the action:

> Just as "(a) person or family may have a spiritual stake in First
> Amendment values sufficient to give standing to raise issues con-
> cerning the Establishment Clause and Free Exercise Clause," so a
> black American has standing to challenge a system of federal
> support and encouragement of segregated fraternal organiza-
> tions . . .
>
> Defendant relies upon the provision of the Declaratory Judg-
> ment Act, 28 U.S.C. §2201, which specifically excepts suits "with
> respect to Federal taxes" from its coverage. In our view, the
> scope of this exception is coterminous with the breadth of the
> Tax Injunction Act, 26 U.S.C. §7421(a), which forbids enjoining
> the collection or assessment of any tax. As originally passed in
> 1935, the Declaratory Judgment Act did not contain the present
> exception for Federal taxes. The exception was added the follow-
> ing year for the explicit purpose of limiting the jurisdiction of the
> courts to issue declaratory judgments in the same fashion as their
> general jurisdiction was limited by the Tax Injunction Act. If the
> injunctive relief requested by plaintiff is barred by the Tax In-
> junction Act so too will relief be barred by the Declaratory Judg-
> ment Act . . .
>
> Plaintiff's action has nothing to do with the collection or as-
> sessment of taxes. He does not contest the amount of his own
> tax, nor does he seek to limit the amount of tax revenue collect-
> ible by the United States. The preferred course of raising his ob-
> jections in a suit for refund is not available. In this situation we
> cannot read the statute to bar the present suit. To hold otherwise
> would require the kind of ritualistic construction which the Su-
> preme Court has repeatedly rejected. Even where the particular
> plaintiff objects to his own taxes, the Court has recognized that

the literal terms of the statute do not apply when "the central purpose of the Act is inapplicable." In the present case, the central purpose is clearly inapplicable. It follows that neither §7421(a) nor the exemption to the Declaratory Judgment Act prohibits this suit.[118]

Later cases, even though denying the plaintiff's substantive claim, such as *Marker v. Schultz*[119] and *McCoy v. Schultz*,[120] did not pause over the standing question.

But this willingness to hear cases involving tax expenditures was undercut by the Supreme Court's decision in *Simon v. Eastern Kentucky Welfare Rights Organization*.[121] The Internal Revenue Service, reversing an earlier position, had ruled that a nonprofit hospital can maintain its tax-exempt status (and receive deductible charitable contributions) even though it does not admit, except to its emergency care unit, patients who cannot meet the financial requirements for admission.[122] The plaintiffs, consisting of welfare organizations and of low-income individuals who had been refused medical services because of inability to pay, sued the Secretary of the Treasury and the Commissioner of Internal Revenue. They contended that the later ruling erroneously interpreted the governing provision of the Internal Revenue Code granting exemption to a hospital and that the earlier ruling requiring a qualifying hospital, to the extent of its financial ability, to accept persons who could not afford to pay, was the correct interpretation. The government, on a motion to dismiss, supported the later ruling and also challenged the plaintiffs' standing. The District Court for the District of Columbia held for the plaintiffs.[123] The Court of Appeals for the District of Columbia agreed that the plaintiffs had standing but also held the later ruling to be a permissible definition of "charitable."[124] Both parties appealed.

The Supreme Court denied standing and therefore did not consider the validity of the new ruling. In denying standing, the majority applied the same tests used in cases challenging direct government actions. Crucially, the majority concluded that the plaintiffs had failed to establish in their complaint that the new ruling produced any "actual injury" to themselves or their members. That is, in the majority's view, it was "speculative" whether the new ruling, if applied, would deny hospital service to the poor or, if overturned, would cause the hospitals to provide services to the poor.[125] In a concurring opinion Justice Stewart stated that he "[could not] now imagine a case, at least outside the First Amendment area, where a person whose own tax liability was not affected could ever have standing to litigate the federal tax liability of someone else."[126] The majority, however, expressly stated that it did "not reach . . . the question of whether a third party ever may challenge IRS treatment of another."[127]

In *Allen v. Wright*,[128] the Supreme Court continued to narrow the ability of third parties to challenge the tax status of another. The plaintiffs, parents of black public school children, sought a nationwide injunction to bar the IRS from granting tax-exempt status to all schools practicing racial discrimination and to direct the IRS to adopt stricter administrative practices to follow in determining whether discrimination existed. The plaintiffs had no interest in having their children admitted to any of the private schools that they listed as practicing discrimination. Instead, they asserted that the financial aid provided through the tax exemption encouraged the operation of segregated white schools, thus depriving black children of the opportunity to obtain a desegregated education. A majority of the Supreme Court held that the plaintiffs had no standing to bring the suit. Relying primarily on *Eastern Kentucky Welfare Rights Organization*, the majority concluded that the plaintiffs had not alleged facts sufficient to establish the requisite injury to support standing. The mere fact that discriminatory private schools receive government financial aid was insufficient to establish an injury to the plaintiffs since they had not been personally subject to discrimination by the schools:

> If the [plaintiffs'] abstract stigmatic injury were cognizable, standing would extend nationwide to all members of the particular racial groups against which the Government was alleged to be discriminating by its grant of a tax exemption to a racially discriminatory school, regardless of the location of that school. All such persons could claim the same sort of abstract stigmatic injury [plaintiffs] assert in their first claim of injury. A black person in Hawaii could challenge the grant of a tax exemption to a racially discriminatory school in Maine. Recognition of standing in such circumstances would transform the federal courts into "no more than a vehicle for the vindication of the value interests of concerned bystanders."[129]

Nor did the plaintiffs' claim that the federal tax exemptions impaired efforts to have the public schools desegregated establish an injury to them that would support standing. Here the fatal defect, in the view of the majority, was that the alleged injury was "not fairly traceable to the Government conduct [plaintiffs] challenge as unlawful."[130] They did not allege that there were enough tax-exempt discriminatory private schools in their communities that withdrawal of tax-exempt status would make any appreciable difference in efforts to integrate the public schools. The causal link between tax exemption and injury to the plaintiffs was thus too weak in the majority's view:

> It is, first, uncertain how many racially discriminatory private schools are in fact receiving tax exemptions. Moreover, it is entirely speculative ... whether withdrawal of a tax exemption from any particular school would lead the school to change its policies ... It is just as speculative whether any given parent of a child attending such a private school would decide to transfer the child to public school as a result of any changes in educational or financial policy made by the private school once it was threatened with loss of tax-exempt status. It is also pure speculation whether, in a particular community, a large enough number of the numerous relevant school officials and parents would reach decisions that collectively would have a significant impact on the racial composition of the public schools.[131]

The majority also concluded that its affirmance of standing in the earlier Green case[132] was not controlling. The Green case involved only one state, was based on findings of the extensive role of private segregated schools in Mississippi, and was brought at a time when the IRS policy was to grant tax exemption to segregated schools. The majority did not hold that standing was erroneously granted in Green; it simply concluded that the case was distinguishable.

Justice Stevens in dissent argued that "tax policy, economics, and pure logic all confirm the conclusion that [plaintiffs'] injury in fact is fairly traceable to the Government's allegedly wrongful conduct."[133] Justice Brennan in dissent asserted that the earlier decision in Green should be controlling and concluded: "What is most disturbing about today's decision, therefore, is not the standing analysis applied, but the indifference evidenced by the Court to the detrimental effects that racially segregated schools, supported by tax-exempt status from the federal government, have on the [plaintiffs'] attempt to obtain an education in a racially integrated school system. I cannot join such indifference, and would give the [plaintiffs] a chance to prove their case on the merits."[134]

It remains to be seen whether *Allen v. Wright* has closed the door on third-party challenges to the tax-exempt status of another. It is possible that complaints may be framed and facts alleged that will satisfy the Supreme Court's standing requirements. But the task confronting plaintiffs' lawyers, even in racial discrimination cases, has obviously been made very difficult.[135]

An important policy question raised by the standing cases is whether it is desirable to permit interested persons to challenge Treasury and IRS interpretations of tax expenditures on the ground that the interpretations improperly allow benefits to certain taxpayers.[136] Challengers likely to bring such suits include parties similar to those in the racial discrimination cases: interested congressmen, public-interest law firms seeking to contain generosity to others whose interests and activities they consider contrary to their clients' goals, and competitors of the beneficiaries. One objection to enactment of a statute giving standing to challenge Treasury and IRS interpretations is the concern that it would add to the already extensive litigation by taxpayers resisting Treasury interpretations and actions that result in the assertion of tax liabilities against them. It is doubtful, however, that a standing statute would add a sufficient volume of cases to overwhelm the courts in tax matters, or even that such cases would constitute a significant percentage of tax litigation.[137] Moreover, the sheer volume of tax expenditures may make it desirable to give concerned citizens an avenue other than Congress by which to check an overgenerous Treasury. One check already exists in the conceded right of taxpayers to protest the assertion of tax liabilities against them if the Treasury interpretation is arbitrary, unreasonable, or whatever standard courts now use. There is thus a judicial safeguard against an *overzealous* Treasury. The unanswered question is whether a judicial safeguard is needed against an *overgenerous* Treasury, or whether the only check should be a complaint to Congress. A realistic view of the congressional agenda, together with the likelihood that overgenerous Treasury action is considerably less frequent than overzealousness, constitutes a strong argument for allowing standing as a safeguard against generosity.[138] For these reasons people having a reasonable claim to be harmed by Treasury generosity to others should be able to challenge tax expenditures in the tax law.

Judicial cases involving constitutional or interpretative issues with regard to tax expenditures should be decided in the same manner as cases involving direct government spending programs. Given the federal government's own assertion that tax expenditures "can be viewed as alternatives to budget outlays, credit assistance or other policy instruments" and the "[tax] expenditures have objectives similar to those programs funded through direct appropriations,"[139] it is difficult to see how this position can be denied. Whether a case involves a First Amendment religious or free speech issue, discrimination on the grounds of race or sex, or a statute providing that the receipt of governmental assistance places undue restrictions on recipients of that assistance, the result should be the same for both forms of assistance.

The same analysis may be applied to the state action doctrine. If the presence of state action or involvement turns on the amount of government assistance or the relation of the assistance to the event involved, whether the assistance is a direct outlay or a tax expenditure should not be a critical factor. The state action doctrines developed under direct assistance should be equally applicable to tax expenditures. Decisions on standing to sue should likewise involve the same procedures and reasoning for both tax expenditures and direct outlays.

Courts and litigants are moving toward recognition of the connection between tax and direct spending programs, as early cases such as Green v. Connally, McGlotten v. Connally, and Nyquist demonstrate. The recent Supreme Court decision in Taxation With Representation is a strong affirmation of the connection.[140] Except for occasional footnote references to articles, judges and lawyers still make no direct use of tax expenditure terminology or of the list of items in the tax expenditure budget.[141] It must be remembered, however, that legislators themselves only recently grasped the significance of tax expenditures, the ease with which a program can be structured as either a direct program or a tax expenditure, and the usefulness of a tax expenditure approach in overcoming legislative or political obstacles to a direct outlay program. It is likely that, as the courts and lawyers become aware of this flexibility and of the interrelationship between tax expenditures and direct outlays, they will maintain a close decisional link between the two. If the courts do not take this view, an absurd governmental process could result. Legislators could simply circumvent judicial barriers to direct outlay programs by passing tax expenditures providing the same assistance, but with judicial sanction. The irrationality of such a process and its consequences for our tax and constitutional systems would be profound.

6

INTERNATIONAL ASPECTS

THE TAX EXPENDITURE CONCEPT can be usefully applied to a variety of international tax matters. This chapter discusses its possible applications in four particularly important areas.

One is the determination of jurisdictional issues under the U.S. tax system. An example is the income tax. The United States taxes the worldwide income of its citizens, residents, and corporations. Policymakers can clarify jurisdictional issues by using the tax expenditure concept to decide what provisions of the tax law establish a normative tax on worldwide income and what provisions are tax expenditures—government assistance. In addition, to accommodate the international system of income taxes, the United States allows a foreign tax credit to avoid double income taxation: a U.S. taxpayer can credit against U.S. tax liability on foreign income any income taxes paid to other countries on income arising in those countries and taxed by the United States. Since the credit is only for a foreign income tax, the tax expenditure concept is a useful means of determining whether the foreign tax is really an income tax or some other type of tax. In the same context, the United States taxes foreigners on income they receive from the United States. The issue is whether a normative standard exists for taxation of foreigners so that tax expenditure analysis may be applied, or whether only ad hoc, essentially pragmatic rules are involved. Finally, the double taxation treaties between the United States and other countries must be scrutinized for the presence of tax expenditures.

A second significant application of the tax expenditure concept involves the resolution of disputes that may arise under the tax clauses in international agreements, such as interpretations of the General Agreement on Tariffs and Trade (GATT) and the Treaty of Rome.

A third significant application involves the rapid development of tax expenditure lists in other countries. These efforts to distinguish normative provisions from tax expenditure provisions increase understanding of the tax expenditure concept and raise other interesting questions.

The fourth significant application involves international comparative analyses of budget expenditures and tax burdens. So far these comparisons have disregarded the government assistance provided by every country through its tax system. This omission seriously distorts the comparisons to the point of unreliability. International use of the tax expenditure concept can produce more realistic comparisons. Although the normative rules and tax expenditures of each country are determined by its own domestic tax history, and the underlying concepts are not governed by the approaches of other countries, for certain international comparisons a tax expenditure classification that harmonizes the tax expenditure lists of all the countries involved is appropriate.

U.S. International Income Tax Provisions
RESIDENCE JURISDICTION

In developing an income tax a country must decide what the international scope of that tax is to be. Basic is the jurisdictional decision how to treat the foreign-source income of its residents. Historically, countries have divided on this choice. Some countries, influenced in part by their history of a "schedular tax system," under which the various types of income each had a separate computation and rate schedule, confine their tax to income arising only within the country and do not tax residents' income from outside the country.[1] Other countries, influenced in part by their history of a "global tax system," under which all types of income and expense are lumped together in one computation to which one rate schedule applies, choose to tax their residents on a worldwide basis, taxing income from both foreign and domestic sources.[2] Some countries fall in between, applying domestic-source jurisdiction to some types of income (and thus not taxing, say, income from foreign branches and dividends from foreign subsidiaries) and worldwide jurisdiction to other types (and thus taxing, say, investment income from abroad, except parent-subsidiary dividends). Again, there is no international rule that forces a particular choice upon a country. Each country's decision about how extensively its income tax will cover foreign-source income is based on broad policy considerations such as trade balances and its own history as a capital importer or exporter. The tax expenditure concept has no relevance to this basic choice. Once the decision is made, it becomes the normative background against which to apply the tax expenditure concept.

The United States from the start in 1913 applied its income tax on a worldwide basis. The decision was in a sense an intuitive one, made without debate. But it determined the normative character of the U.S. income tax. It was to be a tax that exercised worldwide jurisdiction over its citizens and residents, as well as source jurisdiction over foreigners (nonresidents). A country that decides to exercise worldwide jurisdiction must provide a structure to support that decision. It must distinguish residents from foreigners, who are taxed only on income from sources within the country. In making this decision, again without any compulsion from an international norm, a country has a choice of rules. In its treatment of individuals, it may define a resident as a person who is present in the country a certain length of time, a person who has an intention to reside for an indefinite period but not permanently, or a person who is domiciled in the country.[3] Or a country may go further—as the United Stated does—and decide to apply worldwide jurisdiction not only to its residents but also to its citizens wherever they reside.[4]

TAX EXPENDITURES IN THE TREATMENT OF FOREIGN INCOME

The federal budget includes in its tax expenditure list the various special provisions excluding from tax some of the income earned abroad by its citizens and residents living abroad and the special deduction granted to those citizens and residents for housing expenses above a base amount.[5] These provisions are tax expenditures since they deviate from the U.S. norm of taxation of the worldwide income of its citizens and residents. Both the need for these federal subsidies and their efficiency must be evaluated. The tax expenditures are defended on the grounds that they are necessary to enable U.S. companies with operations abroad to employ U.S. citizens rather than foreigners and that employment of U.S. citizens is necessary to meet foreign competition and to increase U.S. exports. Thus the argument rests in part on the contention that U.S. citizens are necessary to the success of overseas activities and in part on the view that U.S. citizens—engineers, managers, and so on—are likely to utilize U.S. rather than foreign subcontractors, machinery, and components, the result being an increase in U.S. exports. The empirical evidence to support these propositions is weak. The arguments are advanced largely by U.S. construction companies operating in the Middle East (which under their compensation arrangements would have to bear the higher U.S. tax if the exclusion and special deduction were not available) or, on different grounds, by U.S. charitable organizations, including churches, having employees abroad. Even if accepted, these arguments do not justify subsidies for the many U.S. citizens working abroad in activities that have no direct bearing on the U.S. economy.[6]

In its treatment of corporations, a country may define as a resident only a corporation incorporated within the country, as the United States does; a corporation incorporated outside the country but managed and controlled from or having its "seat of management" within the country; or it may decide to use both tests to determine which corporations are residents.

Here the decisions as to the normative background become more complex. Although the United States uses place of incorporation as the test of residence, it recognizes that the test is highly artificial, since it is very simple to form a foreign subsidiary that is wholly owned and managed by the U.S. parent. An "incorporation test," coupled with the rule that a corporation is a taxpayer separate and distinct from its shareholder(s), leaves the profits of the subsidiary untaxed by the United States until repatriated as dividends from the subsidiary to its U.S. parent. But this result is contrary to the rule that prescribes immediate taxation of the foreign branches of U.S. companies without regard to any transmission of their profits to the United States.[7] Consequently, the tax expenditure list includes the deferral of U.S. income tax—that is, postponing taxation until a formal repatriation through a dividend—on the income of foreign subsidiaries controlled by U.S. companies ("controlled" subsidiaries are those in which more than 50 percent of voting power is held by U.S. shareholders). For some time (at least up to 1981) the Treasury and some legislators have sought to eliminate this tax deferral provision.[8] The efforts have not met with success in Congress because of opposition by U.S. international business. Business asserts the importance of tax deferral as an incentive to invest abroad, with attendant benefits in the forms of increased U.S. exports and jobs created in producing the exports and managing the foreign subsidiary; and as a form of financial assistance to meet the competition in other countries of foreign companies operating under an exemption approach. Here also empirical supporting data are scant. Indeed, labor organizations claim that foreign investment means a loss of U.S. jobs. Most of those who have studied the issue believe that the income tax law should be neutral in the choice between placing U.S. capital abroad or leaving it at home.[9]

Until its repeal in the Tax Reform Act of 1984, another important tax expenditure was the U.S. deferral of tax on part of the income of a so-called domestic international sales corporation (DISC). DISCs were companies, generally paper corporations, that in form exported the goods of their parent company or received an unearned commission on the export by the parent. The deferral lasted as long as the profits were invested in "export assets," a loose, easily met test. The avowed purpose of the DISC legislation, adopted in 1971 as a result of a Treasury Department proposal, was to provide a tax incentive to increase U.S. exports. The Treasury was required to report annually on the efficacy of the DISC legislation to accomplish its purpose. The reports from 1977 on generally indicated that although the DISC provision cost more than $1.5 billion annually, it did little or nothing to increase exports.[10] Treasury efforts to repeal DISC failed,[11] but the insistence of U.S. trading partners that the provision violated the GATT forced Congress in 1984 to repeal DISC for most companies. DISC, however, was replaced by another tax expenditure to subsidize American business operations abroad, the foreign sales corporation (FSC) provision.[12]

Another tax expenditure involving activities outside the United States is the "tax credit for corporations receiving income from doing business in United States possessions." The principal possession involved is Puerto Rico. The tax expenditure results from long-standing provisions originally designed to help U.S. companies meet foreign competition.[13] In recent years, however, the provisions have been defended on the need to assist Puerto Rican employment by encouraging U.S. firms to invest in Puerto Rico. In the early 1960s Puerto Rico included tax incentive provisions in its income tax in order to attract U.S. investors; the incentives had the effect of eliminating the Puerto Rican income tax on the operations of such investors. At that time the U.S. tax system excluded from taxation the income of U.S. branches in Puerto Rico, and, if a Puerto Rican subsidiary were used, it could be liquidated on a tax-free basis so that the Puerto Rican profits would not be taxed by the United States. Since 1976 the tax expenditure has taken the form of allowing a U.S. corporation a 46 percent foreign tax credit (the U.S. corporate tax rate) against U.S. tax for income from Puerto Rico, even though no income tax has in fact been paid to Puerto Rico.

The Treasury Department must also publish an annual report on the Puerto Rico tax expenditure, which involves a cost of over $1 billion annually. The reports, though cautiously worded, have indicated that the provisions are a bonanza to some U.S. companies with Puerto Rican operations and have done relatively little to increase the well-being of Puerto Rico, especially in terms of the employment of Puerto Ricans.[14] Moreover, the tax subsidy appears too wasteful and poorly designed to achieve its avowed objective. For example, the amount of the tax expenditure per employee in chemical companies was $38,446 in 1978, compared with average per-employee compensation of $14,382. The chemical industry accounted for 57 percent of the total tax expenditure but for only 20 percent of the total employment by the U.S. companies. The food, textile, and apparel industries accounted for only 8 percent of the total tax expenditure but for 34 percent of the total employment. The contents of the reports indicate that the sensible course would be either to eliminate the tax expenditure benefit and to use the funds instead in a direct program constructed to assist Puerto Rico or drastically to restructure the tax expenditure to correspond to an effective direct program. At the very least the reports require an impartial study, uninfluenced by the desires both of the U.S. companies to retain their present tax benefits and of the Puerto Rican officials interested in enticing U.S. investors to maintain the present tax expenditure. In 1982 Congress focused for the first time on the wastage of funds under this tax expenditure and added some restrictions that may somewhat lessen the benefits of using domestic subsidiaries operating in Puerto Rico. The tax expenditure, however, remains basically inefficient.

TREATMENT OF DOUBLE TAXATION

In most countries the basic decision to exercise worldwide jurisdiction entails a corollary need to adopt some mechanism to eliminate the double taxation that would result if both the country of source and the country of residence taxed the income from the source country. Some countries, including the United States, unilaterally use a foreign tax credit mechanism that allows a credit against the income tax of the residence country for the income tax paid to the source country. Other countries use double taxation treaties to provide for such a credit. Countries that exercise only source jurisdiction essentially exempt foreign-source income and thus do not have to address the double taxation problem unless their source rules are such as to reach income arising in another country. The elimination of double taxation through restriction of the income tax to source jurisdiction only, and thus allowing exemption of foreign source income, is sometimes referred to as the application of the "territoriality principle" to international taxation. Again, there is no international norm compelling the use of the foreign tax credit approach, the exemption approach, or of various intermediate approaches that have been developed.

Since the foreign tax credit is an accommodation to the generally accepted international system of seeking in one way or another to eliminate or reduce double taxation, the presence of the credit in the U.S. tax system is not a tax expenditure. Nor would a decision to avoid double taxation by exercising only source (or "territorial") jurisdiction be a tax expenditure.

A foreign tax credit is a complex mechanism and requires a number of normative rules for its operation.[15] Thus, although countries using a foreign tax credit are willing to allow the source country to tax the transaction first, thereby leaving only a residual tax for the country of residence—and often no tax if the tax rate in the source country is equal to or higher than the tax rate in the residence country—no country is willing to allow the credit to diminish the residence country tax on domestic income. Such a diminution could occur if the source country tax were higher than the residence country tax and if the credit for the higher foreign tax were allowed to spill over against the tax on domestic income. To prevent this result, countries using a foreign tax credit limit its application to the level of the domestic tax on the foreign-source income taxed by the other countries. This limit can take a variety of forms: a "per-country" limitation, under which the limit is applied separately to each foreign country taxing income also taxed by the residence country;[16] an "overall limitation"—the general U.S. approach—under which the limit rule is applied collectively to all foreign countries taxing income also taxed by the residence country;[17] a rule that applies the stronger of the two limitations in the particular case; a rule that applies the weaker of the two limitations in the particular case; a rule that attempts to refine the per-country limitation to a transactional approach separating transactions within a country; a rule refining the overall limitation by excluding certain transactions that could disturb that limitation and applying a separate limitation to the particular transaction—the U.S. approach.[18] Here also, there is no single normative rule; each country is free to set whatever limit it chooses on the basic decision to allow the foreign tax credit.[19]

Once a particular limitation is chosen, its application requires subsidiary rules, such as source rules to determine whether there is foreign-source income to support the credit, and rules to determine the allocation of expenses, including expenses in the residence country, to compute the foreign-source net income to which the limitation applies.[20] In most countries, including the United States, the development of these rules is usually a technical matter, involving normative structural provisions; neither tax expenditures nor tax penalties result.[21] In 1981, however, Congress temporarily suspended the technical rules in the Treasury Regulations for allocating research and development expenses incurred in the United States between domestic- and foreign-source income,[22] and provided that all such expenses be allocated to U.S. source income. This legislation, by arbitrarily increasing foreign-source income, increased the availability of the foreign tax credit for certain corporations. The legislation was expressly intended to provide an incentive to multinational corporations to locate their research and development activities in the United States and is therefore a tax expenditure.[23]

QUALIFICATION OF FOREIGN TAXES FOR THE FOREIGN TAX CREDIT

One of the basic problems under the foreign tax credit approach is the determination of which foreign taxes qualify for the credit. Since the credit is allowed against the U.S. income tax, only foreign "income" taxes qualify.[24] There has been debate from time to time over this restriction, with contentions, for example, that foreign excise taxes should qualify for a credit. But the rule restricting the credit to income taxes intuitively makes sense, since the double taxation aimed at is income tax double taxation. Furthermore, because excise taxes are usually passed on in a commodity's price, they should not qualify for a credit against an income tax. The assumption here, of course, is that an income tax is not passed on in price, since if it were the credit approach itself would make little sense.[25]

The basic issue remains how to define "income tax" for the purpose of the credit. Tax expenditure analysis can help answer this question. The general criterion applied in the United States for defining a foreign tax as an income tax is whether the foreign tax has the essential characteristics of the U.S. income tax.[26] Apparently, then, this standard requires that a foreign tax rather closely resemble our normative concept of an income tax. Accordingly, the foreign tax must be imposed on "net gain."[27] Hence a tax on gross income or gross receipts would not qualify as an income tax.[28] Although the foreign tax need not tax "net income" in every case, gross receipts must be reduced to reflect "significant" expenses and capital expenditures.[29]

The standards used to determine an income tax should also recognize that there can be differing responses to particular questions and that each of those responses can constitute part of a normative tax. The Treasury Regulations stress that the foreign tax must meet the requirement that income actually be realized in the U.S. sense, and they permit only a few exceptions.[30] This requirement is acceptable if it is understood as applying to situations involving artificial or fictitious gains, such as the use of "posted prices" as the base of the tax, or other estimated gains. But it would be inappropriate if it were used to deny credit for a general income tax that includes in the base imputed income from owner-occupied homes,[31] or appreciation in value reached annually under an accrual concept. Such a general income tax would be closer to a normative income tax than is the U.S. income tax and should be allowed a credit. Even if a country's income tax contains tax expenditures or tax penalties (as does the U.S. income tax), it should qualify as an income tax for foreign tax credit purposes. Thus the presence of a tax expenditure to encourage oil drilling (allowing the current deduction of intangible drilling expenses rather than their capitalization) or of a tax penalty to discourage oil drilling (denying any deduction for drilling expenses) should not prevent an income tax from qualifying.

Still another issue to be decided in structuring a foreign tax credit is the application of the credit to dividends from a foreign corporation. As was mentioned earlier, most countries, as an exercise of source jurisdiction, impose a withholding tax on dividends paid by their domestic corporations to foreign shareholders. The foreign shareholders may be corporations that are parents of the subsidiary domestic corporation—or they may be portfolio investors, either corporate or individual. These countries will also apply their regular income tax to the domestic subsidiaries of foreign corporations.

A foreign tax credit should be available in the shareholder's country for the tax withheld on any dividends from the foreign subsidiary (the domestic subsidiary in the perspective of the taxing country, as in the preceding paragraph). But should the credit also apply to the income tax incurred by the foreign subsidiary? That subsidiary is an entity in itself, and the foreign income tax legally is being imposed on it and not on the parent. Also, under the U.S. tax deferral rule discussed above, the parent and subsidiary are regarded as separate entities, so that the parent is not currently taxed on the undistributed profits of the subsidiary. But in an economic sense, the parent and subsidiary are linked and the tax on the subsidiary is really being borne by the parent. If the foreign operation were a branch, the company could credit the foreign tax on the profits of the branch. Also, in situations involving a domestic parent and a domestic subsidiary, tax provisions generally prevent a dual imposition of the corporate income tax by not taxing the parent on an intercorporate dividend or by applying only a low tax rate to that dividend. For these reasons, the U.S. foreign tax credit system allows, on the payment of a dividend from a foreign subsidiary to a U.S. parent, a credit for both the withheld tax on the dividend and the foreign income tax borne by the subsidiary. The technical approach is to "gross up" the dividend by the withheld tax and the income tax applicable to the profits represented by the dividend, with the grossed-up dividend included in the parent's taxable income and a credit then allowed for both taxes. The credit for the income tax on the subsidiary is called a "deemed credit" or an "indirect credit."[32]

Although technical details of an indirect foreign tax credit—the percentage of ownership required to qualify, the number of tiers of subsidiaries through which the credit will extend—may differ from country to country, the indirect credit itself is a necessary part of the technical implementation of a comprehensive foreign tax credit system. As such it does not constitute a tax expenditure. Indeed, if a country granted a foreign tax credit for branch operations but denied it for subsidiaries, a tax penalty would be involved.

SOURCE JURISDICTION

In developing an income tax a country must, in addition to making a jurisdictional decision on the extent to which it will tax its own nationals—individual residents (and/or citizens) and corporations—also make a jurisdictional decision on how it should treat foreigners receiving income from the country. Every country with an income tax will tax the foreigner on income from sources within the country. A contrary result would be almost impossible to maintain, since its own tax-payers are being taxed on income earned within the country.

Given that a country will apply its income tax to foreigners deriving income from sources within the country, an interesting issue is whether there is a normative standard applicable to the treatment of the foreigners. The Schanz-Haig-Simons definition of income is the basic element used to structure taxation of a country's own taxpayers, but it does not specify which foreigners should be subject to the income tax and, if they are subject to tax, how they are to be taxed. The Schanz-Haig-Simons definition does not concern itself with source rules. Each country seems to devise its source rules on an ad hoc basis.[33] Despite the efforts of international organizations and tax treaties to harmonize the source rules of various countries, there is not yet a norm establishing the source for all types of income.[34] Countries' rate-setting practices also vary. Generally it is accepted that a country may apply its regular income tax rules and rates to the business net income of foreigners. Usually the investment income of foreigners is taxed by a flat rate on a gross basis. But there are no internationally accepted norms establishing what level of activity constitutes doing business, when investment income should be treated as part of the business income, what flat rate should apply to income taxed on a gross basis, whether all investment income should be subject to the same flat rate, and so on.

Nor is it possible for a country to set a legislative norm for taxation of foreigners, deviations from which constitute tax expenditures. Two examples will show why. Suppose a country decides to treat services performed there by foreign lawyers as domestic source but services performed there by foreign opera singers as foreign source. Neither provision can be classified as a tax expenditure, because there is no norm stating that services must always be sourced in the country where performed nor that all types of services must be sourced under the same rule. Or suppose a country generally applies a 30 percent rate to such income but imposes unilaterally a 5 percent rate on royalties and agrees by treaty to vary the rate from 0 to 15 percent on other types of investment income. Again, it is not possible to assert that any tax expenditure is involved, because there is no norm stating that a country must use a single rate applicable to all types of investment income.

Thus it is clear that rules governing the taxation of foreigners are not susceptible to tax expenditure analysis. In this area, tax legislative draftsmen are not involved in working out the technical rules of a decision on a normative issue. Instead they are supplying rules to implement ad hoc answers to individualized cases. These varying rules involve neither tax expenditures nor tax penalties.[35]

DOUBLE TAXATION TREATIES

TREATY PROVISIONS

Unilateral steps to avoid double taxation fail to solve several issues. For example, differing source rules can produce double taxation not relieved by an exemption or foreign tax credit approach. Also, although double taxation does not exist under the foreign tax credit approach if the foreign tax is at a higher rate than the domestic tax—the excess simply being disallowed under the limitation on the credit—the higher foreign tax can still prevent a neutral decision between domestic investment and foreign investment. Furthermore, even though exemption and credit mechanisms may in some situations eliminate double taxation, countries may regard it as either administratively difficult or as inconvenient to taxpayers to apply a tax at source in every situation. Even when a country is determined to tax at source, it may find itself handicapped, through lack of sufficient knowledge of the entire transaction, in applying its tax. The residence country desiring to tax on a worldwide basis may in turn find itself handicapped by a lack of knowledge regarding the foreign-source income.

To solve these and other problems affecting international income tax transactions, most countries have entered into bilateral treaties "for the avoidance of double taxation and the prevention of fiscal evasion," to use the U.S. treaty phraseology.[36] Over time these treaties have become systematized, so that in general their provisions are quite similar.

The basic issue presented by these bilateral treaties is whether their modifications of a country's unilateral rules constitute tax expenditures or tax penalties. Because the assertion of source jurisdiction and the accompanying detailed rules are an amalgam of experience, pragmatic decisions, the judgment on the need for equitable equivalence to the taxation of residents, and adherence to the international norms that exist, it follows automatically that tax expenditure analysis cannot apply to provisions that modify or otherwise affect the source jurisdiction of the treaty countries. For example, in establishing rates applicable to investment income, most treaties provide for a reciprocal reduction in withholding rates. Generally, countries in their domestic legislation impose a uniform flat rate of tax on source country gross passive investment income. The use of a flat rate on gross income is regarded as a surrogate, administratively necessary, for the application of the regular rate schedule to gross income less actual expenses. The approach makes it unnecessary to determine in the domestic legislation the exact amount of a particular foreign investor's expenses or even the average amount of expenses for a particular class of income. But the treaty negotiators, by closely analyzing comparative data on the average expenses for several classes of income (such as royalties or interest versus dividends), are able to devise withholding rates for particular classes of income that are more refined than the general statutory flat rate. Hence a treaty's reduction in withholding rates is not a tax expenditure, because such reductions are generally attempts to make the tax burden closer to what would be imposed if the regular tax rate schedule were applied to net investment income.

Likewise, tax expenditures are not created by other restrictions on source jurisdiction, such as those on income from business activities and the performance of services. Restrictions on taxation of business activities center on the definition of a "permanent establishment." This definition, a refinement of the usual "engaged in trade or business" requirement, provides certainty and reduces the administrative burden of the foreigner filing a return in the source country. The restrictions on the performance of services by a foreigner in the source country are usually phrased in terms of amount of time spent or amount earned, and are likewise designed to eliminate temporary, minor activity from entanglement with the tax rules of the source country.

A different analysis is required for treaty articles involving residence jurisdiction. Generally the treaties entered into by the United States and by other countries exercising worldwide jurisdiction restrict source jurisdiction but not residence jurisdiction. However, some treaties do reduce the U.S. income tax on its citizens and residents. When such a reduction would result in a tax expenditure if legislated as a statute then a treaty provision producing the same effect should likewise be considered a tax expenditure. The U.S. tax expenditure lists, however, have not yet applied this analysis.

The necessity to apply tax expenditure analysis to such treaty provisions became evident in 1981 when the congressional tax committees wrote to the Senate Foreign Relations Committee, which has jurisdiction over tax treaties, stating that they did not approve using treaties to reduce the tax on U.S. citizens and residents. Such reductions, the tax committees thought, should be a legislative matter.[37] The Senate Foreign Relations Committee concurred. Some of the provisions that generated this congressional concern were:

> A provision in the Morocco treaty making eligible for the foreign tax credit payments of compulsory loans to the government. The treaty was ratified with a reservation limiting the provision to loans made before 1988. The proposed treaty with Israel contained a similar provision.
>
> A provision in the Jamaica treaty excepting Jamaica from Internal Revenue Code rules on the deductibility of expenses incurred in attending conventions outside North America. The treaty was ratified, but the committee indicated its dislike for the provision; approval of the provision largely rested on an earlier personal assurance made by President Reagan to President Seaga of Jamaica—an assurance made, according to Washington reports, without the knowledge of the Treasury Department.
>
> A provision in the Israel treaty permitting U.S. taxpayers to obtain a deduction for direct contributions to charitable organizations in Israel. The committee ratified the treaty but indicated its strong disapproval of including such provisions in future treaties.

Although earlier actions by the Senate Foreign Relations Committee had implied similar disapproval of the use of treaties to reduce the tax on U.S. citizens and residents,[38] firm expression of this above viewpoint was new. In contrast, the committee reports accompanying the Morocco, Jamaica, and Israel treaties stated that "the Director of the Congressional Budget Office has examined the Committee's budget estimate and agrees that the effect on budget receipts will be negligible. In keeping with the spirit of section 308(a) of the Budget Act, and after consultation with the Director of the Congressional Budget Office, the Committee states that the treaty does not provide any new budget authority or any new or increased tax expenditures."[39] The explanation for this claim is that the Congressional Budget Office had simply not considered or used tax expenditure analysis in the context of a treaty. But there is no reason not to apply the analysis in the case of U.S. taxpayers. The classification test to apply is whether the treaty provision, if enacted as an IRC provision, would produce a tax expenditure.

Under this test, the charitable contribution provision in the Israel treaty is no different from the code's charitable contribution tax expenditure. The Jamaica convention provision is somewhat harder to classify, since it involves the borderline between personal and business expenses, and the IRC rules governing foreign conventions have never been listed as tax expenditures.[40] The Morocco treaty provision that a compulsory loan is eligible for the foreign tax credit involves a tax expenditure, since a technical interpretation of the IRC credit would not consider the loan to be an income tax.[41]

In sum, the U.S. tax expenditure lists have correctly omitted any provision dealing with the U.S. taxation of foreign individuals or corporations. The lists, however, need to be refined to include treaty provisions that would constitute tax expenditures if they had resulted from unilateral legislation.

TREATY NEGOTIATIONS

The tax expenditure concept can be usefully employed in tax treaty negotiations, although so far treaty negotiators do not appear to have recognized its potential. Treaty negotiations should consider whether the unilateral statute being modified constitutes a tax expenditure in that country's system or is a part of its normative tax structure. The issue can arise during consideration of the nondiscrimination clause contained in most tax treaties. This clause in general prevents a source country from imposing on nationals of the residence country taxes more burdensome than are applied to its own nationals in the same circumstances and from imposing on enterprises owned by foreigners but operated within that country, whether in corporate or branch form, a tax burden higher than is imposed on domestically owned enterprises.

Although the nondiscrimination clause entitles nationals of the residence country to the benefits of the normative provisions of the source country's tax rules, it does not guarantee them the right to benefit from the source country's tax expenditures. Suppose country A is negotiating a tax treaty with country B. Country A grants a tax credit for research and development but country B does not. Country B employs an investment tax credit but limits it to corporations organized and operated in country B. Country B's tax law also includes a provision permitting businesses to use the last-in, first-out (LIFO) method of inventory valuation if they also use it for financial reporting purposes. The following conclusions emerge:

Country A is not entitled to insist on obtaining a research and development tax expenditure for its nationals receiving income from or doing business in country B if the tax expenditure is not granted by country B to its own residents. Country A would in effect be asking country B to create a tax expenditure for the benefit of country A's nationals.

Country A is not entitled to obtain for its residents the application of the investment credit tax expenditure of country B even if its residents are receiving income from country B. Country B presumably could limit its direct spending provisions to residents of country B, so long as there was no contrary provision in domestic law or other treaties giving nonresidents the same status as residents in respect of such spending. Similarly, if country B decides to use tax expenditures rather than direct spending, the nondiscrimination clause in a tax treaty has no application.

If a resident of country A is engaged in trade or business through a permanent establishment in country B or if residents of country A are the controlling shareholders of a country B corporation, with such permanent establishment or corporation subject to the country B basic income tax, then country A is entitled to obtain the application of the normative tax provisions of the country B income tax for the permanent establishment or corporation. As a result, country A is entitled to insist on the availability of the LIFO inventory method for its nationals' permanent establishments and controlled corporations.

The same analysis can be applied to the troublesome issues arising in negotiations over the international application of a particular country's corporation income tax when that tax involves a form of "integration" with the individual income tax.[42] This problem is especially difficult in negotiations between a country with a classical corporation tax and a country with an imputation system or other form of integration. Suppose country X has a classical corporate tax system (as does the United States), treating the corporate income tax and the individual income tax on shareholders as separate taxes, and country Y has an imputation system, such as a shareholder credit for all or part of the corporate income tax. Country Y, however, grants the shareholder credit only to country Y residents who are shareholders in country Y corporations but denies the credit to shareholders from other countries. The question is whether country X can insist that country Y provide a shareholder credit for shareholder-nationals of country X receiving dividends from country Y corporations. Under the analytic technique employed above, if the shareholder credit is a tax expenditure within country Y's system, then country X is not entitled to assert that country Y must extend the credit to country X nationals on the basis of the nondiscrimination clause. On the other hand, if the imputation credit is part of the normal structure of country Y's tax, then country X could base its argument on the nondiscrimination clause.[43] In this context, it is interesting to note that Canada and France list their corporate integration systems as tax expenditures, while Germany does not; yet France and Canada by treaty have extended their shareholder credits to U.S. nationals, but Germany has refused to do so.

Under existing interpretations, treaty negotiators (and interpreters) appear to view tax expenditures simply as "tax provisions" and hence do apply the nondiscrimination clauses to them.[44] It does seem strange, however, for a country to subject its subsidies to tax treaty nondiscrimination clauses simply because it uses the tax rather than direct spending mechanism. On the other hand, under existing interpretations of the nondiscrimination clause, if the source country (country Y in our examples) had adopted a split-rate structure or a dividend deduction system, then the system would have to be applied to dividends paid to nationals of the residence country (country X), whether the shareholder credit system is regarded as normative or as involving a tax expenditure. The nondiscrimination clause, as now worded, does not require the allowance of the imputation credit to foreign shareholders, at least not if the dividend is paid to a country X corporation that controls the country Y corporation paying the dividend. This rather untidy situation results from the lack of international agreement on (1) whether systems that have partially integrated corporate and personal income tax constitute tax expenditures or form part of the normal structure and (2) how such systems should be applied to foreign shareholders.[45] Use of the tax expenditure concept can help sharpen the analysis if not provide definitive answers to these questions.

The Resolution of International Tax Disputes

A number of important international tax disputes and the solutions so far adopted or available are susceptible to tax expenditure analysis.

Two such disputes involved the General Agreement on Tariffs and Trade (GATT) and the Treaty of Rome.

GATT: DISC AND THE EXEMPTION APPROACH TO INTERNATIONAL DOUBLE TAXATION

The European Community and Canada challenged the U.S. income tax incentive for exports, the domestic international sales corporation (DISC) provision, as being contrary to the prohibition on export subsidies in the General Agreement on Tariffs and Trade.[46] The DISC provisions technically provide a deferral of U.S. income tax on a portion of the profits earned by taxpayers exporting U.S. products.

The GATT Council asked a panel of experts to consider the European challenge to DISC. The panel found DISC to be a proscribed export subsidy within the GATT rules. The panel first examined the economic effect of the DISC legislation and concluded that it "conferred a tax benefit ... essentially related to exports."[47] It then stated that "if the corporation income tax was reduced with respect to export related activities and was unchanged with respect to domestic activities for the internal market this would tend to lead to an expansion of export activity."[48] Noting that, according to the U.S. Treasury, exports had increased as a result of the DISC legislation, and considering that "the fact that so many DISCs had been created was evidence that DISC status conferred a substantial benefit,"[49] the panel concluded that the legislation should be regarded as an export subsidy. In determining whether the deferral of tax under the DISC provisions constituted a remission of tax or an exemption from tax, the panel "was not convinced that a deferral, *simply* because it is given for an indeterminate period, was equal to a remission or an exemption."[50] Nevertheless, the panel noted that no provision was made for the interest component normally associated with a later or deferred payment of tax. As a result, the panel ruled that the DISC legislation constituted a partial exemption from tax and hence a subsidy, leading presumptively to any or a combination of the following consequences in the export sector: "(a) lowering of prices, (b) increase of sales effort and (c) increase of profits per unit. Because the subsidy was both significant and broadly based it was to be expected that all of these effects would occur and that, if one occurred, the other two would not necessarily be excluded. A concentration of the subsidy benefits on prices could lead to substantial reduction in prices. The Panel did not accept that a reduction in prices in export markets need automatically to be accompanied by similar reduction in domestic markets."[51] These conclusions were supported by statements by American individuals and companies about the effectiveness of DISC, and the panel felt that it should take this evidence into consideration.[52] The panel therefore concluded that "the DISC legislation in some cases had effects which were not in accordance with the United States' obligations under Article XVI:4 [of the GATT],"[53] and that "the various options under the DISC legislation for the allocation of profits from export sales . . . could influence the size of the exemption."[54]

It is difficult to see how the panel could have reached any other conclusion. DISC is included in the U.S. tax expenditure budget and is thus recognized as the functional equivalent of an interest-free government loan, potentially unlimited in duration, to U.S. exporters. It is defended by its supporters as an incentive to exports. Those supporters had described in glowing terms its effect in increasing exports, which the Europeans used to bolster their arguments. The U.S. defense before the panel was necessarily a weak one, given the circumstances surrounding DISC, and essentially rested on the assertion that a deferral of tax was not a subsidy. This was clearly an unacceptable argument to the economists on the panel.[55] The panel decision on DISC thus broke no new ground but instead represented a rational acceptance of the strong arguments provided to the Europeans by the origins of DISC, the contentions of its supporters, and the fact that, from its inception, it was regarded by the United States as a tax expenditure.

At the same time, however, the United States had in effect launched a counterclaim by maintaining that the Europeans' tax treatment of exports was also contrary to GATT. The United States pointed out, for example, that France under the territoriality principle in its income tax does not tax the income of foreign branches owned by French companies.[56] Consequently, where a French-owned foreign branch sold goods manufactured by a French company, the profits on the sale by the branch were not taxed by France. In contrast, the United States would tax the company in this situation in the absence of DISC. France, under the territoriality principle, also exempts from its income tax 95 percent of the dividends received from a French-owned foreign subsidiary, the remaining 5 percent being considered as includable in income to offset deductions by the parent of expenses attributable to the dividends. France does tax a French company on its profits on goods transferred to its foreign subsidiary, and thus taxes profits that DISC in effect partially exempts in the United States. In addition, France taxes exports to third parties, which as a result of the DISC provision are not fully taxed in the United States. But France does not, under its income tax, tax the foreign-source income of business taxpayers whose income is derived from a foreign branch or subsidiary.

France, in tax terminology, uses the territoriality principle of source rather than worldwide taxation of income. This principle in effect avoids double taxation of international income by the exemption of foreign income, allowing exclusive tax jurisdiction to the country in which the income arises. With some variations, the Dutch and Belgian tax systems also use the territoriality principle, and hence the exemption approach.

The U.S. tax expenditure budget does not consider the foreign tax credit to be a tax expenditure, but instead regards it as an appropriate accommodation of the U.S. income tax system to the income tax systems of other countries.

Similarly, the French tax expenditure budget does not treat the exemption of foreign-source income as a tax expenditure. Presumably the French regard their territoriality principle as a counterpart to the U.S. foreign tax credit approach, that is, as the accommodation, under the French normative concept of an income tax, to other tax systems to avoid double taxation. Although it may be argued that a foreign tax credit approach is in general a better approach in today's tax world, the exemption system has its supporters. The OECD model for bilateral tax conventions includes it along with the foreign tax credit as an alternative in article 23a, "Methods for Elimination of Double Taxation."[57] Accordingly, the French exemption system is part of its normative tax structure and should therefore not have been regarded as a "subsidy" under GATT.

Despite this analysis, in considering the United States claim that European tax treatment of exports violated GATT, the GATT panel, consisting of the same individuals who made the DISC decision, ruled that the French treatment of foreign income from export sales abroad was a subsidy under GATT. After "examining the effects of the income tax practices before it in economic terms . . . [the panel noted that] the particular application of the territoriality principle by France allowed some part of export activities, belonging to an economic process originating in the country, to be outside the scope of French taxes. In this way, France has foregone revenue from this source and created a possibility of a pecuniary benefit to exports in those cases where income and corporation tax provisions were significantly more liberal in foreign countries."[58] The panel further found that although these "practices may have been an incidental consequence of French taxation principles rather than a specific policy intention, they nonetheless constituted a subsidy on exports because the . . . benefits to exports did not apply to domestic activities for the internal market."[59] Finally, after noting that the French tax treatment of dividends from abroad ensured that the benefits were fully preserved,[60] the panel concluded that "in circumstances where different tax treatment in different countries resulted in a smaller total tax bill in aggregate being paid on exports than on sales in the home market . . . there was a partial exemption from direct taxes."[61] It reached the same decision for the Dutch and Belgian approaches.[62]

The decision is a debatable one. In tax expenditure terms, it appears to rest on the proposition that the territoriality principle and the exemption method of relief against double taxation of exports are not parts of a normative tax system.[63] This interpretation would leave the foreign tax credit method as the only normative approach. If this interpretation were correct, it would equally appear that the exemption method is itself a tax subsidy—though not a GATT export subsidy (unless goods exported from the residence country are involved in the foreign activities)—when applied to exempt from residence country tax either the income of a foreign branch engaged in activities other than export sales or the dividends of a foreign subsidiary earning profits from such activities. The GATT panel decision also supports the U.S. classification of the deferral of tax on controlled foreign subsidiary profits as a tax expenditure, for it really implies that anything short of current taxation of those profits is a tax subsidy—though, again, not necessarily a GATT export subsidy since exports are not directly involved.

It is thus understandable that France and other countries using the territoriality principle and the exemption method cannot accept the decision of the GATT panel.[64] Their primary contention is that, whatever other countries may see as defects of that principle and the exemption method, the approach has a long historical basis in European tax systems. Their defense of the method in the modern world rests on this history and on tax jurisdiction concepts, rather than on the importance of continuing the territoriality principle and the exemption method to provide, in effect, a subsidy for exports and other foreign activities.[65]

THE TREATY OF ROME

Other international organizations may also need to utilize the tax expenditure concept to decide substantive issues of interpretation in the international agreements they enforce. Thus, articles 92-94 of the Treaty of Rome, establishing the European Community, impose limits on "aid" (Beihilfen) granted to a business by a member state "in any form whatsoever" that distorts competition. The Commission of the European Community has taken the position that state aid includes financial benefits provided through preferential tax provisions. This view appears to have been upheld, at least implicitly, by the Court of Justice of the European Communities.[66] The application of the treaty provision would be facilitated by the development of internationally accepted criteria for differentiating provisions that constitute part of the normative structure of the various tax systems employed by Common Market countries, which should not constitute aid under articles 92-94, and deviations from the normative structure, which should constitute aid or tax expenditures within the treaty terms. Classifying a particular provision as a tax aid does not imply that it constitutes a violation of the treaty. It simply means that the same standard treaty test of distortion of competition should be applied to tax aids and to direct aids.

The Tax Expenditure Concept in Other Countries

The tax expenditure concept as developed systematically in the United States is rapidly becoming a subject of interest in the rest of the world. Canada, France, Austria, and Spain now have official tax expenditure lists. Germany has had a list of tax subsidies since 1967. The United Kingdom and Belgium have published government lists of tax expenditures. Sweden, the Netherlands, and Australia are studying the application of the concept to their tax systems. Fiscal scholars in India and Tunisia have conducted studies of tax expenditures.

This widespread interest has largely resulted from the selection of tax expenditures as a principal topic of discussion at the annual meetings of the two major international fiscal organizations.[67] At its congress in Jerusalem in 1976 the International Fiscal Association (IFA) selected as one of its topics "Tax Incentives as an Instrument for

Achievement of Governmental Goals—Their Role in Income Taxation and a Comparison with Alternative Instruments Regarding Both Economic and Social Goals."[68] The IFA directive guiding the preparation of national reports for about twenty countries described the tax expenditure concept, asked whether thinking about the tax system in the various countries had encompassed that concept, and requested the preparation of a tax expenditure budget for each country. The IFA general report noted that the vast majority of reporting countries did not have tax expenditure lists and lacked the requisite data to develop them.[69] The conference discussion concluded that there was a need to define and estimate tax expenditures and to scrutinize them as carefully as other matters of budget and economic policy.[70]

At its Varna congress in 1977 the International Institute of Public Finance (IIPF) also considered tax expenditures as forms of tax relief under the topic "Subsidies, Tax Reliefs, and Prices."[71] The various papers presented at the congress contributed useful observations on the appropriate criteria for choosing between tax assistance and direct assistance, on the political and psychological factors underlying the use of tax assistance, on the almost universal tendency of legislatures to approve tax expenditures more readily than direct assistance, and on the adverse effect on the basic tax structure of incorporating tax expenditures in an income tax system. In addition, the majority of members acknowledged both the absence of this technique in official and academic considerations of tax systems and the need to develop a tax expenditure approach to a tax system.

The consideration and acceptance of the tax expenditure concept at these two international conferences undoubtedly stimulated much of the recent work in countries other than the United States. Initially this work took the form of academic studies.[72] Soon, however, governments began exploring the tax expenditure concept.[73]

CANADA

In Canada a considerable body of literature preceded the Department of Finance's publication of the *Government of Canada Tax Expenditure Account* in December 1979.[74] The government document covers the income tax and the manufacturers' sales tax (Canada does not have a national wealth transfer tax). Its publication placed Canada, along with the United States, in the forefront of countries applying a complete tax expenditure analysis to their budget and tax systems.

Both the analytical discussion and the information imparted are thus of importance not only to Canadians but to other governments and those who work in the public finance field.

FRANCE

There does not appear to have been much discussion in France of the tax expenditure concept before 1979.[75] In January 1980, however, the finance act for 1980 stated in article 32 that every year thereafter, "in the document 'Ways and Means' annexed to the Finance Bill, the Government will trace the evolution of the tax expenditures, showing, in a clear manner, the initial evaluations [estimates], the evaluation based on actual experience, and the results. The tax expenditures shall be classified in detail by nature of the taxes, and by objectives, and by categories of beneficiaries." This requirement was largely prompted by the desire of the Parliament and the executive branch to obtain better fiscal control over the budget and to eliminate some tax expenditures. Accordingly, the 1981 finance bill, introduced in December 1980,[76] contained the French tax expenditure budget. The list extends to all national taxes: individual and corporate income taxes, value-added tax, inheritance tax, and various special taxes. It contains three lists, classified by type of tax, by objectives (similar to the use of budgetary functional classifications, as in Canada and the United States), and by the groups benefited by the tax expenditures.

UNITED KINGDOM

As late as 1978, tax officials in the United Kingdom expressed skepticism about the tax expenditure concept. This attitude was evident in a Treasury memorandum, *Interface of Public Expenditure and Taxation* (TM37), presented to the Expenditure Committee of the House of Commons on February 1, 1978.[77] It appeared, however, that the Expenditure Committee and others desired that the government make available "a list of direct tax allowances and reliefs (known as tax expenditures)."[78] Moreover, the publication of 1978 of Willis and Hardwick's *Tax Expenditures in the United Kingdom*,[79] containing both a discussion of tax expenditure analysis and a list of tax expenditures under the U.K. individual income tax, demonstrated the feasibility of applying the tax expenditure concept. In 1979 the Chancellor of the Exchequer included a list titled "Direct Tax Allowances and Reliefs" in *The Government's Expenditure Plans, 1979–1980 to 1982–83.*[80] Although the document reflected a certain amount of continuing skepticism concerning the tax expenditure concept,[81] the U.K. list of tax expenditures is not too different from that of Canada or the United States. It covers the U.K. income and wealth transfer taxes but not the value-added tax. Nor does it contain any description of the purposes of the items involved and the reason for inclusion or exclusion.[82]

WEST GERMANY

West Germany has had a type of tax expenditure budget since 1966. In its existing form the list is published every two years and is divided into subsidies for business and subsidies for personal activities and relief for hardships.[83]

SPAIN

Article 134.2 of the Spanish constitution and Spain's budget law require that the annual budget provide data on the tax expenditures in the Spanish tax system. The information provided includes the amount of tax expenditures, classified by type of tax, by individuals and corporations, by relations to total revenues, and by activity (activities of a general character, social and community activities, and economic activities).[84] There is no item-by-item enumeration.

OTHER COUNTRIES

Japan legislatively classifies "Special Taxation Measures," and the Ministry of Finance provides the legislature with annual budget estimates of the revenue loss involved in these special measures. The list is not as inclusive as a tax expenditure list would be.

In 1982 Australia's House of Representatives Standing Committee on Expenditure recommended that the government provide comprehensive information on taxation expenditures. The committee report provides a detailed description of the tax expenditure concept and explains its usefulness in promoting an understanding of government spending.[85]

Since 1978 the Austrian Ministry of Finance has included a tax expenditure budget in its annual report on government subsidies. The Netherlands Ministry of Finance has established a commission to consider tax expenditures in that country's tax system.[86] Sweden, New Zealand, Ireland, and Belgium have begun to consider a tax expenditure budget.

Clearly, the tax and budget authorities in other countries increasingly see both the desirability and feasibility of preparing and publishing tax expenditure lists.

International Comparative Data on Budget Expenditures and Tax Revenues

The Organization for Economic Cooperation and Development (OECD) for years has published comparative data on the budgets and tax systems of member countries. With the development of the tax expenditure concept, it has become obvious that these comparisons present an incomplete picture of actual direct spending and revenue collections. The 1976 *General Report* of the IFA congress in Jerusalem contained the following observations:

> The OECD has published comprehensive material on Revenue Statistics of OECD Member Countries; the latest published in 1975 covers 1965–1972. These statistics, following a standard classification established by OECD, indicate tax revenues as a ratio of GNP. The study, however, excludes tax expenditures. Yet tax expenditures can affect such ratios, since one country may finance certain activities through the tax system while another country finances the same activities through the direct budget. The two countries looked at in terms of collected revenues alone may show the same ratio whereas in fact the first country could actually have more relative participation of the public sector in the economy once tax expenditures are included . . . Other comparative studies under consideration by the OECD also require tax expenditure data to make the international comparisons meaningful, and would thus complement a basic tax expenditure study. For example, one set of studies relates to government financing in selected functional areas, such as health, housing, etc. Certainly the extent of financing through tax expenditures is a necessary ingredient. Thus in housing one should look at tax expenditures to individuals for home ownership, to business to construct homes, and to financial institutions to lend funds for

the construction or purchase of homes. These tax expenditures would be joined with other government budget aids such as grants, loans, guarantees and the like to form the complete picture.[87]

The OECD, though presumably recognizing the relevance of these remarks, has been proceeding slowly in its treatment of tax expenditures. But it has taken some initial steps. The Committee on Fiscal Affairs stated in connection with one of its decisions:

> 7. Many countries have in recent years substituted cash transfers for tax allowances or credits. The question is whether such changes should be allowed to affect tax receipts which, in the absence of other offsets, would show an increase, by the amount of tax credits or allowances shifted to cash transfers, or whether the cash transfers should be deductible from tax receipts, thus leaving the level of taxation more or less unchanged. It follows from what has been said . . . that where an expenditure provision is substituted for a tax provision, the change should be reflected in tax receipts shown . . .
>
> 8. Whilst it may at first sight seem paradoxical to show an increase in tax revenue receipts merely because a country has moved from a tax provision to an expenditure provision to subsidise certain citizens or activities, this is the only logical way to treat revenue receipts and it has always been recognised that an inherent drawback of comparisons of tax yields to GDP ratios is that they cannot take into account different relative reliance on tax provisions and expenditure provisions.[88]

Obviously, the situation described in paragraph 8 arises because tax expenditures do exist and are a method of providing government assistance. Hence if direct assistance is substituted for a tax expenditure, a proper presentation would show that government expenditures have not been reduced, only that the avenue of payment has been changed.

On the basic issue of recognizing tax expenditures as government assistance, presumably the OECD has decided to wait until several member countries have developed their own official tax expenditure lists. Five OECD members—Canada, France, the United Kingdom, the United States, and West Germany—now have such lists. Using these as a foundation, the OECD should be able to begin to develop a structure to guide other member countries in preparing their tax expenditure lists.[89] The OECD should also launch a comparative study of the tax expenditure lists. The results could be included in the comparative OECD budget and revenue data.

The Rotterdam Institute for Fiscal Studies of Erasmus University, the Boston College Law School, and the Harvard Law School are currently engaged in an international research project to formulate tax expenditure lists for Canada, France, the Netherlands, Sweden, the United Kingdom, and the United States in forms that will support comparative analysis. A group of fiscal scholars from each country involved first developed guidelines for uniform formulation of the lists. The guidelines cover the income tax, the value-added tax or any other national sales tax used, the transfer tax (estate, gift, inheritance), and the wealth tax. Next they prepared tax expenditure lists for each country in conformity with the guidelines. The lists also indicate the departures from each country's official list. The lists prepared under the guidelines do not vary in a major way from the official lists.[90]

Representatives of the OECD and the EEC are informally associated with the project. The results of the study will enable those organizations to conduct comparative and other studies of revenues and expenditures in general, and of particular aspects of the public sector, on a more informed basis than in the past. Scholars and government officials in the countries involved should also be able to develop studies and analyses based on the material. Both the guidelines and the resulting lists should be valuable resources for other countries that intend to prepare tax expenditure lists.

Once the OECD or EEC develops an organized comparative approach to the use of tax expenditure data and analysis, other regional organizations such as the Organization of American States, the Association of South East Asian States, and the Organization of African Unity should be able to apply that approach to their studies. The United Nations and the International Monetary Fund in their analyses of fiscal systems similarly could assist countries in the use of the tax expenditure concept and advance its application to comparative fiscal studies.

7

CONCEPTUAL ASPECTS OF TAX EXPENDITURE ANALYSIS

THIS CHAPTER explores in detail the conceptual issues involved in tax expenditure analysis and in the formulation of a tax expenditure list. It discusses the definitional issues involved in the analysis of an income tax, the methods used in estimating tax expenditures under an income tax, and the application of tax expenditure analysis to other broad-based taxes.

General Definitional Issues in the Income Tax

In its initial presentation of the concept of tax expenditures in 1968, the Treasury Department described the rationale used to classify items as tax expenditures:

> [The analysis] lists the major respects in which the current income tax bases deviate from widely accepted definitions of income and standards of business accounting and from the generally accepted structure of an income tax ...
>
> The study does not attempt a complete listing of all the tax provisions which vary from a strict definition of net income. Various items that could have been added have been excluded for one or more of several reasons:
>
> a. Some items were excluded where there is no available indication of the precise magnitude of the implicit subsidy. This is the case, for example, with depreciation on machinery

and equipment where the accelerated tax methods may provide an allowance beyond that appropriate to the measurement of net income but where it is difficult to measure that difference because the true economic deterioration or obsolescence factor cannot be readily determined.

b. Some items were excluded where the case for their inclusion in the income base stands on relatively technical or theoretical tax arguments. This is the case, for example, with the imputed rent on owner-occupied homes, which involves not only a conceptual problem but difficult practical problems such as those of measurement.

c. Some items were omitted because of their relatively small quantitative importance.

Other features of our income tax system are considered not as variations from the generally accepted measure of net income or as tax preferences but as part of the structure of an income tax system based on ability to pay. Such features include personal exemptions and the rate schedules under the individual income tax, including the income splitting allowed for married couples filing joint returns or for heads of households. A discussion of income splitting and the dependent's personal exemption is thus considered outside the scope of this study on tax expenditures.

It must be recognized that these exclusions are to some extent arbitrary and some may prefer to add items that we have omitted or to omit items that we have included. The immediate objective, however, of the study is to provide a list of items that would be generally recognized as more or less intended use of the tax system to achieve results commonly obtained by Government expenditures. The design of the list seemed best served by constructing what seemed a minimum list rather than including highly complicated or controversial items that would becloud the utility of this special analysis . . .

The assumption inherent in current law, that corporations are separate entities and subject to income taxation independently from their shareholders, is adhered to in this analysis.[1]

Over a decade of discussion of the tax expenditure concept has demonstrated that the initial Treasury approach was sound. Its basic conceptual framework has enabled tax technicians presenting subsequent tax expenditure lists to maintain a remarkable degree of consistency and, without serious difficulty, to incorporate additional tax expenditures resulting from subsequent tax legislation.[2] The initial Treasury approach and the consistent elaboration developed thereafter have also provided other countries with a useful framework for the preparation of their own tax expenditure lists. Those lists show little departure from the Treasury approach, and the differences that do exist reflect differences in the countries' tax histories.

The first step in tax expenditure analysis of an income tax is to distinguish between its normative, structural component and its tax expenditure component. Only then is it possible to consider the issues involved in the appropriate classification of selected income tax provisions and the reasons behind the classification.

Separating the basic structural provisions from the tax expenditure or tax penalty provisions requires an understanding of the normative structure of the tax: the provisions that establish the tax base, or the definition of income; the tax period and the accounting concepts required to apply that period; the taxable units; the rate structure chosen; application of the tax to international transactions; and appropriate administrative procedures. The remaining provisions constitute tax expenditures and tax penalties for special activities or groups. Congress recognized this distinction when in the Budget Act of 1974 it identified a tax expenditure as a "special" provision[3] that constitutes a "deviation from the normal tax structure."[4]

THE TAX BASE

The crucial structural task of technicians devising an income tax is to define just what income is. The standard used by the Treasury in 1968 was "widely accepted definitions of income" developed by economists over many years and culminating in the Schanz-Haig-Simons (S-H-S) definition, which is accepted by most economists in the United States and elsewhere.[5] That definition, as stated by Henry Simons, is "the algebraic sum of (1) the market value of rights exercised in consumption and (2) the change in the value of the store of property rights between the beginning and the end of the period in question . . . In other words, it is merely the result of adding consumption during the period to 'wealth' at the end of the period and then subtracting 'wealth' at the beginning."[6] Thus income is the increase in net wealth between two specified times plus consumption during that period.

The term "consumption" in the definition covers all expenditures made except those incurred as costs in the earning or production of income. Thus the term is not an independent concept, as it is when used as the base of a general tax on consumption, such as retail sales tax or value-added tax. Instead, consumption is viewed as an arithmetic result of the subtraction process stated above.

There is no equivalent legal definition of income. In the early years of the income tax the Supreme Court essayed a definition in *Eisner v. Macomber:* "Income may be defined as the gain derived from capital, from labor, or from both combined."[7] Later decisions, however, found the definition incomplete.[8] In a decision that included in taxable income punitive damages received by the wronged party, the Court reasoned that the damages were "instances of undeniable accessions to wealth, clearly realized, and over which taxpayers have complete dominion."[9] The Court thus defined income on an item-by-item basis rather than considering the total change in a person's economic position during the taxable period. But, with the exception of the requirement that the gain be "clearly realized," the result closely resembles the S-H-S definition.

Taxable income, as defined in the Internal Revenue Code, is net income and is initially determined by the subtraction from gross income of enumerated deductions, one set of which, in code sections 162, 165, 167, and 212, basically represents the expenditures involved in earning or producing the gross income. This subtraction process is similar to the one used in determining the amount of consumption under the S-H-S definition. But the code excludes from gross income a number of receipt items, such as gifts, interest on state and local government obligations, certain employer payments, and scholarships. Also, it includes a number of other deductions to reach taxable income, such as charitable contributions, interest paid on loans to purchase residences or durable consumer goods, state and local taxes, nonbusiness bad debts, and medical expenses. The basic task of tax expenditure definition is to distinguish between the exclusions and deductions that are essential to a normal structure and those that are tax expenditures.

Although the S-H-S definition is a useful starting point for identifying the normative provisions in an income tax, it cannot be used alone to distinguish normative provisions from tax expenditure provisions. One reason for this is that Simons applied his definition of income to only a few items. He did not discuss the appropriate technical treatment of many receipts (such as government transfer payments, personal damages, and scholarships) or of many expenditures or losses (such as medical expenses, casualty losses, and charitable contributions). A second reason is that the S-H-S definition does not address all the issues involved in framing a normal income tax, such as the taxable period to be used in applying the definition. A third reason, more narrowly applicable to the definition of income, is that the S-H-S definition, though theoretically correct, is too rigid and demanding to be applied comprehensively in a national income tax. It remains an "ideal," a "theoretically pure treatment."[10]

Because the tax expenditure concept is intended to serve as a useful legislative and budgetary tool, the 1968 Treasury analysis tempered the S-H-S definition by also referring to "the generally accepted structure of an income tax." The objective was to exclude from classification as tax expenditures certain items of income that would be covered by the S-H-S definition. These items historically had not been viewed as income in the United States. The Treasury analysis cited only two items as belonging to this second category: unrealized appreciation (during a person's lifetime) in asset values and imputed income from homes or other durable consumer assets. This combined standard—"widely accepted definitions of income" (that is, S-H-S) and "the generally accepted structure of an income tax"—has allowed the preparation of tax expenditure lists in this country to proceed successfully and with useful results.[11]

Some seek to employ definitions other than S-H-S, but these prove inadequate for tax expenditure analysis. The concept of ability to pay, for example, lends itself too easily to treating as appropriate deductions such consumption items as medical expenses or charitable deductions, because it is being used to state what is socially desirable rather than to define economic income.[12] Equally unhelpful are the notions of discretionary income and discretionary economic power.[13]

THE ACCOUNTING PERIOD

The S-H-S definition does not specify the period to be used in calculating income. A normative income tax, to be administratively workable, must specify that period. The U.S. income tax, following financial accounting practices, uses the standard of a year. The taxpayer may use a calendar year, a fiscal year, or a "short year" when a change in the taxpayer's annual accounting period produces less than a twelve-month period.

But tax accounting for a normative tax must also provide rules for allocating items of income and deduction to the appropriate years. Examples are the application of the cash method or the accrual method of accounting, the distinction between current expense and capital expenditure, and the proper allocation over a period of years of capital expenditures. Because the S-H-S definition does not deal with the taxable period, income tax specialists have relied heavily on accounting principles and rules developed and used in financial reporting over the years. The 1968 Treasury analysis thus stated that, in determining the proper accounting periods, it would use "widely accepted ... standards of business accounting."[14] This approach has proved to be appropriate and feasible for distinguishing normative tax accounting from tax expenditure special measures.

On the other hand, the "standards of business accounting" test cannot be applied exclusively, for a number of reasons. First, the objectives of financial reporting and business accounting may in some situations be quite different from those of tax accounting. For example, financial accounting standards may indicate that an expense should be assigned to an earlier period than that for which a deduction is permitted under tax accounting rules. Conversely, in some situations tax accounting may permit an item of income to be reported later than the period for which income is reported for financial accounting purposes. Although divergence between the two accounting methods should signal the need for consideration of the factors that produce the divergence, the divergence does not itself produce a tax expenditure or tax penalty.

Thus, because of the desire to estimate profits as conservatively as possible, financial accounting will often permit reserves to be created in the current year for expenses to be incurred in future years. With a few exceptions, tax accounting does not permit the deductibility of such reserves in the year they are created. The tax accounting rule is not a tax penalty since it is based on tax administration grounds—that is, that taxpayers might try to deduct excessive reserves under the financial accounting principle of conservatism, with resulting excessive revenue losses. On the other hand, tax accounting permits the use of the installment method of reporting gains from property sales in cases in which payments are spread out over a period. Financial accounting rules would not permit such a deferral of income recognition. The installment method for tax purposes is not a tax expenditure since the rule is intended to ensure that taxpayers include an amount in income in the same year in which they received the payment and therefore have the necessary funds with which to pay the tax on the income. Similarly, rules designed to ameliorate the impact of a rigid application of the annual accounting period concept, such as the rules for income averaging and for the carryback and carryover of losses, do not constitute tax expenditures. These rules reflect a judgment from a tax accounting standpoint that it is appropriate to smooth out fluctuations in income over a reasonable period. Thus, the "standards of business accounting" criterion is tempered in tax expenditure analysis by resort to practical concerns of tax collection and tax administration. In situations in which those concerns produce a deviation from financial accounting, neither tax expenditures nor tax penalties are involved.

THE TAXABLE UNIT

After establishing the income tax base and the methods of accounting for receipts and expenditures, policymakers must address the issues involved in specifying the taxable unit; that is, just who or what will be subject to the tax. Typical issues are, for *persons,* whether an individual or the family (which in itself requires definition) is the appropriate unit and how trusts for individuals should be treated; for *businesses,* how partnerships and corporations (which must be defined distinctly from a partnership or a business trust or association) are to be treated; and for more *special situations,* how other organizational forms such as cooperatives, or special lines of business activity such as insurance companies or investment companies, or nonprofit organizations are to be treated.

The tax specialist cannot use tax theory to ascertain whether the taxable unit should be an individual or the family. The tax specialist can only point out the technical consequences that flow from the choice and the technical problems that must be solved. But the choice cannot really be made on these technical grounds. The choice involves, for example, issues of how to tax single persons versus married persons versus single persons supporting a dependent in their households versus single persons living together but not married and how to tax a family with one working spouse versus a family with both spouses working versus either family with working children. These choices depend heavily on such factors as a country's attitudes about marriage, men and women in general and men and women in the work force, the role of children, the family in general, and other social and economic considerations.[15] Those drafting tax legislation therefore need decisions from the government policymakers, for there is no normative tax guideline in this area. Furnished with that decision, the tax expert can properly implement it.[16] The tax expenditure concept, therefore, does not dictate that there is a single normative choice of the taxable unit for individuals. But if a clear-cut policy decision exists, departures from it for incentive or other reasons could produce tax expenditures.

The taxable unit question also arises in the context of family trusts. Should such a trust be treated as a taxable unit separate from its creator and/or its beneficiaries? The problems arise because there are pressures to use the trust device for nontax purposes. If such pressures do affect the tax law, then a tax expenditure classification problem will arise when a family uses the trust device for those purposes but the trustee, viewed from either an economic or practical control standpoint, is a "member of the family." Suppose a living donor establishes a trust for ten years under which the trustee has discretion to accumulate or distribute income or to choose who among a designated class of beneficiaries will receive the distributed income. Under existing tax rules—called the "Clifford rules"—either the trustee or the beneficiaries receiving the income may be taxable but the donor is not if proper precautions are taken. The questions posed by tax expenditure analysis are (1) whether a trust should ever be treated as a taxpayer separate and distinct from its grantor and/or its beneficiaries and (2) whether the trust rules adopted are consistent with the fundamental policy decisions made with respect to the treatment of the family unit.

Similar issues arise with regard to partnerships. Whether the partnership is to be treated as a separate entity or as an aggregate of its individual partners is a policy decision that must be made independent of technical tax theory. Once the decision has been made, as in the United States, to treat that form of business organization as not constituting a taxpaying unit, a series of normative rules must be provided to relate the partnership accounts and activities to those of the partners in order to determine the treatment of the partners. Although the task is a difficult one, it is within the realm of the development of normative tax rules. If the basic policy decision is consistently carried out, tax expenditures are not involved.

THE RATE SCHEDULE

The next issues to be decided are the rate schedule to be used and the level of income at which application of the tax rates should begin.

Are the tax rates to be proportional, progressive, or regressive? Should the tax start at the first dollar of income and, if not, at what level? Here tax specialists fully realize that the answers are not theirs to supply. There is no normative rate schedule or exemption level to guide them. Again, these are matters that policymakers must decide, looking to whatever sources they choose—the political scene; the advice of economists, sociologists, lawyers, accountants, business executives, tax specialists, or their own constituents; their own instincts; history; developments in other countries; and so on. Without these answers, there will be no income tax. Tax expenditure analysis does not extend to the general rates of tax or to the level of exempt income.

Once a general rate schedule is chosen by policymakers, the introduction of special rates for certain activities or groups as tax incentives or tax subsidies creates a tax expenditure. The special tax rate for capital gains is one example. A policy decision to reduce or increase a generally applicable rate, on the other hand, is not a tax expenditure decision.

APPLICATION TO INTERNATIONAL TRANSACTIONS

As was discussed in chapter 6, a country deciding to impose an income tax must also decide whether and how that tax should relate to international transactions. Once again, the basic choice rests with the policymakers. Thus a country may decide to tax only income arising within its borders and then only of its own residents or, more likely, both its own residents and foreigners who receive such income. Or a country may decide to tax the income that individuals and corporations derive from sources outside the country. The latter choice in turn requires defining the individuals and corporations to be so taxed. Are *individuals* to be citizens, domiciliaries, or residents however defined? Are *corporations* to be those incorporated within the country, those incorporated elsewhere but owned by its individuals and corporations, those incorporated elsewhere but managed within the country, or all of these?

Because these decisions rest with policymakers, countries may adopt different approaches, reflecting such factors as the country's view of its role in the world economy, the importance of incoming and outgoing trade and investment, balance of payments considerations, and the desired comity among all nations that impose an income tax. Sometimes the decision will stem from whether the income tax developed as a schedular tax, with separate schedules and rules for each form of income (such as wages and salaries, business income, investment income), an approach likely to lead to nontaxation of income from foreign sources; or whether it developed as a "global tax," with all items of income included in one overall total, an approach likely to lead to taxation of income from foreign sources.

Once policymakers determine the basic approach, the normative implementation of that approach can proceed. In the United States, for example, the normative approach to international income taxation involves (1) taxation of foreigners receiving income from U.S. sources, with the tax applied in accord with international tradition and comity; (2) taxation on the worldwide income of U.S. citizens, wherever they live, and on the worldwide income of corporations incorporated in the United States; and, (3) through the foreign tax credit and bilateral tax treaties, amelioration of double taxation. Special provisions enacted as incentives and departing from this normative implementation are tax expenditures.

ADMINISTRATION

With the structural aspects of the income tax defined—tax base, accounting rules, taxable units, rates of tax, and international application—legislation must specify the appropriate procedures for tax administration. This legislation is unlikely to contain tax expenditures, since the overall method and techniques of administration are not essentially a part of the tax expenditure concept. A variety of administrative approaches is available, and the final decisions will be based on factors prevailing in the particular country.

The problems of tax administration, however, may force some departures from the technical precision of the normative rules. Thus, although the normative rules may determine the net income base through a subtraction of proper deductions from gross income items, inadequate record keeping in certain segments of the community— perhaps in agriculture or small business—may force administrators to use other methods to determine net income. One possible method is a "*forfait* system," a presumptive determination of the net profit that an enterprise can be expected to earn, given its location, size, activity, and so on. When this approach is genuinely utilized as the only available method to apply an income tax and is designed so as to reach as close an approximation of actual net profit as possible, no tax expenditure results. But if the approach is designed to create an incentive and thus produces a lower tax result than would prevail with properly kept records, the distortion becomes a tax expenditure.

Tax administrators may also create a tax expenditure through an interpretation of the statutory law that initially appears to be correct but on later analysis is seen to be a departure from the proper application of the normative statutory rule. If policymakers continue, for incentive or relief purposes, to' use the erroneous interpretation, so that it becomes a special provision in itself, a tax expenditure results. In the United States, the longtime complete exclusion from gross income of Social Security benefits, which was a nonstatutory rule traceable to an early decision by tax administrators, is an example of such a development.

CONCEPTUAL CONFUSION: 1983 SPECIAL ANALYSIS G

Before publication of the 1983 Special Analysis G, the tax expenditure lists prepared by the staff of the Joint Committee on Taxation (JCT), the Congressional Budget Office (CBO), and the Office of Management and Budget (OMB) were identical. This unanimity prevailed because those responsible for preparing the lists worked together and, more crucially, applied the type of analysis previously described to determine the proper classification of specific provisions. In the 1983 Special Analysis G, however, OMB used a different conceptual framework and produced a tax expenditure list that differed in several important respects from those published by CBO and JCT. The OMB action produced both conceptual and budgetary confusion.

The conceptual framework articulated by OMB is highly idiosyncratic and is inconsistent with tax theory, tax expenditure analysis, and the statutory definition adopted by Congress in the 1974 Budget Act.[17] Instead of beginning with the normal structure of an income tax (as described in the preceding discussion) and then determining whether a particular provision represents a deviation from that structure, OMB formulated a "reference tax" structure and then identified deviations from that structure. OMB described the reference tax concept as follows:

> The reference tax provisions are those which deal with the basic structural features of the Federal income tax. These features include such concepts as the definition of income subject to

tax; taxable units and their threshold levels of taxability; the relationship between the taxation of corporations and their shareholders; the tax rate schedules; the basic tax accounting rules; the treatment of international transactions; and the system of tax administration. All of these structural features must be dealt with in some manner in order to have an operational income tax. In contrast to such reference provisions, it would be possible to have a fully operational income tax that did not contain any of the special provisions that give rise to tax subsidies.

While the distinction between the reference and special provisions of the Code may be clear as general concepts, there are numerous difficulties encountered when applying these concepts to obtain an actual list of tax subsidies. The inclusion of wages in the tax base is a clear example of a reference tax provision; the exclusion of fringe benefits is due to special provisions, and therefore clearly constitutes a tax subsidy. On the other hand, a less clear example is provided by the capital gains provisions, which apply to a broad class of transactions and taxpayers, but are exceptions to the general rules governing taxation of income from all other sources . . .

For a provision to involve a tax subsidy, two conditions are necessary:

—The provision must be "special" in that it applies to a narrow class of transactions or taxpayers; and
—There must be a "general" provision to which the "special" provision is a clear exception.

If these two conditions are satisfied, the special tax provision clearly has the characteristics of a direct outlay program—a program objective and a method of reimbursing program costs.[18]

The defects in this definition are numerous. First, OMB provided no guidance on how to identify a "reference tax" provision. Certainly nothing in existing tax literature or in the Budget Act provides a clue, since the term was invented by OMB. Second, the definition really provides no standard at all. The statement that a "special" provision must apply to a narrow class of transactions or taxpayers is meaningless and, ultimately, nonsensical. Would OMB, for example, really not treat as a tax expenditure a provision excluding from income the first $1,000 of wages received by all workers? Third, as the examples below will demonstrate, the attempt to identify "general" provisions has produced some bizarre classifications (and nonclassifications) in OMB tax expenditure lists.

The 1985 Special Analysis G appears to have recognized some of the more obvious defects of the reference tax approach. In a studied understatement, OMB noted that the lack of conformity between its list and those of CBO and JCT had produced "a condition some have found confusing."[19] OMB's solution to the confusion it had created was to provide separate revenue estimates for an item classified as a tax expenditure under the "normal tax" approach but not so classified under the "reference tax" approach. This modest step does help clear up some of the budgetary confusion, but conceptual confusion remains. The 1985 Special Analysis G contained a short essay describing the reference tax rules, but the discussion does not address conceptual issues. There is still no explanation of how OMB determines which provisions in the code are reference provisions. For example, it states that corporations and shareholders are treated as separate taxpayers under the reference rules; hence it concludes that the deferral of tax on income earned by controlled foreign shareholders is not a tax expenditure. But why is that the reference provision? Why are not the indirect tax credit and subpart F provisions—which treat foreign subsidiaries and their U.S. parent as one taxpayer—the reference provisions? If they are not, how are they to be classified? Special Analysis G offers no answers to such obvious questions.

The lack of any articulated defensible conceptual basis for the OMB reference tax approach forces reliance on the specific examples in which that approach produces a result different from the normal tax structure approach. These examples are considered in the following discussion.

Specific Issues

Several specific definitional questions have arisen since the 1968 Treasury presentation of the tax expenditure concept. The fact that there is debate about the classification and/or presentation of a particular item does not mean that the tax expenditure concept is fundamentally flawed. The tax expenditure concept requires a dynamic and continuing analysis of the provisions in a tax system. As the tax expenditure concept compels closer consideration of the role of a specific tax provision (or nonprovision) in the overall tax system, new studies are undertaken, new data are developed, and continual rethinking of positions is required. Especially with respect to borderline issues, unanimity of opinion on classification issues is rare. But the debates and analyses are themselves important contributions to the continuing improvement of a country's tax and spending structures. Moreover, the number of classification or presentation issues that have inspired debate is insignificant in relation to the number of items on the tax expenditure list about which there is no disagreement.

DEFINING THE TAX BASE

IMPUTED INCOME FROM OWNER-OCCUPIED HOUSING AND CONSUMER DURABLES

Under the S-H-S definition, income should include the imputed rental value of owner-occupied housing and consumer durables (such as automobiles and household appliances). The U.S. tax expenditure lists have not included this item, and some have criticized the omission. In one respect, the issue may simply involve the amount of revenue that should be reflected in the tax expenditure list. That is, tax expenditure lists to date have always shown the revenue loss arising from the deductions for home mortgage interest, property taxes on residences, consumer interest, and deductions for property taxes on consumer durables. If the tax expenditure list were changed to show the nontaxation of net imputed rental income from owner-occupied residences and consumer durables, these items currently in the tax expenditure list would disappear, since they would be proper deductions in arriving at net imputed rental income.

The current U.S. tax expenditure lists do clearly identify the federal subsidies for home ownership and consumer durables. The initial Treasury decision to show the individual deductions associated with home ownership and consumer durables as tax expenditures, rather than as imputed rental income, was based on the belief that since imputed income had never been subject to tax in the United States, it would be confusing to show that item in a tax expenditure list. More recently, Special Analysis G has taken the position that nontaxation of net imputed income may be justified on the basis of the administrative difficulties that would be involved in attempting to reach such income. Both of these justifications appear sensible. For members of Congress and the general public, it is likely that the existing practice is the best and most useful way to present information concerning the tax subsidies that are provided to owners of personal residences and consumer durables. However, it would certainly be appropriate for preparers of tax expenditure lists to include as an information item the budget costs associated with the broader concept of the nontaxation of imputed rental income. The Canadian tax expenditure budget shows the revenue costs associated with the nontaxation of net imputed rental income. But both the U.S. and the Canadian presentations rest on the same conceptual ground. That is, the U.S. decision to list the deductions associated with home ownership and consumer durables as tax expenditures is based on the view that these costs are associated with the production of income that is not included in the tax base; the Canadian approach views the noninclusion of income as the fundamental item and thus does not show the deductions associated with it as tax expenditures.

THE REALIZATION REQUIREMENT

The U.S. tax expenditure list has also been criticized because it does not treat as a tax expenditure the exclusion from income of annual unrealized appreciation from assets. Under the S-H-S definition, annual gains in property constitute income, whether those gains are realized or not. The decision not to include the nontaxation of unrealized gains in the U.S. tax expenditure list was based on two factors. First, the concept of realization has played a large part in the legal definition of income since the inception of the U.S. income tax. Second, it is likely that most legislators and members of the general public do not view gains from property as income until some step has been taken to realize on that gain, such as by a sale or by an exchange of the property. To these factors may also be added the administrative difficulties involved in imposing a tax on annual accrued gains, especially in the case of property such as real estate and closely held businesses.

But as the public and legislators become more knowledgeable about the effects of the policy decision to defer taxation on gains until realized,[20] the initial Treasury decision to exclude this item from the tax expenditure list should be reexamined. The nontaxation of accrued gains in effect constitutes an interest-free loan to the holder of appreciating property, and this fact is becoming more widely recognized, both in and out of Congress. This issue involves no real conceptual dispute between preparers of the U.S. tax expenditure list and those who have criticized the noninclusion of unrealized gains in the list.

The appropriate response to the growing public awareness of the role played by the realization rule would be to include in future tax expenditure lists, as an informational item, the revenue cost of the nontaxation of annual accrued gains. The Canadian tax expenditure list includes the nontaxation of unrealized gains as a tax expenditure but provides no revenue estimate for the item. Simply listing the item with no associated revenue estimates appears to be of little or no value. Thus, the U.S. practice to date appears to be a sound one from the standpoint of budget presentation. But those preparing the tax expenditure list should periodically reevaluate that practice to ensure that meaningful data are available to provide a more comprehensive picture of the revenue cost involved in nontaxation of annual accrued gains.[21]

CAPITAL GAINS AT DEATH

The U.S. tax expenditure lists have included one important item involving accrued gains: the nontaxation of accrued gains in property transferred by gift or at death. Under existing rules, in the case of a transfer of appreciated property at death, the accrued gain is forever exempt from tax; in the case of gifts, tax on the gain is deferred until a sale by the donee. The revenue estimate represents the revenue loss resulting from the failure to tax the gain to the donor or in the decedent's final income tax return.

The 1983 Special Analysis G continued to list the capital gains at death provision as a tax expenditure but changed the method for estimating the revenue cost. Under the OMB approach, the revenue loss is not reflected until the asset is actually sold by the recipient of the property. In addition, OMB shows the cost of the capital gains at death tax expenditure as only 40 percent of the amount of revenue that would have been realized under full taxation of such gains. The other 60 percent of the gain is treated as part of a tax expenditure for the general capital gains exclusion. Over the long term, the revenue cost under the OMB method and under the method used by CBO and JCT will be the same. However, an important conceptual difference underlies the two methods of revenue estimation. In effect, the OMB technique asserts that the normative method for treating gains in property transferred by gift or at death is carryover basis to the recipient. On the other hand, the traditional method used by CBO and JCT assumes that the normative rule is taxation of the appreciation at the time the property leaves the taxable unit. Although carryover basis is more sound than the rule exempting gains at death, the CBO and JCT approach appears to rest on firmer conceptual ground. Although the realization requirement may justify omission from the tax expenditure list of an item for the nontaxation of annual accrued gains, it cannot extend to nontaxation once the property has left the owner's hands. The 1983 Special Analysis G presentation of the capital gains at death item introduces unnecessary conceptual confusion and produces no offsetting budgetary gain.

The tax expenditure lists have not included the nontaxation during life of unrealized gain, but the nontaxation of realized gains, when provided as an incentive or a subsidy, is a tax expenditure. Thus the lists have included the deferral of tax on the realized gain from the sale of a residence. They should also include the tax-free rollover of realized gain on the sale of stock to an employee stock ownership plan (ESOP), as provided in the Tax Reform Act of 1984. On the other hand, because of the basic acceptance of the nontaxation of unrealized gain, the postponement of tax on reinvestment of gain resulting from involuntary conversions and on certain mergers and other reorganizations is not classified as a tax expenditure. These rules do not seem to be grounded in incentives. A more doubtful instance is the nontaxation of gain on the exchange of like-kind properties, especially real estate. Although this rule may have its origin in supposed technical valuation difficulties, its basis today closely approximates a desire to encourage investment in real property. Repeal of the current rule is warranted in view of its judicial expansion to permit three- or four-party arrangements that essentially involve sales and purchases rather than an "exchange" of properties.[22] The defenses advanced for retaining the rule in its current form would help determine its classification if it were to remain.

GIFTS AND BEQUESTS

Under existing U.S. rules, the amount of a gift or bequest is not included in the recipient's income. The nontaxation of these receipts is not treated as a tax expenditure even though such items would constitute income under the S-H-S definition.[23] The appropriate treatment of gifts in an income tax has been the subject of extensive discussion among tax theorists. There are three ways in which gifts could be treated under an income tax: (1) the donee should include the gift in income and the donor should not be allowed a deduction for the gift; (2) the donee should include the gift in income and the donor should be allowed a deduction for the gift; (3) the donee should not be required to include the gift in income and the donor should not be allowed a deduction for the gift. The United States uses the third approach. Apparently, no country has adopted either of the first two approaches.

Advocates of the first approach ground their view in the S-H-S definition. The receipt of the gift or bequest produces an increase in the net worth of the donee. From the standpoint of the donor, making a gift or bequest is not a cost of producing income; hence no deduction should be allowable.

Advocates of the second approach assert that the S-H-S definition did not really explore the appropriate treatment of the donor. Focusing on the term "consumption" in the S-H-S formula, they assert that a gift is not consumption by the donor; the only consumption occurs when the donee spends or uses the gift for such purposes. A simple example illustrates this point. A earns $100, then gives it to B, who spends it on food. The total amount of consumption in the economy is $100. The first approach, however, produces the result that the $100 gift has created $200 of consumption in the economy, a result that is manifestly not so in monetary terms and would not be so reflected in the national income accounts. Many advocates of the second approach concede that the rule might give rise to tax avoidance devices in a system in which progressive income tax rates are employed and the donee is a child of the donor who is in a lower income tax bracket. Accordingly, they view the third approach as a second-best solution that produces the correct conceptual result of including the amount of the gift in the income tax base only once.

The historical U.S. exclusion of gifts and bequests from the income of the donee (but without allowing a deduction to the donor) does not indicate clearly whether the normative treatment of gifts and bequests in this country should be regarded as involving the first or the third approach. Accordingly, the current exclusion of the nontaxation of gifts and bequests to donees from U.S. tax expenditure lists can be supported on theoretical as well as on historical grounds.

SCHOLARSHIPS AND FELLOWSHIPS

Beginning with the 1983 Special Analysis G, OMB has omitted the nontaxation of scholarship and fellowship income as tax expenditures on the theory that they constitute "gifts": Since gifts are not included as tax expenditures, neither are scholarships. With respect to fellowship receipts, the OMB change has no conceptual basis. Under existing tax rules, fellowships in excess of $3,600 per year are includable in income. It is clear that this provision is an exception to a general rule of income inclusion and thus constitutes a tax expenditure. In the case of scholarships, the gift analogy simply breaks down in several important respects. Many scholarships are funded from investment and related business income of the donor institution. Others are funded from government grants and must be treated as government subsidies, as will be discussed below. Finally, the recipient of a scholarship may well view it as a reward for the performance of personal services, like a prize or award. And the current exclusion for certain prizes and awards is itself a tax expenditure (presumably it has not been shown on tax expenditure lists because of the small amount of revenue involved).

DIRECT GOVERNMENT SUBSIDIES AND TRANSFER PAYMENTS

The federal government and state and local governments provide a diverse set of expensive subsidies to individuals and corporations. The subsidies may be divided into several types: direct cash or in-kind grants related to business activities, direct cash grants in the nature of welfare transfers, loan subsidies, technical assistance, and general public services.

1. *Direct cash or in-kind grants related to business activities.* Grants made to corporations or individuals in business activities should be reflected in taxable income. Under the Internal Revenue Code and related court decisions, if the grant is in return for services, it is included in gross income. If made to a corporation and regarded as a nonshareholder contribution to capital, the grant is initially excluded from gross income but is included over time through the requirement that the cost basis for depreciation be reduced.[24] Failure to follow these rules produces a tax expenditure, as in the provisions for the exclusion of payments (including those from government agencies) in aid of construction of water and other utilities and the exclusion of government cost-sharing agricultural payments. The CBO and JCT lists have consistently followed this analysis. The 1983 Special Analysis G, however, treated payments in aid of construction and government cost-sharing payments as part of the reference structure (and therefore not as tax expenditures). Although a basis reduction for true contributions to capital does not create tax expenditures, the Internal Revenue Service had consistently ruled that these types of payments were for

services rendered or property acquired. Accordingly, they properly had to be included in income under existing code and court decisions. The 1983 Special Analysis G therefore represents an incorrect analysis of both the economic and the legal nature of the payments.

2. *Direct cash grants in the nature of welfare transfers.* Grants that are welfare payments to individuals should be included in taxable income, but Revenue Rulings and the Internal Revenue Code exclude some of these welfare payments.[25] As a result the tax expenditure list includes several of these. Examples are the untaxed portion of Social Security benefit payments, untaxed unemployment insurance benefits, workmen's compensation benefits, and public assistance benefits. The treatment of these items as tax expenditures is in accord with the views of most tax theorists that welfare payments constitute income.[26]

The federal budget included untaxed government cash transfer payments in its tax expenditure lists until publication of the 1983 Special Analysis G. OMB has not clearly explained the reason for the change in classification. Two somewhat different justifications are briefly mentioned. The first is that " 'gifts' or unilateral transfers from governments" are not tax expenditures.[27] The OMB reasoning seems to be that since the nontaxation of recipients of gifts is not listed as a tax expenditure, untaxed government welfare payments should not be classified as tax expenditures either. But the conclusion is erroneous. Although the current classification of gifts is arguably correct, few taxpayers would regard the payment of required taxes as the equivalent of making a gift to one of their children or grandchildren. In paying taxes for welfare purposes, taxpayers may well be implicitly seeking a social return in the form of, say, civil tranquillity. In any event, the involuntary action of paying taxes can hardly be equated with the gratuitous and completely voluntary action of making a gift. Possibly the OMB also had in mind the fact that welfare payments are derived from nondeductible taxes and hence, like nondeductible gifts, are included in the overall tax base. The problem with this view is that it would lead to the conclusion that any payment received that came from nondeductible taxes should be nontaxable, and, as OMB itself recognizes, this cannot be the case.

The second ground for the OMB classification of public assistance benefits appears to be its view that cash grants (and also in-kind grants) constituting price reductions for specific uses of the grant are properly not includable in income.[28] Thus if the government provided "housing cash grants" (or "housing vouchers") to prospective homeowners, the OMB view would classify the program as similar to one under which lenders were given subsidies on mortgage lending, and thus as only a price adjustment. (The lender would have to include the subsidy in its income, but this fact alone does not justify the OMB classification; all personal consumption expenditures wind up in someone's income.) But unless the lender is required to pass the subsidy directly to the borrower, there may or may not be a price effect equivalent to the subsidy. If the lender is required to pass the subsidy in full to the borrower, then the lender is only a conduit and would not be taxable on the subsidy (or would receive an offsetting deduction). The tax issue would thus revert to the proper treatment of targeted government direct consumption subsidies to individuals, such as those for housing. As noted above, the predominant view is that such payments are properly includable in the recipient's income, just as untargeted subsidies (unemployment benefits) or benefits (Social Security payments) should be included in the recipient's income—on which point there seems to be no disagreement. The lists published by CBO and the JCT staff have correctly continued to treat the nontaxation of both types of benefits as tax expenditures.

3. *Direct in-kind grants in the nature of welfare transfers.* Some direct welfare transfer grants are made not in cash but in kind, such as food stamps and Medicare or Medicaid payments. The 1968 Treasury presentation did not discuss the treatment of these in-kind government transfer programs. As 1982 Special Analysis G stated: "The dividing line is not clear cut between nontaxable government benefits that result in tax expenditures and those that do not. Food stamps, for example, are so nearly the equivalent of cash that their exclusion from income subject to tax might be considered to result in a tax expenditure, but in this analysis they are not so considered."[29] The issue, of course, extends to the proper treatment of general government services, such as public education, subsidized transportation, police and fire protection, public parks, and national defense. It seems clear that because of the impossibility of properly measuring and allocating the value of these generally provided benefits, they cannot be included under an income tax. The nontaxation of such benefits has properly been excluded from tax expenditure lists. On the other hand, the nontaxation of these general government services does not justify the current nontaxation of the targeted and measurable in-kind payments enumerated above.[30]

Although it is difficult to draw a distinction between appropriately nontaxable in-kind general public benefits and appropriately taxable in-kind benefits, so far the U.S. tax expenditure lists have erred on the side of noninclusion. An in-kind benefit program targeted to a specific group, such as poverty-level individuals (food stamps and Medicaid) or the aged (Medicare), should be included in income. Correspondingly, nontaxation of the benefit should be shown as a tax expenditure.[31]

4. *Loan subsidies.* Some direct government programs involve loan subsidies, either through providing interest rates lower than market rates or through providing loan guarantees. Whether these loan subsidies are to businesses, either corporate or individual, or to nonbusiness individuals, their benefits should be included in taxable income. The problem here is one of measurement of the revenue cost rather than of classification, and is discussed below. These loan subsidies were not considered in the original 1968 tax expenditure analysis and have not been analyzed in subsequent lists.

5. *Technical assistance or welfare services.* Some government programs involve the provision of government technical assistance services to those engaged in business activities or some welfare assistance services for individuals. Presumably the value of these services would be excluded from taxable income because of measurement and administrative problems. The exclusion from income of these technical or welfare-type assistance services has not been considered a tax expenditure.

6. *General public services.* The provision of general government services—public education, police, and so on—is not considered a part of taxable income, and tax expenditure analysis lists accordingly do not include such items.

VARIOUS PERSONAL EXPENSES

Some writers who have considered the tax expenditure concept have difficulty accepting the classification of certain personal expenses as tax expenditures. The usual targets are the deductions for charitable contributions and medical expenses.[32] Some of the critics do not consider these as consumption items. Yet most economists have little trouble viewing them as such.[33] Hence these deductions are properly classified as tax expenditures. Some critics of the tax expenditure concept, using an "ability to pay" approach, usually list medical expenses[34] and casualty losses[35] as examples of misclassification. But these items are clearly not costs of producing income;[36] hence their classification as tax expenditures is correct.

TRAVEL AND ENTERTAINMENT EXPENSES

Tax expenditure lists to date have not included the deduction for travel and entertainment expenses. This omission should be corrected. Presumably the noninclusion of travel and entertainment expense items in income resulted from consideration of only the payor's side of the transaction. That is, the current rules governing the deductibility of travel and entertainment expenses could be viewed as an attempt by the Congress to draw a somewhat arbitrary line between nondeductible consumption and deductible business costs. However, this analysis covers only half the transaction. Even when the expenditure is a proper business expense for the payor, the value of the consumption item should be included in the income of the beneficiary. Thus, when a business provides a meal in a luxury restaurant to a customer, the customer should include the value of the meal in income. What is clear under existing rules is that a large amount of consumption is excluded from the tax base by rules providing for deductibility of the costs to the payor and nontaxation of the benefit to the recipient. Either deductibility or noninclusion is a tax expenditure and should so be reflected in the tax expenditure list. Since income inclusion is generally not administratively feasible,[37] it would seem preferable to view deductibility as the tax expenditure. This conclusion is buttressed by the congressional debate in 1978 over President Carter's proposals to limit the deduction for business entertainment. Most of the congressional debate turned on the adverse effects of the proposals on commercial sports activities, luxury restaurants, the arts, the attraction of travel to New York City, and the like; defenders of the deduction thus claimed that it was a necessary incentive to maintain those endeavors.[38]

FRINGE BENEFITS

Similar administrative issues arise with regard to the exclusion of certain employee fringe benefits from gross income. The difficulty is to separate "working conditions" (such as a desirable office or protection from kidnapping) and benefits administratively difficult to value and collect (such as certain employee discounts) from benefits that are essentially compensation though in kind (such as free air travel for airline employees, personal use of company airplanes by executives, and personal use of company cars by automobile salesmen).[39] (The statutory exclusions in this area, such as employer-purchased life insurance, employer contributions to pension plans, employer-provided health care, and employer-provided meals and lodging, are all listed as tax expenditures.) Tax expenditure lists to date have not included any item concerning the untaxed fringe benefits. But the classification of fringe benefits will have to be examined in light of the general fringe benefit legislation enacted in 1984. Under this legislation, fringe benefits are not included in income if they qualify under one of five categories: (1) a working condition fringe benefit; (2) an employee discount if offered to employees on a nondiscriminatory basis up to a specified amount; (3) a fringe benefit that does not require the employer to incur any additional cost to provide the benefit to the employee; (4) a fringe benefit that is insignificant in value; and (5) a tuition reduction plan offered by educational institutions for employees of the institution. In addition, the value of certain parking and eating facilities provided to employees, on-premises athletic facilities, and demonstration cars provided to auto salespersons is not included in income. In some cases the value of the benefits is excluded even if they are available to members of the employee's family.[40] Some of these exclusions qualify as tax expenditures. Examples are fringe benefits qualifying under the no-additional-cost provision, the employee discount rules, the tuition reduction plans, and the parking and meals exclusions. All result in a permanent exclusion of consumption from the tax base: the income is not taxed to the employee, yet the employee obtains a deduction for the items. In none of these special cases does the provision employ income tax concepts to determine excludability. The working conditions fringe benefit is a proper income determination test and an insignificant-value rule can be justified on the grounds of administrative convenience. But the fact that an employer incurs no additional cost in providing a service to an employee (such as free airline seats for airline employees) does not mean that the employee has not thereby realized additional compensation income. Indeed, the availability of such benefits has been reported to be an important factor in setting the cash pay scale for such employees. Again, the difficulty of determining the taxable income of employees may indicate that it would be administratively more feasible to deny a deduction to an employer for benefits that represent nondeductible consumption to the employee but cannot readily be includable in the employee's income. Future tax expendi-

ture lists should include either the nontaxation of fringe benefits that
are excluded from income on nonincome definition grounds or the deductibility of such items by employers.

INFLATION

As a result of persistent inflation in the United States in recent years,
increasing attention has been focused on how that inflation affects the
income tax system.[41] Proposals have been advanced to index the tax
base. Up to now, the tax system has used nominal cost in the computation of taxable income—a dollar is a dollar—even though the value
of a dollar has risen (or fallen) in relation to the value measured at the
time the cost was incurred. Indexation of the tax base would involve
an adjustment of the various items affected by inflation (such as depreciation, inventory, and debt) to reflect the effect of inflation (or deflation) in computing taxable income—a dollar is not a dollar but is a
dollar adjusted for the effect of inflation (or deflation).[42] Tax expenditure analysis does not indicate whether the correct choice is indexation or nonindexation.[43] Tax expenditure analysis does indicate,
however, that once a government has decided to index elements in the
tax base for inflation, indexing must be applied consistently to all
items in the tax base affected by inflation, or tax expenditures result.
So far the United States has decided not to adjust the tax base for inflation on an automatic basis. That decision is, of course, subject to review and change. But so long as the current policy is in effect, any
action to index a particular item in the tax base for inflation will create
a tax expenditure. For example, the House version of the Revenue Act
of 1978 included a provision to adjust gain realized on the sale or exchange of certain capital assets for the inflationary element, if any, inherent in the gain.[44] This proposal constituted a tax expenditure
benefiting holders of particular types of investments. Excluded from
the proposal were debt instruments, savings accounts, the cash value
of life insurance and annuity contracts, inventories, and other assets,
all of which are also adversely affected by inflation.

Tax expenditure analysis therefore indicates that proponents of inflation adjustment for capital gains are suggesting a tax expenditure
whose adoption would have to be justified on the ground that the proposal is a proper subsidy viewed as a federal spending program. Critical issues in analyzing such a proposal include the questions whether
inflation in the United States is high enough to make any subsidy nec-

essary to offset its effect; whether data indicate that sellers of capital assets are in greater need of a federal subsidy than those whose investments are in the form of savings accounts or bonds; whether this federal subsidy might accelerate inflationary trends; and how the benefits of the subsidy would be distributed among income classes.

Advocates of inflation adjustments usually focus on the taxability of gains attributable to inflation or on the reduced value of depreciation deductions resulting from not indexing the basis of assets. But they fail to mention that inflation produces untaxed gains for many of the same persons, notably for borrowers repaying debt with inflated dollars. The defense some invoke for this position is that since both debtors and creditors have the same marginal tax rate, the gains of debtors are balanced by the losses of creditors so that the Treasury comes out even and an inflation adjustment for borrowing is therefore not required. This defense involves both a heroic assumption and a disregard of the fact that a discussion of the effects of inflation must consider income tax liabilities separately for each taxpayer. It is no comfort to the taxpayer with a disallowed inflation loss (a creditor) that another taxpayer did not have to include an inflation gain in income (the debtor). The essence of an income tax is to measure the contributions required to the national fisc on the basis of the impact of economic and other forces on the *separate* incomes of the various taxable units.

ACCOUNTING AND THE TAXABLE PERIOD

ACCELERATED DEPRECIATION

The current tax provisions for depreciation are both diverse and complex. The tax law allows a taxpayer to use depreciation methods that need not be used in the taxpayer's financial reports.[45] The permitted divergence produces a tax expenditure if the taxpayer chooses a faster tax depreciation write-off that lowers taxable income but then follows a slower depreciation write-off to show higher book profits.

Over the past three decades, depreciation for federal income tax purposes has generally been guided more by the norm of economic depreciation than by financial accounting techniques. Until recently, economic depreciation has been difficult to reflect in administrable tax rules because of the problem of determining actual price declines each year for the large number of assets that must be covered by the depreciation rules. But there has been a continuing search for depreciation rules that are reasonably good surrogates for economic depreciation.

Thus, in the case of machinery and equipment, studies have found that the declining balance method of depreciation over the asset's useful life is a fairly close approximation of economic depreciation. In the case of depreciable real estate, straight-line depreciation over the property's useful life has been accepted as the norm that most closely correlates with economic depreciation.

For tax expenditure classification purposes, depreciation rules providing for depreciation deductions in excess of those that would be permittted under either the accounting or economic norm have been classified as tax expenditures. For example, when the asset depreciation range (ADR) system was introduced in 1971 to permit a taxpayer depreciating machinery and equipment to elect a useful life that was 20 percent shorter than the guideline lives established by the Treasury, a tax expenditure resulted: the ADR system in effect permitted a taxpayer to take depreciation faster than the norm of declining-balance depreciation over the useful life of the asset. The provisions permitting a taxpayer to use a declining-balance method of depreciation for buildings also constituted a tax expenditure, since these rules allowed deductions faster than would have been the case under the norm of straight-line depreciation.

In 1981 Congress adopted the accelerated cost recovery system (ACRS). The ACRS method places machinery and equipment in a three-, five-, or ten-year class and permits the taxpayer to write off the cost of an asset on a declining-balance method within the applicable period. For real estate a fifteen-year (now eighteen-year) write-off period was established, again with a declining-balance method. ACRS thus permitted even faster depreciation than had been permitted for machinery and equipment under the ADR system and for buildings under the declining-balance methods of depreciation. The CBO and JCT tax expenditure lists appropriately treated both the excess of ACRS over the declining-balance method for machinery and equipment and the excess of ACRS over straight-line depreciation for buildings as tax expenditures.

The congressional reasons for introducing ACRS were to "provide the investment stimulus that was felt to be essential for economic expansion," to compensate for inflation, and to reduce the complexity of existing depreciation rules.[46] The first two justifications are those used for federal spending programs (since the congressional concern about inflation extended only to one group of assets affected by inflation). The third justification was presumably based on difficulties experienced in measuring useful lives and in determining economic depreciation. But this congressional perception ignores the existing state of economic analysis of depreciation and is refuted by the fact that techniques have been developed to ensure that a taxpayer takes no more and no less than economic depreciation.[47]

The 1983 Special Analysis G departed from the CBO and JCT lists by treating ACRS as a part of the reference tax structure, thereby eliminating it from tax expenditure classification. But other documents produced by the administration showed clearly that ACRS cannot be considered a normative depreciation rule. The 1982 *Economic Report of the President,* for example, showed that ACRS produced highly varying effective rates of tax among industries and among companies within the same industry.[48] A tax provision that produces such a result cannot, by definition, be part of the normal tax structure. Moreover, when ACRS was combined with the investment credit, it produced a negative income tax rate for the income generated by certain kinds of investments; that is, for some assets the after-tax rate of return was greater than the before-tax rate of return (or, put another way, some taxpayers were better off under ACRS than if there were no income tax at all!). Again, a normative tax depreciation rule simply cannot produce those results. The failure of OMB to classify ACRS as a tax expenditure is demonstrably wrong both in light of the legislative history of the provision and in terms of economic and tax theory.

RESEARCH AND DEVELOPMENT COSTS

For tax accounting purposes, research and development costs may be either deducted immediately or amortized over a five-year period. The immediate expensing option has been treated as a tax expenditure; yet for financial accounting purposes, research and development costs must be expensed in the year incurred. The reason given by the Financial Accounting Standards Board for the change from capitalization to expensing of research and development costs was that when a business is incurring a large number of research and development costs on a recurring annual basis, it is likely that the expenses do not have a benefit beyond the year in question (in this respect, the accounting profession views such costs as similar in nature to advertising expenses). From the standpoint of tax expenditure analysis, the issue raised by the change in accounting standard is whether the reasons were sufficient to justify removal of the immediate deduction for research and development costs from the tax expenditure classification.

The financial accounting change, however, should not change the tax expenditure classification for the immediate deduction. The financial reporting standard applies only to large business taxpayers incurring substantial research and development costs on an annual recurring basis. A significant number of taxpayers deducting research and development costs do not fit within this category. One notable example is the one-shot research and development tax shelter, in which a single partnership is formed for a specific amount or for a specific type of research project. Given both the rule's inapplicability to a significant number of taxpayers who incur research and development costs and the avowed congressional purpose of encouraging research and development activities through the immediate expensing option, tax expenditure classification continues to be appropriate for the item.

DETERMINING THE TAXABLE UNIT

EXEMPTIONS FOR DEPENDENTS

Under current U.S. tax rules, parents are entitled to a $1,000 personal exemption for each dependent child. On the other hand, the income earned by the child is not included with that of the parents to determine the total taxable income of the family unit. Suppose a grandparent sets up a trust for a grandchild, and the income is distributed to the grandchild currently. The grandchild computes tax on the trust income in his or her separate return, but the grandchild's parents are nonetheless entitled to take a dependent's exemption if they have provided more than 50 percent of the child's support.

U.S. tax expenditure lists have shown neither of these provisions as a tax expenditure. Attention has focused on the dependents' exemptions, and those preparing the tax expenditure lists have taken the position that the dependents' exemptions are in effect a part of the rules defining the point at which positive tax rates should begin for the family unit. The logical result of this line of reasoning is that all members of the family unit for whom an exemption is granted should be included in the family unit for income determination purposes. Under this view, then, the failure to include the income of a dependent in that of the family unit's total income represents a tax expenditure.

On the other hand, it can be argued that the dependents' exemptions are really the functional equivalents of children's allowances. Many countries utilize direct children's allowances, and it is possible to convert a direct children's allowance to a dependent's exemption and vice versa. Under this view, the dependent's exemption should be classified as a tax expenditure, and the treatment of the child as a separate taxable unit should be considered an acceptable policy judgment that does not involve the creation of tax expenditures.

Clearly either a dependent's exemption or the provision treating a dependent as a separate taxable unit constitutes a tax expenditure. Given the fact that a decision to include a dependent in the taxable unit would be based on broad social policy grounds involving the prevailing view of the family, the relationships between parents and children, and the like, it seems likely that the decision to treat the child as a separate taxable unit is not a tax expenditure. Moreover, the close correspondence between direct children's allowance programs in other countries and the dependents' exemptions buttresses the view that the exemptions represent tax expenditures and should be so reflected in the U.S. tax expenditure lists.

THE TWO-EARNER FAMILY

In 1981 Congress adopted a deduction equal to 10 percent of the lesser earned income of a spouse in a two-earner family, with a ceiling of $30,000 of that spouse's earned income. This deduction was a response to the view that the tax schedule rates adopted for a married couple in 1969 produced a "marriage penalty": when two persons, each with earned income, married, they paid more taxes than the total of their previous separate taxes as single people. The tax committees gave the following reasons for the 1981 change:

> The Congress believed that alleviation of the marriage penalty was necessary because large tax penalties on marriage undermined respect for the family by affected individuals and for the tax system itself. To do this, the Congress was obliged to make a distinction between one-earner and two-earner married couples. The simplest way to alleviate the marriage penalty was to allow a percentage of the earned income of the spouse with the lower earnings to be, in effect, free from income tax.

> The provision also alleviates another effect of the prior system on all married couples—high effective marginal tax rates on the second earner's income. Recent studies have shown that these high marginal rates had a significant adverse effect on second earners' decisions to seek paying jobs. The ten-percent reduction in marginal tax rates for second earners provided by the new de-

duction will reduce this work disincentive. In addition, some contend that two-earner couples are less able to pay income tax than one-earner couples with the same amount of income because the former have more expenses resulting from earning income, as well as less free time. Under this concept, the new deduction will improve equity by reducing the tax burdens of two-earner couples compared to one-earner couples.[49]

The so-called marriage penalty has two different aspects. First, because imputed income from household services is not included in the tax base, a couple with one cash producer will pay less tax than a couple with two cash producers even though the two couples have the same total economic income. A deduction for the lower cash producer in two-earner families can thus be seen as an adjustment to compensate for the administrative difficulty of taxing the imputed income in one-earner families. The problem is that this marriage penalty effect is not confined to situations in which the cash is produced by personal services; it also exists when the cash results from passive investments. This argument would seem to require that an unlimited deduction be granted for the second cash producer in a two-earner family. In addition, there is a host of imputed income-producing activities, such as washing one's own car. It is safe to say that there would be general astonishment if a deduction were granted to an individual who paid to have his car washed and the deduction were not treated as a tax expenditure on the ground that it offset the failure to tax the imputed income of the person who washed his own car.

Second, the two-earner provision could be seen as a measure to adjust the relative tax burdens between two different types of taxable units: married couples and single persons. Thus the 1969 action, in reducing the rates for single persons vis-à-vis married couples, did not involve a tax expenditure. The two-earner deduction readjusts that relationship for two-worker couples. Again, the problem is that the solution is confined to earned income, whereas the problem of the appropriate relationship exists whether the income is from services or investments.

The two-earner deduction as adopted in 1981 is not sufficiently general in its coverage to be regarded as part of the technical structure necessary to implement decisions concerning the taxable unit. On balance, therefore, classification of the provision as a tax expenditure appears correct.

CORPORATION-SHAREHOLDER RELATIONSHIPS

Many public finance theorists hold the view that only individuals should be subject to an income tax, that an income tax should not apply to corporations, just as it does not apply to partnerships. In this view, a corporation is not a taxpaying unit but rather, as in the case of a partnership, the income of the corporation (whether or not distributed) must be considered the income of the shareholders and allocated among them. If this "full integration" approach were the basic national policy, tax experts presumably could develop the appropriate technical or normative rules to work out the tax solutions necessary to implement the decision. Other public finance theorists, however, consider the corporation as in itself a taxable unit.[50] Also, social and political forces in a country might determine that, because of the nature of the corporation and its role in society, a corporation should be subject in itself to the income tax.[51] If this "classical" separate approach were the basic national policy, tax experts could likewise develop the necessary normative rules to handle the tax relationships between a corporation and its shareholders.

Both the full integration approach and the classical separate approach are acceptable as national policies. Tax theory does not posit either as normative. But once a policy decision has been made for either approach, it is possible to identify tax expenditures. Because the United States has chosen the classical separate approach toward corporation and shareholder, the exclusion of $200 of dividends ($400 on joint returns), generally defended as an incentive to savings, is a tax expenditure.

Certain types of entities that are corporations under applicable state law are treated in effect as partnerships for federal income tax purposes, with the result that no corporate-level tax is imposed on the income of the entity. The only tax is at the shareholder level. Among the beneficiaries of this treatment are so-called S corporations (in general, corporations with thirty-five or fewer shareholders), mutual funds, and real estate investment trusts. U.S. tax expenditure lists have not included shareholder-level taxation of these types of entities. The decision appears appropriate, since Congress in effect has determined that for income tax purposes the entities involved are more akin to partnerships than to corporations. Conversely, federal income tax rules also treat as corporations certain entities that constitute partnerships under state law. The imposition of corporate-level taxes on these entities does not constitute a tax penalty, since again the state law classification has not been deemed appropriate for federal income tax purposes.

Under the existing U.S. tax rules, a business that is organized and operated as a cooperative for the benefit of its patrons (owners) is exempt from the corporate income tax to the extent that it distributes dividends or issues certificates representing "rights" of the patrons to the earnings of the cooperative. This dividend deduction technique renders the business organization exempt from the corporate income tax. In accordance with earlier tax expenditure lists, the CBO and JCT lists include the dividend deduction for cooperatives. This treatment is based on the view that under applicable principles for classifying an organization as a corporation rather than as a partnership, cooperatives belong to the former category and thus should be subject to the corporate income tax.

Beginning with the 1983 Special Analysis G, however, the OMB tax expenditure list has omitted the tax treatment of cooperatives. At first glance there appears to be some support for the OMB position, in view of the fact that organizations such as S corporations, real estate investment trusts, and mutual funds are likewise not subject to tax at the entity level. The situation of S corporations, however, is distinguishable in that the S corporation rules apply to all kinds of businesses whereas the cooperative rules are specifically confined to the agricultural sector. The distinction between the farmers' cooperatives and the mutual funds and real estate investment trusts rests on the fact that farmers' cooperatives are engaged in active businesses whereas the other types of organizations are confined to passive investments. They are thus more like large investors' clubs that have pooled their resources for investment purposes. That is, when three or four neighbors join together to form an investment club, it would not seem appropriate to treat them as a corporation and impose a corporate-level and a shareholder-level tax. Extension of this model to the mutual funds and real estate investment trusts appears appropriate under the rather tight rules that govern those organizations. On the other hand, if three or four neighbors join together to conduct an active business, the enterprise must be subject to the normative rules for distinguishing partnerships from corporations; under these tests, farmers' cooperatives constitute cooperations. Accordingly, the failure to impose a corporate-level tax on these organizations produces a tax expenditure, acknowledged in the CBO and JCT lists.

Although no major industrialized country has adopted the full integration approach for corporate income, several countries have adopted "partial integration" rules. The effect of these systems is to reduce the overall corporate and shareholder tax on dividend distributions. The reduction in tax is sometimes made at the corporate level through a deduction for dividend distributions and sometimes at the shareholder level through a credit against the shareholder's individual tax for all or a part of the corporate income tax attributable to the dividend distribution. Several countries have had to consider whether the partial integration rules constitute tax expenditures. The Canadian tax expenditure list includes the partial integration rule on the ground that the basic Canadian policy remains the classical approach, which Canada used until the adoption of the partial integration rules. On the other hand, Germany does not view a similar partial integration approach as a tax expenditure. There the reasoning is that the shift from a classical system to the partial integration system in 1977 involved a fundamental policy change. Under this view, presumably the remaining corporate-level tax in Germany should be viewed as a tax penalty (although the German tax expenditure lists to date have not shown any tax penalties).

Although it may seem strange that the same provision can constitute a tax expenditure in one country and a tax penalty in the other, in fact both the Canadian and the German approaches are consistent with tax expenditure analysis. The treatment of the provision depends on what the country's basic policy is deemed to be; thereafter, deviations from that policy constitute tax expenditures. The differences in the Canadian and German lists occur because, in making its basic taxable unit decision regarding corporations and shareholders, each country has taken into account several considerations other than purely tax ones, such as the role of corporations in the economy, the social view of corporate economic power, and historical and legal views of corporations. If those preparing the U.S., Canadian, and German tax expenditure lists have correctly determined the basic policy adopted in each country, they have applied tax expenditure analysis appropriately to the departures from those policies.[52]

DEFERRAL OF TAX ON INCOME OF FOREIGN SUBSIDIARIES OF U.S. CORPORATIONS

As was discussed in chapter 6, the deferral of tax on the income of U.S.-controlled foreign subsidiaries constitutes a tax expenditure because for foreign tax credit purposes these subsidiaries are considered part of the same taxable unit as the parent U.S. corporation. Since the U.S. parent corporation is given a credit for foreign taxes incurred by its subsidiary, on the theory that the two corporations in effect constitute a single taxable unit, the failure to tax currently the income of the foreign subsidiary must constitute a tax expenditure. This is the approach adopted by the CBO and JCT lists. The OMB's failure to show the deferral as a tax expenditure, beginning with 1983 Special Analysis G, is incorrect. This conclusion derives added strength from the fact that the OMB list does not show the indirect foreign tax credit as a tax expenditure. Even under the OMB view, one or the other of the two items must constitute a tax expenditure.

TRUSTS

U.S. tax expenditure lists have not included any item involving family trusts. Moreover, none of the discussions accompanying the lists have mentioned the standards used to classify the various provisions governing family trusts.

In cases in which the grantor of the trust is still living, the critical issue is whether the grantor has sufficiently parted with control over the property placed in trust to justify inclusion of the trust income in the income of the beneficiaries. Although the current rules governing these situations may be criticized on the ground that they permit the grantor to retain too much control over the trust property while shifting the income tax burden to the beneficiaries, nonetheless the rules are aimed at drawing this critical line. It thus appears appropriate to classify the grantor trust rules as normative components of the income tax rather than as tax expenditures.

In cases in which the grantor has shifted control of the trust property to the trustee, either by complying with the rules governing lifetime transfers or because the grantor is deceased, the issue is whether it is appropriate to treat the trust itself as a separate taxpayer if not all the trust income is distributed to the beneficiaries. When the trust distributes the income to the beneficiaries, they are taxed currently and no tax expenditure issue arises. When the trust accumulates income for later distribution to beneficiaries, it is treated as a taxpayer with respect to the accumulated income. However, upon distribution to the beneficiaries, a special "throwback" rule requires the beneficiaries to recompute their income for the five years preceding the distribution and to pay the average increase in tax that would have resulted had the income in fact been distributed to them. They receive credit for the taxes paid by the trust. If the beneficiary is in a higher tax bracket than the trust during the years of accumulation, then tax deferral results. The reverse is true if the beneficiary is in a lower income tax bracket than the trust. Although it would seem appropriate to impose an interest charge in situations involving tax deferral, as is done in the case of foreign trusts created for U.S. beneficiaries, the absence of the interest charge does not appear to warrant tax expenditure classification. Nontax considerations affect decisions by trustees to distribute or accumulate income or to apportion it among various beneficiaries, and the existing rules, which provide a deferral benefit to some beneficiaries but a penalty to others, seem to be a rough trade-off based on tax simplification and administrative grounds. As the American Law Institute has recognized, the entire trust area is badly in need of thorough analysis and restructuring. But the very fact that this needed study is being undertaken by the technical experts involved in the American Law Institute project indicates the appropriateness of the current view that the trust rules are normative rather than tax expenditure provisions.

TAX-EXEMPT ORGANIZATIONS

U.S. tax expenditure lists have not included any item related to nonprofit, tax-exempt organizations, nor have they given any reason for this omission. As the following analysis indicates, the U.S. tax treatment of nonprofit organizations should be classified as a tax expenditure.

Under U.S. tax rules, the "related" business income of a qualifying organization is exempt from tax. In addition, for most tax-exempt organizations, investment income is also exempt from tax. To the extent that this exempt income is utilized to provide consumption for the beneficiaries of the organizations, and to the extent that the consumption is untaxed, significant amounts are excluded from the tax base. In such situations, tax expenditures result from the exemption.

Some tax-exempt organizations appear to conform to the model of the typical for-profit corporation. Hospitals represent one rather clear example of this type. When the corporate model is appropriate, the tax expenditure list should include the nontaxation of the business and investment income of the organization. Under this approach, no deduction should be allowed to the organization for distributions to beneficiaries, because it is not administratively feasible to include the charitable benefits in the income of the various beneficiaries. This treatment is akin to the second-best approach adopted for certain types of corporate gifts and fringe benefits.

On the other hand, some exempt organizations may appropriately be viewed as partnerships of individuals joining together for a common purpose. The social club is a typical example. In such cases, the value of the untaxed consumption to those who benefit from the organization's business and investment income should be classified as a tax expenditure.

Because it is likely that the revenue cost of the exemption for nonprofit organizations is substantial, the omission from the U.S. tax expenditure lists is a serious one and should be rectified.

THE RATE STRUCTURE

BASIC PERSONAL EXEMPTIONS AND THE ZERO BRACKET AMOUNT

The personal exemption allowed for each taxable unit is simply a way of defining an amount of income taxed at a zero rate. A zero rate bracket is appropriate in a general rate structure, so long as it applies to all types of income and thus does not constitute a tax expenditure any more than does any other rate of tax below the top rate. Similarly, the "zero bracket amount" in U.S. tax rules is not a tax expenditure since it too provides an additional level of income that is available to all taxable units and is taxed at a zero rate. Indeed, as is done in the tax tables, the personal exemptions and the zero bracket amount can be combined into a single figure for each taxable unit. Just as changes in the general positive rates do not involve tax expenditures, neither do changes in the zero bracket amount or basic personal exemptions. This is the view consistently adhered to by those preparing the U.S. tax expenditure lists.

INDEXING TAX BRACKETS AND BASIC EXEMPTIONS FOR INFLATION

In 1981 Congress provided that the tax brackets, the personal exemptions, and the zero bracket amount would be indexed for inflation. When implemented, indexation of these items will not involve tax expenditures. Indexation of items in the rate structure represents general rate reductions in an inflationary economy. Congress can and has attained the same results through ad hoc rate reductions. Similarly, a decision to index, say, only the zero bracket amount would not constitute a tax expenditure.

CORPORATE TAX RATES

Until 1978 all tax expenditure budgets treated the corporate surtax exemption as a tax expenditure, thus regarding the normative corporate tax to be a flat-rate tax.[53] The lower rates, provided within the corporate surtax exemption range, traditionally were justified as aids to small business and accordingly were included in tax expenditure lists. In the Revenue Act of 1978, the normal tax and surtax structure was repealed and replaced by a five-step rate structure on corporate taxable income, with rates ranging from 17 (now 15) to 46 percent for taxable income in excess of $100,000. The House Ways and Means Committee report stated: "With respect to business taxpayers, the basic corporate tax structure is changed and taxes are reduced, but the committee does not consider a new tax structure to be a tax expenditure, even though the change reduces tax liabilities. The Congressional Budget Office does not agree."[54] In some respects, the committee's justification of the changed rate structure is consistent with its view that the change simply implemented a new rate system for corporations. The committee was concerned that the former "abrupt jump in tax rates" from 22 to 48 percent was undesirable.[55] Moreover, it argued that the new system of graduated rates would reduce the impact of the tax provisions on the selection of the form in which to operate a small business.

These arguments appear to be based on structural grounds rather than on subsidy considerations. However, the committee also stated that it was making the change because tax relief was "especially needed for small companies."[56] The focus on small business was highlighted by the committee's decision to halt the progression of the rates at $100,000 of taxable income, since 78 percent of corporate net income and 93 percent of corporate taxes are attributable to corporate income above $100,000. Despite the committee's statement, the tables on changes in tax expenditures provided in the tax committee reports treated the revenue loss from the lower corporate rates on the first $100,000 of taxable income as a tax expenditure.[57]

The 1978 changes in the corporate rate structure present an interesting conceptual issue. Certainly, tax expenditure analysis does not imply that a country can adopt only a flat-rate corporate tax. Progressive rates have traditionally not been applied to corporations, because a progressive rate schedule has largely been justified on an "ability to pay" rationale, and such a rationale has little relevance to corporations. A country could choose, however, to have a truly graduated and progressive rate scale for corporations. But the 1978 legislation does not represent such a structure. The benefits of the new rate schedule are largely confined to small business because of the failure to extend the five-step rate schedule farther up the income scale. Moreover, the changes amount to only a $7,750 reduction in tax on the first $100,000 of income. This seems a relatively minor revenue change and not significant enough to justify removal of the four-step lower corporate tax rates from the tax expenditure category, in which the previous two-step system was included. On balance, therefore, the CBO and JCT classification of the graduated rate system for corporations as a tax expenditure program for small business is correct. Beginning with the 1983 Special Analysis G, OMB has treated these graduated corporate rates as part of the reference tax structure rather than as tax expenditures.

TAX PENALTIES

Tax expenditures represent departures from a normative income tax and provide government financial assistance through the income tax system. Other provisions also depart from the normative structure but penalize the taxpayer by requiring a greater tax payment than would be due under the normative rules. Just as it is appropriate in the tax expenditure budget to reflect government interventions in the economy through tax expenditures, so it is also appropriate to reflect in the tax expenditure account government interventions in the economy through these tax penalty provisions.

An analysis of the tax penalty provisions reveals that they are the functional equivalents of direct government regulatory or financial penalty rules. In the United States, for example, businesses are denied deductions for fines paid to government entities.[58] This statutory provision embodies earlier court decisions that denied deduction for fines on the ground that they were not "ordinary and necessary" business expenses since "a finding of 'necessity' cannot be made if allowance of the deduction would frustrate sharply defined national or state policies, proscribing particular types of conduct, evidenced by some governmental declaration thereof."[59] But under normative tax (and accounting) principles, these business costs should be deductible because they are costs of producing income. Disallowance of the deduction increases the amount of the fine that is imposed directly (just as the exclusion of a particular item of income from tax increases the cost of the direct program). Suppose a state imposes a fine on trucks that exceed the maximum weight laws, and the federal government wishes to add a fine for the violation. It can do so directly, or it can deny deductibility (the converse situation in the tax expenditure area is the increase in federal revenue sharing by allowing deductions for state sales taxes). Once a tax penalty has been identified, it must be analyzed in the same way as any direct federal penalty program in terms of its necessity, effectiveness, and correspondence to other direct penalty programs. Such analysis immediately reveals, for example, that tax penalties imposed on proprietorships or partnerships have an upside-down effect; the amount of the penalty imposed rises with income. Comparison of this program with the treatment of direct penalty programs will reveal whether such an effect is rational.

As another example, a business is not allowed to deduct expenditures for lobbying for or against legislation, for political campaigns (including the support of or opposition to any candidate for public office), or for propaganda (including advertising) related to any of those activities.[60] Again, the denial of the deduction is equivalent to the imposition of a fine for carrying on the proscribed activity. This tax penalty raises some interesting constitutional issues with respect to free speech.

It might be argued that a normative income tax should be designed to mesh with criminal laws imposing financial penalties. In this view, it would be normative to deny deductions for fines or other monetary penalties, since otherwise the monetary impact of the penalties is reduced under the progressive rates of tax. In addition, it would be difficult to devise a monetary penalty that took account of the deductibility of that penalty. Under this logic it could then be argued that a normative income tax should also be designed to complement laws expressing deeply held moral or public policy positions, such as laws against murder, bribery, and lobbying. But in a sense every law regulating conduct or imposing financial, regulatory, or criminal sanctions expresses some public policy. Thus it seems quite impossible to distinguish between public policies that can be accompanied by "normative" deduction denial provisions and public policies for which the denial of a deduction constitutes a tax penalty. On balance, therefore, denials of deductions for the costs of producing income should be classified as tax penalties since the result is to tax more than net income.

The tax penalty items should be reflected in a combined tax expenditure and tax penalty list, as was discussed in chapter 2. Correspondingly, analysis of the need for and rationality, effectiveness, and efficiency of these tax penalty provisions should proceed in the same way as the analysis of tax expenditure provisions. The following is a list of the tax penalty provisions now present in the Internal Revenue Code:

> Limitation on deduction for business lobbying costs
> Disallowance of deduction for bad debts of political parties
> Disallowance of deduction for indirect contributions to political parties
> Disallowance of deductions for demolition of certain historic structures
> Limitation on the deduction for business wagering losses
> Disallowance of deduction for illegal bribes and kickbacks
> Disallowance of deduction for business fines and penalties
> Limitation on deduction of treble damage payments under the antitrust laws
> Limitation of ordinary business deductions to amounts at risk
> Reduction of foreign tax credit for participation in an international boycott
> Accumulated earnings tax
> Personal holding company tax

In analyzing tax penalties, it is important to keep in mind that not all limitations imposed on deductions constitute tax penalties. Thus limitations on tax expenditure deductions simply define the scope of eligibility for the program and do not constitute tax penalties. Subpart F, for example, currently taxes a U.S. parent on the income of certain U.S.-controlled foreign subsidiaries. The general deferral of tax for foreign subsidiaries constitutes a tax expenditure; the deferral is granted to enable U.S. subsidiaries to be competitive in the country in which they are organized. Subpart F withdraws the deferral privilege for a foreign subsidiary that has dealings with its parent or other subsidiaries and realizes its income outside the country of incorporation. In this case it is engaging in competition in countries other than that in which it is incorporated, and Congress has determined that it is not prepared to subsidize that kind of activity. Subpart F therefore establishes the limits on the subsidy program provided through deferral and is not a tax penalty. Similarly, the minimum tax on tax preferences is not a tax penalty; rather, it imposes a limit on the advantage a taxpayer can take of multiple tax expenditure provisions. Whether or not the limitations imposed on the tax expenditure programs are rational when viewed from a spending perspective, they must be analyzed as limitations and not as tax penalties.

The "at risk" rules represent provisions that simultaneously limit tax expenditures and impose tax penalties. Under the at risk rules, when a taxpayer purchases an asset utilizing nonrecourse debt, deductions for depreciation or other costs are allowed only for his own actual investment, the extent to which the taxpayer is "at risk." Historically, U.S. taxpayers were allowed to take deductions based on the full cost of the purchased assets, even when the borrowing was in part represented by nonrecourse financing. The at risk rules, when they are applicable, require the taxpayer who utilizes nonrecourse financing to defer deductions attributable to that financing until such time as he has invested his own funds in the project. To the extent that the at risk rules defer the deduction for tax expenditure items, they function simply as limits on the tax expenditure programs. That is, Congress has decided that the federal subsidy is not to be made available except to the extent that the taxpayer has his own funds invested in a particular project.

The at risk rules, however, extend their effect beyond the tax expenditure provisions. They can also operate to defer deductions that represent costs of producing income under normative rules. It could be argued that the at risk rules represent the first step in a change in the normative U.S. rules regarding the treatment of nonrecourse debt. That is, the rules may reflect a changing attitude toward the historic position that the cost of an asset, for depreciation and gain computation purposes, should include both the taxpayer's own funds and funds represented by nonrecourse debt. At present, however, it is impossible to establish that such a fundamental change has occurred. The at risk rules do not apply to real estate, and the basic rule that nonrecourse debt is to be reflected in a taxpayer's cost basis in the asset was quite specifically left unchanged when the at risk rules were adopted. Accordingly, for now it seems appropriate to classify the at risk rules as a tax penalty to the extent that they defer the otherwise deductible costs of producing income.

The definition of tax expenditures in the 1968 Treasury presentation, in subsequent legislation, and in critical comment has presented interesting but not insurmountable conceptual problems. These problems have arisen with regard to borderline situations, which are few in relation to the huge number of existing tax expenditures, and which are inevitable for any useful concept.[61] Continuing experience with the tax expenditure concept, both in the United States and in other countries, will undoubtedly disclose new matters for analysis and a need to examine earlier analyses of some items. The fact remains that the ability to define tax expenditures is essential to a country's control of its tax and budget policies.

Estimates of Tax Expenditures

Tax expenditure analysis requires a means of estimating the cost of each tax expenditure item. The general estimating methods used in supplying tax expenditure data are the same as those used before 1968 to determine the revenue effects of changes in the tax laws. The Treasury economists had always prepared for the executive branch and Congress estimates of the annual revenue loss or gain involved in proposals for changes in the tax laws. These economists continually refined their estimating techniques as new data became available, as economic tax analysis developed, as computerization of tax return information proceeded, as sampling techniques improved, and so on. When the first tax expenditure list was developed in 1968, these economists chose the *revenue loss* produced by a tax expenditure item as the standard of measurement for the tax expenditure budget.

The analytical problems involved in estimating tax expenditures are the same as those involved in estimating revenues for any proposed legislative tax changes. These problems include: the handling of an estimate for one item when the item is affected by changes in other items—the so-called stacking of changes in interrelated items; the assumption that economic behavior remains unchanged if an item is eliminated—the so-called first-order estimates; and the assumption that economic conditions remain unchanged by microeconomic measures. The economists who supply the revenue estimates for tax revision proposals are the same individuals who furnish the tax expenditure estimates. Hence, any criticisms of the tax expenditure estimates are essentially criticisms of the basic revenue-estimating procedures used by the Treasury and Congress, not of the tax expenditure concept itself.

The 1982 Special Analysis G described the basic estimating methods used in obtaining the estimates for revenue losses from the expenditures:

> The tax expenditure estimating procedure uses the same implicit assumption that governs estimates of out-year budget outlays, namely that the existing tax structure and all other institutional determinants of resource costs are given. In effect, the estimating procedure answers the question, "How much

more tax liability would be incurred by taxpayers if the preferential tax rule were not in force, but all other features of the tax system, including the structure of rates, remained the same?" When the special tax rule involves an extraordinary deduction or exclusion of income receipts, the tax expenditure is estimated to be the excess deduction or excluded income times an applicable marginal tax rate. However, in the case of individual taxpayers, account is taken of the likelihood that some will no longer have remaining deductions sufficient to itemize and, hence, would elect the standard deduction, absent the preferential deduction in question. When the special tax rule is a preferential credit against taxes otherwise due, the tax expenditure estimate is equal to the credits claimed by all taxpayers.[62]

Behind this straightforward explanation lie some significant issues with respect to the measurement of tax expenditures.

THE USE OF A FIRST-ORDER APPROACH

All U.S. tax expenditure estimates have assumed that there are no "second-order" effects; that is, "taxpayer behavior" is "assumed to be unaffected by the assumed deletion of a tax expenditure provision."[63] The first-order estimates indicate the revenue change that would result in the first round of effects following the elimination or addition of a tax expenditure or a change in the item. The Treasury uses the same general rule in making estimates on specific tax provisions.

In recent years some critics of Treasury estimates have contended that the estimates disregard the "feedback" effects of changes in taxpayer behavior consequent to the tax change. The critics argue that the allegedly altered taxpayer behavior might lead to revenue losses in other areas (so that no net gain might occur if the tax expenditure were dropped) or result in other taxpayer action that would require an increase in direct government expenditures.[64] This criticism overlooks the fact that all Treasury estimates follow the same approach precisely because, as the critics themselves acknowledge, it is very difficult to predict taxpayer reaction to changes in revenue provisions. Consequently, the Treasury and the Congress have thought it safer, in most situations involving the estimation of revenue loss or gain from a tax change, to use a first-order estimate, which is in effect a "snapshot" of existing economic conditions with this one change made.

Those preparing data on direct spending items also use a first-order approach: a calculation that x dollars could be saved if a direct program were dropped is based on current cost of the program; no conjecture is made as to any ripple effect. It is worthwhile to attempt to learn more about ripple effects consequent to tax law changes. But the consideration of those effects properly occurs in connection with the analysis, in cost-benefit terms or otherwise, of the wisdom or effectiveness of a particular tax expenditure. The tax expenditure estimates themselves simply follow the currently accepted approach used by the Treasury and Congress for both general revenue estimates and direct expenditure programs. The General Accounting Office has emphasized these points as follows:

> The "other-things-being-equal" approach to estimating costs has attracted criticism. Business interests, for example, maintain that the investment tax credit does not cost the Government revenue but creates it. They estimate how much employment and profits have increased in response to the investment credit and conclude that the increased taxes in wages and profits are greater than the direct costs of the credit . . .
>
> However important these questions may be in appraising the costs and benefits of tax expenditures, they do not discredit the tax expenditures budget. Secondary and "ripple" effects become a part of the budgeting process only after initial costs have been established. The U.S. Budget does not record the costs of the social security programs net of the welfare payments that might be required if there were no such programs. The budget of the Public Health Service is not presented net of the taxes on the wages of the workers its programs have kept healthy enough to work. These are important in deciding whether to undertake or continue a program, but they are not relevant to the question of how many resources the program consumes. The same is true of tax expenditures.[65]

THE TREATMENT OF TAX EXPENDITURE ITEMS PROVIDING A DEFERRAL OF TAX

Some tax expenditures—such as ACRS depreciation, nontaxation of the profits of foreign subsidiaries until repatriated as dividends, and the DISC treatment of exports—provide a deferral of tax rather than a complete and final tax reduction in the year the item is deducted. The effect is twofold. One, a loan is granted through the tax system, since the tax payment is deferred, with the loan being "paid" when the deferral ends; because this loan is not taxable, only its amount need be shown. Two, the loan is interest free.

The tax expenditure estimates for such deferrals follow the "cash flow" approach used in all Treasury estimates. They show as the current revenue loss the net of the "loans" made each year (from the tax deferral provision) in excess of "payments on the loans" (resulting from the ending of deferral) for that year. The tax expenditure estimates have not included any figure for the subsidy inherent in the interest-free effect.

The 1981 Special Analysis G suggested an alternative method for handling these deferral tax expenditures:

> An alternative method of measuring tax expenditures that involve deferral would be to compute for each year the present value of the tax savings associated with the preference items. This method would make it easier to compare the values of subsidies that result from tax preferences that postpone tax liability—with the values of those that reduce it permanently. Such a present value calculation would avoid the anomalous negative estimates that result when tax revenues calculated on a cash flow basis are higher than they would have been without the tax expenditure. This occurs in situations where taxpayers whose tax liabilities were reduced in earlier years have larger tax payments in later years than they otherwise would have.[66]

However, the cost to the government of *direct loan programs* that are made at below-market interest rates is not, for direct budget outlay purposes, computed on a "present value" basis.[67] Thus the treatment of tax expenditure loans and direct government loans is consistent for budget purposes.

The present value approach to estimate the cost of interest-free tax loans would involve several problems. One is that for some deferrals (such as the deferral of tax on profits of foreign subsidiaries) there is no way of knowing precisely how long the deferral will last. Another is that it would be difficult to determine the appropriate interest rate to use.[68] Bank windows are available on different items to different taxpayers and are closed to some would-be borrowers. But the Treasury "bank window" on tax expenditure deferrals is open regardless of credit standing; accordingly, the interest-free aspect of the loan that this Treasury window affords might be difficult to estimate. The cash flow method does show that a loan is being made through the tax system. But it does not measure the value of the interest-free element. The 1985 Special Analysis F did provide present-value cost estimates for below-market direct loans. Now OMB must determine if it can apply the same estimating techniques to interest-free tax expenditure loans. If so, the more refined estimates for these loans would be useful.

TOTALING THE ESTIMATES FOR THE SEPARATE TAX EXPENDITURE ITEMS

Since 1981, Special Analysis G has warned against a simple totaling of the estimates for the separate tax expenditure items to obtain the total revenue loss arising from the presence of tax expenditures:

> Tax expenditure estimates cannot be simply added together to obtain totals for functional areas or a grand total. However, where tax expenditures for both individuals and corporations result from the same tax code provision, such as the investment tax credit, the two estimates may be added together.
>
> Simply adding tax expenditures produces inaccurate totals because tax expenditures affect the value of other tax expenditures. This interaction may be demonstrated by comparing the result of deleting two tax expenditures simultaneously to that of deleting them separately. In some cases, the revenue gained from the deletion of two tax expenditure items simultaneously would be greater than the sum of the gains from the deletion of the two items separately. For example, if interest income from State and local government securities were made taxable and capital gains were taxed as ordinary rates, many more individuals would be pushed into higher tax brackets than if just one of these sources of income became fully taxable; the combined effect on revenue would be greater than the sum of the two separate effects. In other cases, the revenue gain from the deletion of two items together would be smaller than the sum of the gains considered separately. For example, if the deductibility of mortgage interest payments and homeowner property taxes were both repealed and the standard deduction were left unchanged, more individuals who now itemize their deductions would opt for the standard

deduction than if only one preference were repealed. The revenue gain would therefore be lower from repealing both preferences together than the sum obtained from repealing each one separately.

In general, elimination of several itemized deductions would increase revenue by less than the sum of the revenue gains measured by eliminating each item separately because more taxpayers would use the standard deduction. Conversely, elimination of multiple items that are exclusions from adjusted gross income would increase revenue by more than the sum of the individual gains because taxpayers would be pushed into higher tax brackets.[69]

Tax expenditure estimates have never indicated whether the overstatement effect (resulting from the interaction between itemized deductions and the zero bracket amount) or the understatement effect (resulting from the fact that repeal of exclusions or deductions from income could move taxpayers into a higher tax bracket) is the greater. Presumably the reasons for this omission lie in technical estimating problems. More fundamentally, however, the same interaction effects are present in direct outlay programs. The CBO cited one example: "if veterans' college benefits were ended, outlays would probably rise in the basic educational grant program."[70] If the interaction effect does not prevent the computation of direct budget totals, it should not prevent the computation of tax expenditure totals.[71]

OUTLAY EQUIVALENT ESTIMATES

The 1974 Budget Act requires that the tax expenditure estimates show the revenue loss caused by the tax expenditure. Another approach, introduced in 1983 Special Analysis G, is to estimate an "outlay equivalent" for each tax expenditure. This amount represents the outlay (before-tax) cost of a direct program structured to produce the same after-tax result of the tax expenditure. Obtaining the same after-tax result requires two steps: (1) since the programs in the direct outlay budget are expressed in before-tax numbers, the tax expenditure programs must be stated in the same terms; (2) the recipient of the direct program must be as well off after tax as under the existing tax expenditure program. Accordingly, the revenue cost of the tax expenditure program must be grossed up to include the tax that would have been paid had the subsidy been in the form of a taxable direct outlay. An example in the 1985 Special Analysis G illustrates this process:

> The budget outlays for certain housing and meal allowances of military personnel are not includable in their income and therefore understate the cost of this National Defense budget element. If this form of compensation were treated as the generally applicable reference or normal tax rule as income taxable to the employee, the Defense Department would have to make larger cash payments to its military personnel to leave them as well off after tax as they are now with nontaxable allowances. Only when the existing tax subsidy is added to the tax-exempt budget outlay is this element of National Defense expenditure comparable with other defense outlays.[72]

The outlay equivalent measurement can provide useful information. It is applied in part 5 of the federal budget, "Meeting National Needs: The Federal Program by Function," so that the tax expenditure numbers under each function are before-tax figures and thus correspond with the direct outlay figures. The development of the outlay equivalent approach to estimating the costs of tax expenditures has increased the value of the tax expenditure list.

There are, however, some rather important limitations to the outlay equivalent approach that need to be mentioned. Most important, the amounts shown in the outlay equivalent estimates are crucially dependent on the proper income tax treatment of the comparable direct outlay program. If the funds received under the comparable program should be included in taxable income, then gross-up is necessary and the outlay equivalent number should be larger than the revenue loss figure. If the funds are not taxable under normative income tax principles (for example, loans), gross-up is not necessary and the two numbers are the same. In some instances, the errors made by OMB in its reference tax approach carry over to understate the revenue cost of specific items under the outlay equivalent measurement technique. For example, 1985 Special Analysis G treats the nontaxation of direct government grants for consumption items as properly nontaxable income under the reference tax. Accordingly, there is no gross-up for the revenue cost of this item. But that conclusion with respect to direct government outlays is contrary to generally accepted tax theory and the outlay equivalent approach for the item is therefore understated.

Second, the outlay equivalent approach presupposes that Congress would replace each tax expenditure program with a direct outlay program that exactly duplicates the distribution of the tax expenditure program by income classes. This assumption is unrealistic. The equivalent direct programs would be quite expensive, and their upside-down effects would be obvious. On the other hand, the outlay equivalent approach, if applied to studies showing the distribution of tax expenditures, would make the upside-down effects of most tax expenditure programs even more dramatic than they are under the revenue loss estimation method. Thus, although the outlay equivalent assumption is a little strained, it nonetheless highlights the peculiar distributional effects of most tax expenditures as discussed in chapter 3. The outlay equivalent approach requires the preparation of distributional tables, a step not yet taken by OMB and the Treasury.

Experience indicates that reliable tax expenditure estimates can be developed. The problems of estimation are quite similar to those involved for direct expenditures. Failure to develop such estimates has profound consequences. Without them, a country's policymakers cannot know how much particular programs cost the government. In short, the country would have no control over its tax policy or its budget policy.

Application of Tax Expenditure Analysis to Other Broad-based Taxes

Most of the discussion in this and earlier chapters has been in terms of an income tax, because tax expenditure analysis in the United States was developed in relation to that tax. But tax expenditure analysis is applicable to any broad-based, or global, tax. Possible candidates include the estate and gift taxes, now styled "wealth transfer taxes"; a value-added tax or other general sales tax (such as a retail sales tax or manufacturer's sales tax); state taxes; and, at the local level, a real property tax intended to be comprehensive.[73] Special excise taxes, being inherently limited in scope, involve no normative provisions and thus are not candidates for such analysis.

ESTATE AND GIFT TAXES (WEALTH TRANSFER TAXES)

The first federal tax expenditure list for taxes other than the income tax was prepared in 1976–77. Senator Edward Kennedy, in testimony before the Senate Finance Committee in 1976, submitted a list of tax expenditures prepared for the estate and gift taxes that were in effect before the Tax Reform Act of 1976.[74] A revised list of tax expenditures under the estate, gift, and generation-skipping taxes reflects the changes made by the 1976 act.[75] The method used to determine the current list of tax expenditures effected through the income tax appears equally applicable to the transfer taxes.[76] Table 6 presents bud-

Table 6. Wealth transfer tax expenditure budget estimates, by function, fiscal years 1982–1986 (millions of dollars)

Function	1982	1983	1984	1985	1986
Agriculture					
Deferral of estate tax payments (farms)	15	15	15	20	20
Preferential valuation for real property (farms)	320	640	730	850	950
Commerce and transportation					
Deferral of estate tax payments (closely held business)	8	8	8	10	10
Preferential valuation for real property (closely held business)	8	12	13	15	15
Education, training, employment, and social services					
Deductibility of charitable contributions (education)	510	530	555	570	620
Deductibility of charitable contributions (social services)	375	395	410	425	460
Exclusion for tuition payments for benefit of nondependents	a	a	a	a	a
Health					
Deductibility of charitable contributions (health)	400	420	435	450	485
Exclusion for medical payments for benefit of nondependents	a	a	a	a	a
Income security					
Exclusion for annuities from qualified retirement plans	80	80	80	80	75
Failure to tax all generation-skipping transfers	820	855	890	915	980

Table 6. (*continued*)

Function	1982	1983	1984	1985	1986
Exclusion for life insurance proceeds on which decedent paid premiums	12	12	13	12	12
Preferential treatment for lifetime gifts (failure to gross-up gifts made more than 3 years before death)	17	30	40	50	60
General government					
Exclusion for gifts to political organizations	3	3	3	3	3
Revenue sharing and general purpose fiscal assistance					
Credit for state death taxes[b]	355	385	425	450	455
Interest					
Bonds redeemable at face value ("flower bonds")	175	185	200	210	225

Source: Gerald R. Jantscher, Assistant Director, U.S. General Accounting Office, Washington, D.C. Estimates for fiscal years 1977–1981 may be found in Stanley S. Surrey, William C. Warren, Paul R. McDaniel, and Harry L. Gutman, *Federal Wealth Transfer Taxation* (1977), 844.

a. Less than $1 million.

b. Estimates are of maximum tax expenditures. Actual tax expenditures, including an offset for an undetermined amount of tax penalties, would be less.

get estimates for transfer tax expenditures for fiscal years 1982–1986. Just as the income tax is designed to encompass all net income, a normative transfer tax is designed to cover all net wealth transferred by the donor or the decedent for less than adequate consideration.

To incorporate the transfer tax into the federal list of tax expenditures, the definition in section 3(a)(3) of the Budget Reform Act of 1974 could be modified to read: "The revenue losses attributable to provisions of the Federal tax laws which allow a special exclusion, exemption, or deduction from gross transfers or which provide a special credit, a preferential rate of tax, or a deferral of tax liability."

A normative transfer tax seeks to tax all wealth transfers by an individual for less than adequate consideration. A normative transfer tax structure would require the application of the tax to a net transfer tax base, ascertained by including all items transferred and allowing as deductions those items necessary to determine the *net* transfers that the individual had the power to make. In addition, a taxable unit must be determined, an appropriate rate schedule and exemption level applied to the tax base, an appropriate period selected for application of the tax, and appropriate administrative provisions provided.

The first task, then, in establishing a tax expenditure list for the transfer tax system is to identify provisions that do not help to define some part of the normal transfer tax structure, but instead effect government spending through the transfer tax system. As in the income tax expenditure list, the enumeration of these tax expenditures does not reflect a judgment as to whether the items themselves are worthwhile or not. The goals are purely informational: identification of the tax expenditure items, quantification, and determination of the relationship between the tax expenditure items and direct budget items.

From the standpoint of tax expenditure analysis, it is unlikely that there would be much dispute over the inclusion of the items shown in table 6 in a transfer tax expenditure list. Usually, as in the case of the income tax, the defense advanced for a particular provision discloses whether its supporters treat it as a tax incentive or tax subsidy or instead are really urging that the provision overcomes a structural distortion that would otherwise exist in the working out of the proper transfer tax structure. Thus supporters of deferred tax payments and special valuation rules for farms and small businesses assert that such preferential treatment is required to provide financial assistance to farms and small businesses for the payment of the estate tax, assertedly for the purpose of preventing their sale outside the family. The deduction for charitable contributions is uniformly defended on the ground that it is a necessary inducement for wealthy individuals to transfer property to charitable organizations. The continued preferential treatment for lifetime gifts—the failure to gross up gifts by the gift tax paid on gifts made more than three years prior to death—is generally supported on the ground that it is economically desirable to encourage acceleration of transfers from older to younger and presumably more aggressive hands.

The failure to tax life insurance proceeds on which the decedent has paid the premiums constitutes a form of federal subsidy for a particular method of providing financial security to the insured's surviving spouse and/or dependents. The exclusion for gifts to political organizations operates as an inducement for political campaign contributions. The credit for state death taxes is a form of revenue sharing with state governments.

Classifying as a tax expenditure the failure to tax all generation-skipping transfers requires more explanation. Some assert that a transfer tax system contains an inherent requirement of periodicity as the measuring device of the appropriate tax period. Others argue that it does not; they assert that the object of the tax is a transfer, and that if the transfer is taxed it is irrelevant whether the transferee is in an earlier, concurrent, or later generation. These arguments are obviously structural rather than incentive or subsidy arguments.

Some argue that the taxation of generation-skipping transfers under the normal pattern of generation-to-generation devolution of property would interfere with valuable estate planning tools that provide needed flexibility for family financial planning. This appears to be an argument not for a proper structural provision in the transfer tax system, but for a form of federal subsidy to provide financial security for the decedent's family through a particular type of estate planning mechanism. As such, the exclusion for generation-skipping transfers constitutes a tax expenditure of the same type as the exclusion of life insurance proceeds from policies on which the decedent has paid the premiums.

Congress, in the Tax Reform Act of 1976, appeared to accept that the equity and structural considerations inhering in the concept of taxing wealth through a wealth transfer tax mechanism require the imposition of the transfer tax at least once each generation so as not to differentiate in the tax burden between families simply because they have different financial planning objectives.[77] Congress failed to adopt the rules necessary to effectuate this policy in full. But the legislative history does indicate that the current failure to tax all generation-skipping transfers is more than just a defective structural component of the transfer tax system; rather, it contains elements of incentives to certain trust and family planning devices.[78] Therefore, that failure should be included in the tax expenditure list.

The transfer tax expenditure list does not include the 5 percent reversionary interest rule in section 2037, use of which can result in the avoidance of transfer tax. This 5 percent rule appears to constitute a structural defect that can and should be remedied. On the other hand, an analysis of the arguments advanced by supporters of the provision might reveal that in fact the provision constitutes a tax expenditure.

The right to use the alternate valuation date is not included in the tax expenditure list. The provision appears to be a response to the often difficult problems and sometimes arbitrary results created in a world of changing values by the necessity of valuing assets on a particular date, in this case the date of death. As such, the provision is akin to an averaging device. The fact that the pre-1984 rule always provided a taxpayer benefit did raise a question whether it should be regarded as a tax expenditure,[79] but the same is true of the averaging mechanism in the income tax, and the income tax expenditure list does not include this item.

The estimates in the tax expenditure list for amounts spent through the transfer tax system are expressed in terms of the revenue losses involved for the various items and are based on the same techniques used for the income tax. Each item is estimated separately under the assumption that the item is deleted and all else remains the same, including the rate schedule. Exceptions are the estimate for deferrals of tax liability, which is based on the current revenue loss, and the estimate for "failure to tax all generation-skipping transfers," under the "Income Security" budget category. The latter includes both the revenue losses attributable to the structural gaps in the provisions adopted in 1976 (such as failure to tax outright gifts and "layered" trusts, and the $250,000 exemption for grandchildren) and those attributable to the failure of Congress to apply the generation-skipping tax to existing generation-skipping trusts. The combined amount is the continuing tax expenditure as the result of the 1976 changes.

CBO, JCT, and OMB should develop an official list of tax expenditures under the wealth transfer taxes to provide a complete picture of the extent of spending effected through the federal tax system.[80]

GENERAL CONSUMPTION TAXES

Although the United States has no general federal consumption tax, the tax expenditure concept can be applied to such a tax, whether it is in the form of a value-added tax or a tax at one or more of the levels of manufacture or sale. Canada applies its tax expenditure analysis to its manufacturers' level sales tax. France extends its list to its value-added tax, but the United Kingdom does not.[81]

STATE AND LOCAL TAXES

Those concerned with state and local taxes are gradually coming to apply tax expenditure analysis to such taxes. Since 1975, for example, the budget submitted annually by the governor of California has contained a list of major tax expenditures effected through the principal taxes employed by the state. For 1979–80 these tax expenditures amounted to more than $9 billion. The discussion in the Governor's Budget Summary also acknowledges the relationship between traditional tax reform efforts and tax expenditure analysis.[82]

Apart from special tax provisions written in by the states themselves, many states automatically adopt all or parts of federal tax expenditures. This result occurs whenever a state bases its income tax on the federal income tax. This automatic adoption of federal tax expenditures may have marked effects on the state's own fiscal policy, possibly resulting in expenditures of state funds for purposes or in amounts that would never be approved as direct programs by its legislature. A list of these "passive" tax expenditures has been prepared for the state of Colorado.[83] Massachusetts took the next logical step in 1984 and in its tax expenditure budget included tax expenditures that resulted from its own special provisions and those that resulted from adoption of federal income tax rules.[84]

Since the introduction of the tax expenditure concept in the United States in 1968, its implications and uses have expanded more widely and rapidly than could have been envisioned. The concept has opened new vistas in tax and budget policy. As developments in recent years have demonstrated, the dynamic nature of the concept holds the promise of still greater understanding of the effects of using a tax system as the vehicle for implementing government spending programs.

NOTES

1. THE TAX EXPENDITURE CONCEPT

1. For a description of the development of the Treasury's analyses, see Stanley S. Surrey, *Pathways to Tax Reform* (Cambridge, Mass.: Harvard University Press, 1973).

2. For example, the Canadian tax expenditure list includes the manufacturing sales tax, and the French list includes the value-added tax.

3. George von Schanz, "Der Einkummensbegriff und die Einkommensteuergesetz," 13 *Finanz-Archiv* no. 1, 1–87 (1896); Robert M. Haig, "The Concept of Income—Economic and Legal Aspects," in *The Federal Income Tax*, ed. Robert M. Haig (New York: Columbia University Press, 1921) 7; Henry Simons, *Personal Income Taxation* (Chicago: University of Chicago Press, 1938) 50.

4. *Annual Report of the Secretary of the Treasury on the State of the Finances for Fiscal Year 1968* (1969) 326.

5. Congressional Budget Office, 97th Cong., 1st Sess., *Tax Expenditures: Budget Control Options and Five-Year Budget Projections for Fiscal Years 1983–1987* (1982) 12–15. (The annual Congressional Budget Office studies are hereafter cited as, for example, 1982 CBO Study, by year of publication.)

6. Ibid. at 15.

7. Eric Kierans, "The Tax Reform Process: Problems of Tax Reform," 1 *Canadian Taxation* 22 (1979).

2. BUDGET POLICY

1. P.L. 93-344 (1974) (hereafter cited as Budget Act). On the budget process generally, see David J. Ott and Attiat F. Ott, *Federal Budget Policy*, 3d ed. (Washington, D.C.: Brookings Institution, 1977) chap. 3; Allen Schick, *Congress and Money* (Washington, D.C.: Urban Institute, 1980).

2. Canada implemented a similar procedure after adopting its first tax expenditure budget in 1979. See Richard M. Bird, "Current Reading," 28 *Canadian Tax Journal* 124 (1980).

3. 1982 CBO Study at 14–15.

4. Ibid. at 14.

5. 125 *Congressional Record* S48 (1979) (hereafter cited as *Cong. Rec.*). To balance the fiscal 1981 budget, Senator Baucus proposed an across-the-board 3 percent cut in both direct and tax expenditures. See 126 *Cong. Rec.* S2345 (March 6, 1980).

6. *Message from the President of the United States,* H.R. Doc. 290, 96th Cong., 2d Sess. (1980), reproduced in 126 *Cong. Rec.* H2350 (March 31, 1981).

7. See *Budget of the United States Government, 1981* (1980) at 315–352. (The basic budget documents are hereafter cited by fiscal year, as, for example, 1983 Budget.)

8. *Special Analyses, Budget of the United States Government, Fiscal Year 1976* (1975), Special Analysis F at 101–117. Beginning in 1979, tax expenditure budgets appeared in Special Analysis G. (Special analyses are hereafter cited by fiscal year.)

9. The lists from 1968 on are collected in Stanley S. Surrey, William C. Warren, Paul R. McDaniel, and Hugh J. Ault, *Federal Income Taxation,* vol. 1 (Mineola, N.Y.: Foundation Press, 1972) 242–245; 1975 supp. at 101–105; 1977 supp. at 123–126; 1979 supp. at 127–133; and 1983 supp. at 98–108.

10. 1981 Special Analysis F at 104–205.

11. Ibid. at 189.

12. Ibid. at 189–192. See also 1985 Special Analysis F at F-34.

13. 1981 Special Analysis H at 239–275.

14. Ibid. at 249–250.

15. 1985 Special Analysis H at H-11.

16. 1985 Special Analysis K at K-1.

17. See 1976–1978 Special Analyses F.

18. See 1977 CBO Study.

19. 1979 Special Analysis G at 160.

20. H. Rept. 95–1173, 95th Cong., 2d Sess. (1978).

21. See 1982 Special Analysis G at 229–230.

22. Robert W. Hartman and Joseph A. Pechman, "Issues in Budget Accounting," in *Setting National Priorities: The 1978 Budget,* ed. Joseph A. Pechman (Washington, D.C.: Brookings Institution, 1977) 425, 434, argue that treating the refundable portion of the tax credit as a tax expenditure may have a practical political effect. Presidents tend to talk about limiting federal spending, by which they mean direct outlays. Thus, including the refundable portion as a direct outlay may reduce the amounts available for other federal programs. As discussed later in this chapter, full budgetary integration of tax and direct spending programs appears to be the real answer to the problem.

23. For a detailed discussion of these differences, see Stanley S. Surrey and Paul R. McDaniel, "The Tax Expenditure Concept: Current Developments and Emerging Issues," 20 *Boston College Law Review* 225, 300–336 (1979).

24. 1981 Special Analysis G at 214. Other techniques could be employed to reflect the tax loan programs in the tax expenditure budget. It would be possi-

ble, for example, to compute the current value of the tax savings for each deferral item; see 1981 Special Analysis G at 215. Or the budget could show the gross amount "loaned" each year and the gross amount repaid (as a negative figure). The basic problem is that budget experts have not yet agreed upon a uniform method of treating below-market interest loans in the direct expenditure budget. In some instances only the net of loan disbursements and loan repayments is shown as an outlay; in others the gross amounts are shown separately; and in still others neither the loans nor the repayments show up in the budget. 1981 Special Analysis F and the 1981 Budget itself at 17–22 mark the beginning of extensive efforts to quantify, control, and integrate federal credit programs into the budget. The techniques that are ultimately developed to present the direct federal loan programs in the budget should also be employed in the tax expenditure budget for loans effected through the tax system.

The budget treatment of below-market loans made by government should parallel that of original issue discount bonds, with the amount the borrower receives composed of two parts: a loan that must be repaid and a government grant that need not be repaid. Suppose the government makes a $100 interest-free loan for a term of one year and the prevailing interest rate is 10 percent. The current value of the interest-free loan is $\frac{100}{1+.10} \times \$100 = \$90.91$. The borrower will repay the government $100 after one year, consisting of $90.01 principle and $9.09 interest. But the $9.09 received at the time the funds are received is an outright grant and should be included in income (or the basis of assets reduced). The fact that the interest payment is deductible does not affect the analysis, because the grant portion should be included in income when received and the interest deduction can be taken only as it is paid or accrued. From a budget standpoint, therefore, below-market budget loans should be reflected as a combination of budget outlays and loans; loan repayments should reflect both interest and principal payments. This is the approach taken in 1985 Special Analysis F with respect to direct below-market interest loans. The tax expenditure budget should treat in the same way loans effected through the tax-deferral mechanism. For additional analysis of some of the measurement problems involved, see chapter 7. See also Congressional Budget Office, *New Approaches to the Budgetary Treatment of Federal Credit Assistance* (1984).

25. See, for example, 1981 Special Analysis G at 231.

26. The use of negative numbers for spending programs is not confined to the tax expenditure budget. For example, when receipts from oil production at the naval petroleum reserves in California and Wyoming exceeded outlays, the net figure was shown as a negative "outlay," not as a budget receipt; see 1981 Budget at 132–133.

27. 1981 Special Analysis G at 215.

28. 1979 Special Analysis G at 154.

29. The items in part 1 were set forth in Congressional Budget Office, 95th Cong., 2d sess., *Five-Year Budget Projections: Fiscal Years 1979–1983, Supplement on Tax Expenditures* (1978) 27, table 5. Joseph A. Pechman adopted a

similar approach in "Tax Expenditures," in *Setting National Priorities: The 1980 Budget,* ed. Joseph A. Pechman (Washington, D.C.: Brookings Institution, 1979) 226.

30. Budget Act §§ 101, 102

31. Ibid., §§ 101(c), 102(a).

32. 3 *Tax Notes* 10 (July 8, 1975). The Senate Finance Committee discontinued its task force after 1976.

33. Budget Act § 201.

34. Ibid., §§ 301, 308(b), (c).

35. Ibid., § 301(c).

36. Ibid., § 308(a)(2).

37. The Budget Act specifies the timetable in § 300; §§ 301–311 detail the procedures described in the text.

38. For a detailed discussion of the legislative process issues described in the text, see Stanley S. Surrey and Paul R. McDaniel, "The Tax Expenditure Concept and the Budget Reform Act of 1974," 17 *Boston College Industrial and Commercial Law Review* 679, 709–720 (1976); and Surrey and McDaniel, note 23 above.

39. Budget Act § 202(f)(1).

40. See, for example, Joint Committee on Taxation, 98th Cong., 1st Sess., *Estimates of Federal Tax Expenditures for Fiscal Years 1983–1988* (1983). (These documents are hereafter cited by year of publication, as, for example, 1980 Joint Committee Staff Estimates.)

41. In addition, the CBO has periodically issued reports analyzing specific tax expenditures. See, for example, the following publications by that agency: 96th Cong., 2d Sess., *State Profits on Tax-Exempt Student Loan Bonds: Analysis and Options* (1980) and *Tax Subsidies for Medical Care: Current Policies and Possible Alternatives* (1980); 96th Cong., 1st Sess., *Tax-Exempt Bonds for Single-Family Housing* (1979); 95th Cong., 2d Sess., *Federal Aid to Post-Secondary Students: Tax Allowances and Alternative Subsidies* (1978); 95th Cong., 1st Sess., *Real Estate Tax Shelter Subsidies and Direct Subsidy Alternatives* (1977).

42. Budget Act § 301. The same section contains similar requirements for the Second Budget Resolution.

43. Ibid., § 301(a)(2).

44. See note 38 above.

45. Each bill was introduced in the First Session of the Ninety-sixth Congress (1979). Congressman Giaimo discussed his bill at 125 *Cong. Rec.* 34813 (1979) and in a letter to the editor of the *Wall Street Journal* (March 3, 1980) at 19. For testimony on the legislation, see *Federal Spending Limitation Proposals: Hearing before the Task Force on Federal Spending Limitation Proposals of the House Rules Committee,* 96th Cong., 2d Sess. (1980). A resolution with a similar approach to that of the Jones and Holt bills was introduced in the Senate in 1980, 126 *Cong. Rec.* S2180 (March 4, 1980).

46. Indeed, Congressman Jones coupled his proposal to limit direct outlays

with a proposal to provide a $60 billion tax expenditure for business by 1984 via an accelerated depreciation scheme.

47. Staff of Joint Committee on Taxation, 96th Cong., 2d Sess., *Summary of H.R. 3919, Crude Oil Windfall Profit Tax Act of 1980* (1980) 28–29.

48. Ibid.

49. For a description of such proposals, see Karen Davis, *National Health Insurance: Benefits, Costs, and Consequences* (Washington, D.C.: Brookings Institution, 1975) 81–85.

50. 1985 Special Analysis G at G-39.

51. 1981 Special Analysis G at 216.

52. 1981 Special Analysis G did estimate that the sum of separate itemized deductions exceeded by $14.4 billion the revenue gain that would result from repeal of all such deductions. Since itemized deductions account for only 25 percent of the tax expenditure budget, it seems likely that the understatement in revenue gains from repeal of the other 75 percent of the budget would more than offset this figure. If anything, therefore, adding individual estimates probably understates rather than overstates the total tax expenditure budget.

53. See Stanley S. Surrey, William C. Warren, Paul R. McDaniel, and Harry L. Gutman, *Federal Wealth Transfer Taxation* (Mineola, N.Y.: Foundation Press, 1977) 884.

54. See Statement of Senator Muskie, 125 *Cong. Rec.* 4451, 4457–58 (1979). See also 1981 Special Analysis F at 141.

55. Examples are § 120 (exclusion for qualified group legal services plans effective in 1977 and originally scheduled to expire after 1981) and § 44C (residential energy tax credit effective in 1977 and scheduled to expire after 1985).

56. *The Government Economy and Spending Reform Act of 1976: Hearings before the Subcommittee on Intergovernmental Relations of the Senate Government Operations Committee*, 94th Cong., 2d Sess. (1976). See Michael J. McIntyre, "The Sunset Bill: A Periodic Review for Tax Expenditures," 4 *Tax Notes* 3 (Aug. 9, 1976).

57. The Sunset Act of 1977, S. 2 § 401(a), 95th Cong., 1st Sess. (1977), reproduced in 123 *Cong. Rec.* 500 (1977).

58. Ibid., § 411.

59. Title VII of H.R. 2, The Sunset Act of 1979, 96th Cong., 1st Sess. (1979).

60. See, for example, Reginald Jones, "Sunset Legislation," 39 *Tax Foundation's Tax Review* 51 (December 1978). Similar views were expressed by representatives of the National Association of Manufacturers and the National Chamber of Commerce in *Sunset, Sunrise and Related Measures: Hearings on H.R. 2 and H.R. 65 before the Subcommittee on the Legislative Process of the House Rules Committee*, 96th Cong., 1st Sess. (1979). The chairman and ranking minority members of the House Ways and Means Committee supported the views of the business community in a communication to Representative Gillis Long, Chairman of the Subcommittee on the Legislative Process; ibid. at 665.

61. See also Senator Long's testimony in *Sunset Act of 1977: Hearings on*

S. 2 before the Subcommittee on Intergovernmental Relations of the Senate Committee on Governmental Affairs, 95th Cong., 1st Sess., 465–466 (1977): "How many people here want to go out and tell people, 'I support the sunset bill. Let me tell you what that does to you, Grandma. That guarantees you an automatic tax increase.' 'Let me tell you what it means, Mr. Homeowner. It guarantees you a tax increase on your home.' 'I support the sunset bill. Let me tell you what that does to you, little widow woman. It means you are going to pay taxes on that social security check that you have been receiving since your husband died.' 'I support the sunset bill. Let me explain what that means to you, Mr. Veteran. It means hereafter you will pay a tax on your veteran's disability pension check.' " As was mentioned earlier, a number of tax expenditure provisions have been adopted with automatic termination dates. Senator Long did not say why the automatic tax increase argument was not equally applicable to such provisions.

62. Concerns about staff sizes and committee workloads were among the factors that caused the Senate Rules Committee subsequently to abandon the automatic termination requirement and substitute a review procedure. See S. Rept. 924, 96th Cong., 2d Sess. (1980) 4–7.

63. Some from the business community understand the points raised in the text. See, for example, "How Tax Loopholes Widen U.S. Deficit," *U.S. News & World Report* 63 (June 18, 1979).

64. *Sunset Act of 1977: Hearings on S. 2,* note 61 above at 109–111. Not surprisingly, Senator Long used the problems cited by the Treasury in his argument recommending that Title IV be deleted altogether from S. 2; ibid. at 484. When the full Government Operations Committee considered the bill in June 1977, Title IV was modified on the motion of Senate Finance Committee members Roth and Danforth. Under their motion, tax expenditures would be reviewed periodically, but no automatic termination date would be established. Feeling that review was no improvement on existing procedures, Senator Glenn, the sponsor of Title IV, moved to drop it from the bill entirely in order to seek its passage in its original form on the Senate floor. See "Sunset Process for Tax Loopholes," 8 *In Common* 14 (Summer 1977); "Tax Expenditures Dropped from Sunset Bill," 5 *Tax Notes* 7 (July 4, 1977). Accordingly, as reported by the committee and as subsequently approved by the Senate Rules Committee, S. 2 contained no provisions governing tax expenditures. S. Rept. 326, 95th Cong., 1st Sess. (1977); S. Rept. 981, 95th Cong., 2d Sess. (1978).

65. Statement of Daniel I. Halperin, Deputy Assistant Secretary of the Treasury (Tax Policy), in *Sunset, Sunrise and Related Measures,* note 60 above.

66. See 124 *Cong. Rec.* S17357–73, 17475–500, 17536–43, 17729–36, 17819 (Oct. 6, 7, and 9, 1978). Senator Glenn subsequently offered an amendment that would have subjected to the sunset process the tax expenditures adopted in the Revenue Act of 1978. That amendment was tabled; ibid. at S17969–72 (Oct. 10, 1978). Adopting a change in the basic Muskie sunset bill, the Glenn amendment provided for a ten-year cycle in which all tax expenditures would be reviewed.

Some aspects of the Glenn amendment are notable. First, the refundable portion of the earned income credit (and any future refundable credit) was treated as an "outlay" and would accordingly have been subject to sunset procedures for direct spending programs even in the absence of a tax expenditure component of sunset legislation; see 124 *Cong. Rec.* S17485 (Oct. 7, 1978). Second, the tax-writing committees were given considerably more discretion as to which tax expenditures would be subjected to sunset review than the authorizing and appropriations committees would have with respect to direct expenditures. The amendment specified a two-step procedure: the Congressional Budget Office, working with the tax-writing committees, would prepare an "inventory" of tax expenditure items; the tax-writing committees would then submit for congressional approval a resolution establishing a review timetable for items in the inventory that the tax-writing committees had determined should be subjected to sunset; see 124 *Cong. Rec.* S17363–64 (Oct. 6, 1978).

The second step would have enabled the tax-writing committees to exempt any tax expenditure item from the sunset process. Of course, Congress could override the committees' recommendations, but it seems undesirable to give initial discretion for exemption to the tax-writing committees. Some direct spending programs such as Social Security would have been exempt from sunset, but this would have been a congressional decision, not a decision of the authorization-appropriations committees. Those committees would not have been given the "exemption privilege" for the direct spending programs that would have been granted to the tax-writing committees under the Glenn amendment.

67. After passing the Revenue Act of 1978, the Senate passed the basic sunset bill, S. 2, 95th Cong., 2d Sess. (1978). The bill as approved by the Senate, however, did not include the Glenn tax expenditure title, and Senator Glenn did not offer his amendment. See 124 *Cong. Rec.* S18145–97, 18211–21 (Oct. 11, 1978). With the conclusion of the Ninety-fifth Congress, S. 2 died, the result expected when it was passed by the Senate. Subsequent sunset legislation has not received a floor vote in either house.

68. 96th Cong., 2d Sess. (1980).

69. Statement of Congressman Gillis Long, 125 *Cong. Rec.* H10533 (Nov. 9, 1979). See also *Sunset, Sunrise and Related Measures: Hearings before the House Rules Committee on H.R. 5858, Sunset Review Act of 1979*, 96th Cong., 1st Sess. (1979).

70. The Senate Rules and Administration Committee reported its version of sunset legislation (S. 2) in a form that closely followed the approach in H.R. 5858; see S. Rept. 924, 96th Cong., 2d Sess. (1980). The review procedure bills ultimately suffered the same fate as the sunset legislation preceding them.

71. See *Hearings on Tax Expenditures before the Subcommittee on Oversight of the House Ways and Means Committee*, 96th Cong., 1st Sess. (1979).

72. Legislation to implement this suggestion was introduced by Senator Moynihan, 128 *Cong. Rec.* S4225 (April 28, 1982), and by Senator Bradley, 128 *Cong. Rec.* S5774 (May 21, 1982).

73. See S. 2285, 98th Cong., 2d Sess. (1984), introduced by Senator Biden, which would require the appropriate legislative committee to write authorizing legislation for a tax expenditure, as is required for direct spending measures; 129 *Cong. Rec.* S1234 (Feb. 9, 1984). For Senator Kennedy's proposal to subject tax expenditures to the appropriations process, see 125 *Cong. Rec.* S48 (1979). See also 1980 CBO Study at 11–17 for a discussion of various techniques for subjecting tax expenditures to greater control under the budget process.

74. Congressman Stark has pointed out that the investment credit for dairy farmers provides a subsidy to encourage dairy herd expansion. On the other hand, a direct government subsidy program guarantees that the federal government will purchase all surplus milk. In this case, each subsidy is obviously feeding the other in a spiraling cost effect; see Statement of Congressman Stark, 130 *Cong. Rec.* E207 (Jan. 31, 1984). For a discussion of how tax and direct expenditure programs for agriculture can produce completely conflicting economic results, see Paul R. McDaniel, "Tax Expenditures in the Second Stage: Federal Tax Subsidies for Farm Operations," 49 *Southern California Law Review* 1277, 1301–8 (1976).

3. TAX POLICY AND ADMINISTRATION

1. In general, see the following articles by Stanley S. Surrey: "Reflections on the Tax Reform Act of 1976," 25 *Cleveland State Law Review* 303 (1976); "Current Tax Developments in Perspective," 11 *Creighton Law Review* 657 (1978); and "Reflections on the Revenue Act of 1978 and Future Tax Policy," 13 *Georgia Law Review* 687 (1979) (hereafter cited as "Reflections"). For earlier legislation, see Stanley S. Surrey, *Pathways to Tax Reform* (Cambridge, Mass.: Harvard University Press, 1973).

2. See U.S. Treasury Department, *High Income Tax Returns: 1974 and 1975* (1977) and *High Income Tax Returns: 1975 and 1976* (1978).

The tax expenditure concept posits the exchange of two checks between the taxpayer and the Treasury Department: the check from the taxpayer to the Treasury is for the full amount of the tax computed on economic income (which we shall call the "economic tax check"); the second check is from the Treasury to the taxpayer for the amount representing the subsidy provided through the tax expenditures for which the taxpayer qualifies. Of course, the two checks are not actually exchanged; instead, the taxpayer computes and remits to the Treasury only the net difference between the economic tax check and the tax subsidy check. For example, if the tax rate is 40 percent, the taxpayer's economic income is $100,000, and a tax expenditure in the form of a $20,000 deduction is provided, then the taxpayer's economic tax check is $40,000, his tax subsidy check is $8,000, and the net actual check sent to the government is $32,000.

One of the traditional forms of intertaxpayer analysis has been to compare the effective tax rate incurred by each taxpayer. The effective tax rate has been computed by comparing the amount of tax paid by the taxpayer with the taxpayer's economic income. In a tax system in which there are no tax expenditures, this method is unexceptionable. But economists and others have continued to apply the term "effective tax rate" in the realm of tax expenditures by comparing taxpayers' net checks to the government with their economic income. Thus, in the example above, the taxpayer's effective tax rate will be shown to be 32 percent. Under tax expenditure analysis, however, the true effective tax rate is 40 percent, that is, the ratio of the taxpayer's economic tax check to economic income. The 32 percent figure is simply the net of the economic tax check and the tax subsidy check compared with economic income.

Differing effective tax rates for two taxpayers with the same economic income computed in the traditional manner simply reveal that the taxpayers have received different amounts of tax subsidies from the government; they do not indicate any differing amount of tax burden, since the latter figure under the tax expenditure concept will always be the same for both taxpayers.

It would clarify analysis if the term "effective tax rate" were confined to a comparison of the economic tax check owed by the taxpayer with the taxpayer's economic income. This figure would compare the tax due under the rate schedules with economic income. The ratio of the net check to the Treasury to economic income should be given a different name, if the ratio is to be used at all. It would seem more meaningful to use the inverse of the traditional effective tax rate number to show the amount of tax subsidies two taxpayers receive as a percentage of their economic incomes. That is, in the example above, it would seem more meaningful to show that the taxpayer has a "tax subsidy rate" of 8 percent (derived by subtracting the $32,000 net check from the $40,000 true economic tax). The tax subsidy rate would then permit comparison of the amount of subsidies that each taxpayer receives through the tax system.

3. Expanded gross income is adjusted gross income plus tax preferences subject to the minimum tax. It does not include items of excluded income that do not appear on tax returns, notably interest from tax-exempt bonds.

4. For a 1978 breakdown of tax expenditues by five income classes—under $10,000, $10,000–$20,000, $20,000–$30,000, $30,000–$50,000, and over $50,000—see Nonna A. Noto, *Tax Expenditures: The Link between Economic Intent and the Distribution of Benefits among High, Middle, and Low Income Groups,* Congressional Research Service, Report no. 80–99E (1980); also Statement of Senator Baucus, 127 *Cong. Rec.* S1811–1821 (March 5, 1981). The Noto material also contains distribution of tax expenditures by items, totals, and income groups among four categories: investment (25 percent of total), consumption (36.2 percent), employment (25.1 percent), and need (13.5 percent). Only in the "need" category does the income group under $10,000 have top ranking. In the same year, 31.3 percent of taxpayers were in the under-$10,000 group, 36.5 percent in the $10,000–$20,000 group, 20.1 percent in the $20,000–$30,000 group, 9.4 percent in the $30,000–$50,000 group, and 2.6 percent in the over-$50,000 group. John F. Witte, "The Politics and Development of the Federal Income Tax" (University of Wisconsin–Madison, 1984), provides details on the distribution

of tax expenditures and also an allocation by categories that uses a somewhat different framework from that of Noto.

5. See also Allen D. Manvel, "Tax Expenditures by Income Class," 7 *Tax Notes* 55 (July 17, 1978).

6. The data are from a November 20, 1982, release of the Joint Economic Committee. For a distribution by adjusted gross income classes of some selected items, see Congressional Budget Office, 97th Cong., 2d Sess., *Tax Expenditures: Budget Control Options and Five-Year Budget Projections for Fiscal Years 1983–1987* (1982), tables E-1 and E-2, using data from the same Treasury source as the Joint Economic Committee release. See also a study by the Congressional Research Service reproduced in Statement of Senator Baucus, note 4 above at S1811.

7. Joseph A. Pechman, ed., *Setting National Priorities: The 1983 Budget* (Washington, D.C.: Brookings Institution, 1982) 256.

8. For a comparison of Canadian tax expenditures and direct programs, see Allen M. Maslove, "The Distributive Effects of Tax Expenditures: A Suggested Methodology and an Example," 2 *Canadian Taxation* 225 (1980).

9. For a study of home ownership tax expenditures and their economic effects, see Congressional Budget Office, 97th Cong., 1st Sess., *The Tax Treatment of Homeownership: Issues and Options* (1981). See also Frank deLeeuw and Larry Ozanne, "Housing," in *How Taxes Affect Economic Behavior*, ed. Henry J. Aaron and Joseph A. Pechman (Washington, D.C.: Brookings Institution, 1981) 283; John Meyer and Leslie Meyer, "The Impact of National Tax Policies on Homeownership" (Joint Center for Urban Studies, MIT and Harvard University, 1981); Jane G. Gravelle, *Tax Subsidies to Housing, 1953–83*, Congressional Research Service, Report no. 82-178E (1982); Allen D. Manvel, "Homeowner Tax Preference," 9 *Tax Notes* 503 (1979).

10. See Manvel, "Homeowner Tax Preference."

11. For earlier data see Congressional Budget Office, 96th Cong., 1st Sess., *Tax-Exempt Bonds for Single-Family Housing* (1979), a study prepared for the Subcommittee on the City of the House Committee on Banking, Finance and Urban Affairs. See also Joan Williams, "It's High Time to Get Homeowners' Deductions under Control," 12 *Tax Notes* 963 (1981).

12. Although some would quarrel with this statement and say that we cannot be sure that Congress would not favor upside-down direct programs, they give no explicit examples of upside-down programs they believe Congress would approve. A group that came closest was the Filer Commission, *Report of the Commission on Private Philanthropy and Public Needs: Giving in America* (1975) 106–14, 127–34, which offered a defense of the upside-down charitable contributions deduction. Yet it remains questionable whether this commission would have been prepared to risk a congressional vote on a direct spending program allocating to individuals, on an upside-down basis, funds earmarked for distribution by them to charitable organizations of their choice.

Although it is not necessary at this point to maintain that no direct program would be structured in an upside-down manner, those who defend upside-down tax expenditures should acknowledge openly that the programs are indeed upside down and should also be required to bear the burden of proof as to the appropriateness of such a result.

13. See Nonna A. Noto, *The Impact of Demographic Changes on the Revenue Cost of the Mortgage Interest Deduction*, Congressional Research Service, Report no. 79-204E (1979) 9. 11; reprinted in *Studies in Taxation, Public Finance, and Related Subjects—A Compendium*, vol. 4 (Washington, D.C.: Fund for Public Policy Research, 1980) 336. The paper discusses the age and income distribution of the benefits of the housing tax expenditures.

14. See Commerce Clearing House, 83 (10) *Standard Federal Tax Reporter* ¶8605, for 1982 data on average itemized deductions.

15. Another upside-down medical assistance tax expenditure program is the exclusion from an employee's income of employer contributions for medical insurance premiums and medical care. Higher-paid employees receive the greater benefit from the exclusion

16. One defense advanced for the upside-down aspect of tax expenditures is that it merely reflects the progressive individual rate structure. See, for example, Morgan Guaranty Trust Company, "What You Get to Keep May Be a 'Tax Expenditure,'" *Morgan Guaranty Survey* (December 1975) 13: "Inescapably, of course, if Congress wishes to achieve an economic or social goal by means of 'tax expenditure,' it must rely most heavily on those most able to finance that goal: those with the most discretionary funds, i.e., those in upper-income brackets." This is quite a sentence. Either it merely explains the upside-down character of tax expenditues (though it neglects to point out the funds made available are government funds involved in the tax expenditure), or it says that because we have a progressive income tax it is only right that those who pay the largest taxes should have the largest control over the spending of government funds.

17. Gerard M. Brannon, "Tax Expenditures and Income Distribution: A Theoretical Analysis of the Upside-Down Subsidy Argument," in *The Economics of Taxation*, ed. Henry Aaron and Michael J. Boskin (Washington, D.C.: Brookings Institution, 1980) 87.

18. A legislator defending the former $200 interest exclusion combined these claims in a letter to one of the authors.

19. Brannon, "Tax Expenditures and Income Distribution," note 17 above at 94. The deduction for charitable contributions is the only example Brannon appears to use to justify upside-down tax expenditures. Brannon also argues at 98 that the way to counter the upside-down aspect is to increase tax rates on the well-to-do, so that the tax expenditures become not a subsidy for the rich but a burden on rich taxpayers who do not qualify for the tax expenditures. This approach is one that is often suggested, but it lacks a real-world basis. Tax rates are generally reduced on the rich as well as on others—sometimes even more so, as in the reduction of the top bracket from 70 percent to 50 percent in the 1981 act. Also, the presence of tax expenditures seems to have no effect on congressional determination either of specific rates for the rich or of

the general degree of progressivity in the tax rate schedule. The wide disper-
sion of the use of tax expenditures within income classes seems to indicate the
impracticality of raising the rates on all members of a class to reach those with
excessive use of tax expenditures.

20. See Paul R. McDaniel, "Study of Federal Matching Grants for Charitable Contributions," in *Research Papers Sponsored by the Commission on Private Philanthropy and Public Needs,* vol. 4 (Washington, D.C.: Department of
the Treasury, 1977) 2417.

21. Boris I. Bittker, "Effective Tax Rates: Fact or Fancy?" 122 *University of
Pennsylvania Law Review* 780, 808 (1974). The child care analysis is in idem,
"Reflections on Tax Reform," 47 *University of Cincinnati Law Review* 185,
195-201 (1978).

22. As is discussed in chapter 4, it is possible to eliminate the upside-down
effect of most tax expenditure programs by using credits against tax that are
(1) refundable and (2) themselves included in income. Such a structuring
would provide a proper assistance program from the standpoint of normative
tax provisions, though administered by the Internal Revenue Service.

23. It is clear that the problems of restructuring efficient tax expenditure
programs parallel those of structuring efficient direct subsidy programs; for
example, it is often difficult to avoid creating a windfall element in direct programs. This similarity holds true for all the efficiency issues discussed in this
section.

24. See Department of the Treasury, *The Operation and Effect of the Domestic International Sales Corporation Legislation,* annual reports. For an
analysis suggesting that even the modest benefits cited in the Treasury studies
are overstated, see the Congressional Research Service report to Representative Fortney H. Stark, *Review of the Treasury Department's Annual Reports
on Domestic International Sales-Corporations (DISC)* (Document 82-11584 in
Tax Notes microfiche service).

25. See Department of the Treasury, *The Operation and Effect of the Possessions Corporation System of Taxation,* annual reports. Stricter eligibility
requirements in 1982 somewhat reduced the benefits of the Puerto Rican tax
expenditure, but even so the tax expenditure continues to cost the federal government far more than it produces in jobs in Puerto Rico.

26. See "Carter Administration's Proposal on Tax Exempt Bonds, Statement of Treasury Secretary Blumenthal," in *President's Tax Reduction and
Reform Proposals: Hearings before the House Ways and Means Committee,*
95th Cong., 2d Sess. (1978) 31, 160. Senator Danforth later proposed an alternative approach with the same economic result but a different political cast; an
individual receiving interest on a tax-exempt bond could elect to include the
interest in income and then take a 40 percent credit against his income tax. See
note 43 below. For a study on industrial revenue bonds, see Budget Office, 97th
Cong., 1st Sess., *Small Issue Industrial Revenue Bonds* (1981).

The ramifications of using tax-exempt bonds are extensive. See, for example, Congressional Budget Office, 96th Cong., 2d Sess., *State Profits on Tax-*

Exempt Student Loan Bonds: Analysis and Options (1980); and idem, 97th Cong., 2d Sess., *Mortgage Subsidy Bond Tax Act of 1980: Experience under the Permanent rules* (1982), discussing IRC § 103A, which imposed restrictions on state and local tax-exempt mortgage subsidy bonds for owner-occupied homes. IRC § 25, added by the Tax Reform Act of 1984, provides for a "mortgage credit certificate" program that local governments could elect to adopt in lieu of exempt mortgage subsidy bonds. Under the program, a purchaser would be entitled to a tax credit for a portion of the interest incurred on a mortgage on his or her principal residence. The credit thus reduces the homeowner's interest cost dollar for dollar rather than indirectly through lower interest charges as under the tax-exempt bond program. The tax credit eliminates part of the middleman commission involved in the bond program, but not all, because the amount of the credit is not included in the income of the homeowner.

27. The current expensing of construction interest and taxes, which previously was a significant part of the real estate tax shelter, was reduced in 1976 for individuals and closely held corporations on a phased-in schedule to ten-year amortization (section 189); the full requirement applicable to subsidized low-income rental housing was to take effect in 1988. The 1981 act permanently excluded such rental housing from the amortization requirement. The 1982 act extended the ten-year amortization requirement to all corporations.

28. See Paul R. McDaniel, "Tax Reform and the Revenue Act of 1971: Lesions, Lagniappes, and Lessons," 14 *Boston College Industrial and Commercial Law Review* 813, 825 (1973) (hereafter cited as "Tax Reform"); idem, "Tax Shelters and Tax Policy," 26 *National Tax Journal* 353 (1973); Jerome Kurtz, "Real Estate Tax Shelter—A Postscript," 26 *National Tax Journal* 341 (1973).

29. McDaniel, "Tax Reform," note 28 above at 830. Constant statutory changes in tax shelters can affect their use and profitability. Thus the 1976 and 1978 acts introduced the "at risk" rules for deductions, and the 1981 act extended them to the investment credit, but the same acts also reduced or eliminated some tax expenditures that produced various shelters. The 1981 act, for example, eliminated many of the commodity straddle tax shelters and increased the cost of being caught in a "leaky shelter" by imposing a penalty for a tax underpayment resulting from overvaluation of an asset and by increasing the negligence penalty. The same act also increased the amount of interest due on all deficiencies to reflect the prime rate charged by commercial banks, and the 1982 act required that the interest be compounded daily. The 1982 act added monetary penalties for those who in promoting tax shelters make false statements about the benefits available or grossly overstate valuations regarding any material matter and permitted injunctions to be brought against those promoting "abusive tax shelters." The same act provided a 10 percent penalty on any substantial understatement of income tax. This penalty can be avoided if the treatment of the item involved is supported by "substantial authority" or if the tax return disclosed all relevant facts; for tax shelter items the penalty may be avoided only if the taxpayer both meets the substantial authority re-

quirement and believes the treatment of the item was "more likely than not" the proper treatment. The 1981 act's reduction of the top marginal rate from 70 percent to 50 percent has affected to some extent both the pricing of and benefits from shelters. None of these changes, however, appears to have affected significantly the volume of tax shelter offerings. Ingenious investment advisers, tax experts, and others continue to devise and promote new types of tax shelters.

30. The 1981 act also adopted a 25 percent tax credit for incremental research and development expenditures as an incentive to research. This credit, however, can be used only to offset the amount of tax attributable to income from the taxpayer's interest in the business conducting the reseach. Thus the credit can be used only against income arising from the tax expenditure activity and not against other income, such as investment or professional income. If this approach were followed for other tax expenditures, the world of tax shelters might start to crumble.

31. Alvin C. Warren, Jr., and Alan J. Auerbach, "Transferability of Tax Incentives and the Fiction of Safe Harbor Leasing," 95 Harvard Law Review 1752 (1982); Paul R. McDaniel and Stanley S. Surrey, "Tax Expenditures: How to Identify Them; How to Control Them," 15 Tax Notes 595, 620 (1982).

32. Alvin C. Warren, Jr., and Alan J. Auerbach, "Tax Policy and Equipment Leasing after TEFRA," 96 Harvard Law Review 1579 (1983).

33. Marvin Chirelstein, "Note: What Is the True Value of a Tax Preference?" in Federal Income Taxation, 3d ed. (Mineola, N.Y.: Foundation Press, 1982) 325 (concession at last paragraph on 331); Boris I. Bittker, "Equity, Efficiency, and Income Tax Theory: Do Misallocations Drive Out Inequities?" 16 San Diego Law Review 735, 739–744 (1979) (concession at 743 and 744, but not in third paragraph on 744, which seems to imply that most tax expenditures level out); idem, "Reflections on Tax Reform," note 21 above at 185, 201–203, where the concession to the real world appears in stronger terms. In the 1979 article Bittker apparently failed to recognize the misallocations of resources resulting from the tax expenditure programs when they are restated as direct spending programs; an example is the assertion at 746 that there is no misallocation of resources in the additional personal exemption for blind persons; but it is questionable whether a direct program would give no assistance to blind persons who are below the starting level of the income tax and the greatest assistance to the wealthy blind. The lack of equity in these tax expenditures is an indication both of their inefficiency and of a misallocation of resources. At this point equity and efficiency analysis can converge, contrary to the apparent assumptions in Bittker's article.

34. See, for example, Statement of Emil M. Sunley, Deputy Assistant Secretary of the Treasury, in Review of Selected Tax Expenditures: Hearings on the Investment Tax Credit before the Subcommittee on Oversight of the House Ways and Means Committee, 96th Cong., 1st Sess. (1979); Staff of Joint Committee on Taxation, 95th Cong., 1st Sess., Tax Policy and Capital Formation (1977) 18, prepared for the Task Force on Capital Formation of the House

Ways and Means Committee; Jane G. Gravelle and Donald W. Kiefer, "The Investment Tax Credit: An Analytical Overview," in *Studies in Taxation*, note 13 above, vol. 3 (1979) 14.

35. See, for example, the various papers by Jane G. Gravelle in *Studies in Taxation*, note 13 above, vols. 3, 4, and 5 (1981).

The ACRS depreciation scheme, adopted in 1981 but modified in 1982, illustrates the extreme distortion in investment decisions that can occur under a generous tax expenditure. See, for example, *Economic Report of the President* (1982) 122–124; Eugene Steuerle, "Interpretation of Effective Tax Rates on New Depreciable Assets" (U.S. Treasury Department, Office of Tax Analysis, Nov. 17, 1982).

36. See Staff of Joint Committee on Taxation, *Tax Policy and Capital Formation*, note 34 above at 32; Joseph J. Minarik, "Conference Discussion," in *What Should Be Taxed: Income or Expenditure?* ed. Joseph A. Pechman (Washington, D.C.: Brookings Institution, 1980) 297–302. See also Martin Feldstein and Daniel Feenberg, *Alternative Tax Rules and Personal Savings Incentives: Microeconomic Data and Behavioral Simulations*, NBER Working Paper no. 681 (Cambridge, Mass.: National Bureau of Economic Research, 1981).

37. For studies of job tax incentives, see Robert Tannenwald, "Are Wage and Training Subsidies Cost-Effective?—Some Evidence from the New Jobs Tax Credit," *New England Economic Review* (September–October 1982) 25; Michael J. McIntyre, "Jury Still Out on Jobs Tax Subsidy Programs," 11 *Tax Notes* 307 (1980); John Fisk, "The Economic Rationale for the Targeted Jobs Credit," in *Studies in Taxation*, note 13 above, vol. 5 at 164; Robert H. Haveman and John L. Palmer, eds., *Jobs for Disadvantaged Workers: The Economics of Employment Subsidies* (Washington, D.C.: Brookings Institution, 1982), especially at 14–15, 276–284; Congressional Budget Office, 97th Cong., 2d Sess., *Improving Youth Employment Prospects: Issues and Options* (1982) 31. For a legislative history of the jobs credit, see Emil M. Sunley, "A Tax Preference Is Born: A Legislative History of the New Jobs Tax Credit," in *The Economics of Taxation*, note 17 above at 391.

A study by the National Science Foundation, *Tax Policy and Innovation: A Synthesis of Evidence*, PRA Research Report 82-1 (1981), concludes that the utility of tax incentives for research has not been proved; see also George Carlson, *Tax Policy toward Research and Development*, OTA Paper 45 (Washington, D.C.: U.S. Treasury Department, Office of Tax Administration, 1981). For an analysis of agricultural tax incentives see C. Davenport et al., *The Effects of Tax Policy on American Agriculture*, Department of Agriculture, Agricultural Economic Report no. 480 (1982). For residential energy credits, see Allen D. Manvel, "The Residential Energy Tax Credit: Two Years' Experience," 14 *Tax Notes* 854 (1982); see also Lee Hanson and Michael S. Kaufman, "The National Energy Tax Act of 1978: Taxation without Rationalization," 3 *Harvard Environment Law Review* 187 (1979); Salvatore Lazzari, "An Economic Evaluation of Federal Tax Credits for Residential Energy Conservation," in *Studies in Taxation*, note 13 above, vol. 7 (1983) at 8. For a description of tax and direct expenditures to encourage the production of alcohol fuels, see Nancy E. Shurtz, "Promoting Alcohol Fuels Production: Tax Expenditures? Direct Expenditures? No Expenditures?" 36 *Southwestern Law Journal* 597 (1982).

38. See chapter 7.

39. A similar analysis of incidence of benefits should also be used for direct budget expenditures. Under direct programs, however, there should be no difference between the broad category of intended beneficiaries and those who actually receive the benefits of the direct programs. Nor should there be a middleman distortion under direct programs.

40. This third level of beneficiary description is the subject of Michael J. Graetz, "Assessing the Distributional Effects of Income Tax Revision: Some Lessons from Incidence Analysis," 4 *Journal of Legal Studies* 351 (1975). Graetz's analysis tries to pursue the tax-exempt trail beyond the second level. The analysis indicates that assumptions are likely to become too hard to control. For another discussion along similar lines, see George Fallis, "The Incidence of Tax Expenditures: A Framework for Analysis," 2 *Canadian Taxation* 228 (1980). See also Nicholas LePan, "Measurement of the Revenue and Distributive Effects of Tax Expenditures," 2 *Canadian Taxation* 220 (1980).

41. See Carl Shoup, "Surrey's *Pathways to Tax Reform*—A Review Article," 30 *Journal of Finance* 1329, 1334 (1975), quoting Boris I. Bittker, "Accounting for Federel 'Tax Subsidies' in the National Budget," 22 *National Tax Journal* 244 (1969).

42. Shoup, "Surrey's *Pathways,*" raised the question whether government subsidies should be given to a business that is currently not operating at an economic profit. Apparently this question has not been much discussed by economists considering subsidies. It has been raised, however, by proposals to make the investment credit refundable (see, for example, Statement of Senator Kennedy, 122 *Cong. Rec.* 7151 [1976]) and by the safe harbor leasing provision of the 1981 act. For a related discussion, see Nonna A. Noto and Dennis Zimmerman, "Federal Assistance to Troubled Firms? An Analysis of Business Failure Data," in *Studies in Taxation*, note 13 above, vol. 5 at 191. The question is also directly linked to tax shelters, since tax expenditures that cannot be directly used by a business currently operating at a tax loss can nearly always be made available to it through tax shelter device, such as bank equipment leasing. See McDaniel, "Tax Reform," note 28 above. If government assistance is to be given only to profit-generating enterprises, then this factor must be among the criteria considered in choosing between the tax route and the direct route; the issue here would be which route can more readily distinguish between losing ventures and profitable ones. Professor Shoup also mentions the aspect of promptness in the government's payment of assistance; this factor, too, should be a criterion, involving studies comparing the promptness with which tax and direct subsidies can be paid, as well as the consequences of subsequent checks, through audits, under both routes.

43. See U.S. Treasury Department, *The President's 1978 Tax Program, De-*

tailed Descriptions and Supporting Analysis for the Proposals (1978). Senator Danforth proposed an optional tax credit to bondholders who include in taxable income the interest on otherwise tax-exempt bonds; Senate Finance Committee, *Revenue Act of 1978*, S. Rept. 1263, 95th Cong., 2d Sess. (1978) 143–150. The proposal was deleted on the Senate floor pending future study. See also Statement of Senator Danforth, 125 *Cong. Rec.* 8776 (1979), explaining his proposal, and the discussion in note 26 above.

44. See House Ways and Means Committee, *The Municipal Taxable Bond Alternative Act of 1976*, H.R. Rept. 1016, 94th Cong., 2d Sess. (1976), a report on H.R. 12774, which provided for a direct subsidy to the issuing government. The proposal was not considered by the full House.

45. In the Revenue Act of 1976 Congress did eliminate, without substitute programs, the tax expenditures involved in western hemisphere trade corporations and in the failure to gross up dividends from subsidiary corporations in developing countries for foreign tax credit purposes. In the Tax Reform Act of 1984, however, DISCs were replaced by another tax subsidy, foreign international sales corporations (FISCs).

46. Robert S. McIntyre, "Lessons for Tax Reformers from the History of the Energy Tax Incentives in the Windfall Profit Tax Act of 1980," 22 *Boston College Law Review* 705 (1981), argues that tax expenditure adherents focus too strongly on the budgetary aspects and instead should use traditional tax reform arguments, such as the distortion that tax expenditures produce for horizontal and vertical tax equity. He urges that tax reform arguments should emphasize tax fairness. Tax fairness arguments, however, especially in periods when economy in government is the goal, are unlikely to be as effective as spending arguments against the strong and well-directed lobbying groups that now influence much congressional activity. They also essentially miss the point that spending programs, not tax provisions are at issue.

47. For a compilation of materials, see Paul R. McDaniel, "Federal Income Tax Simplification: The Political Process," 34 *Tax Law Review* 27 (1978).

48. See, for example, remarks by the Honorable Edwin S. Cohen, Assistant Secretary of the Treasury for Tax Policy, to the American Bar Association National Institute on Tax Reform at San Juan, Puerto Rico, January 23, 1970, in 23 *Tax Lawyer* 417, 424 (1970); Boris I. Bittker, "Tax Reform and Tax Simplification," 29 *University of Miami Law Review* 1, 2–3 (1974).

49. Of course, the degree of complexity depends on the structure of the direct program. If, for example, repeal of the itemized deduction for state and local property taxes were accompanied by a HUD program to assist homeowners, presumably the level of detail for aid recipients would increase—though perhaps no more than it would in an appropriately focused tax expenditure program involving, say, a tax credit for the property taxes. On the other hand, if the repeal were accompanied by increased federal revenue-sharing aid to state and local governments, presumably complexity would decrease at the federal level—though not at the state level. See Nonna A. Noto and Dennis Zimmerman, "Limiting State-Local Tax Deductibility in Exchange for In-

creased General Revenue Sharing: An Analysis of the Economic Effects" (Congressional Research Service, 1983), prepared for the Senate Subcommittee on Intergovernmental Relations of the Senate Committee on Governmental Affairs.

50. Although a particular tax expenditure may in itself appear simpler than its counterpart direct program, its inclusion as an item on a tax return makes the entire return more difficult to handle. Thus while a tuition tax credit in itself may look simpler than direct educational assistance—"just a line on the tax return"—when the credit becomes, say, credit number 15 on the tax return and perhaps requires an additional separate schedule or form or, at the least, more instruction material, the added complexity of that one line becomes significant. On the proliferation of credits for individuals and the resulting complexities, see Bruce L. Balch, "Unification of Credits: A TEFRA Update," 17 *Tax Notes* 971 (1982).

51. On the flat rate approach and alternatives, see, for example, Joseph J. Minarik, "The Future of the Individual Income Tax," 35 *National Tax Journal* 231 (1982); Joint Committee on Taxation, 97th Cong., 2d Sess., *Staff Analysis of Proposals Relating to Broadening the Base and Lowering the Rates of the Income Tax* (1982); *Flat-Rate Tax: Hearings before the Senate Finance Committee,* 97th Cong., 2d Sess. (1982); *Flat-Rate Tax: Hearings before the Subcommittee on Monetary and Fiscal Policy of the Joint Economic Committee,* 97th Cong., 2d Sess. (1982); release from the office of Senator Bradley, Aug. 5, 1982 (on his proposal for a broadened base but with some rate progression).

52. Commissioner of Internal Revenue Jerome Kurtz, "Tax Simplification: Some Observations from a Retrospective View of the United States Experience," address to the Eleventh General Assembly of the Inter-American Center for Tax Administrators, reproduced in 123 *Cong. Rec.* 16123 (1977).

53. See H.R. 1739, H.R. 7896, H.R. 9325, 95th Cong., 1st Sess. (1977), proposing tax expenditures to provide financial aid to the arts and to artists.

54. See Commission on Federal Paperwork, "Final Report on Federal Taxation: Findings and Recommendations" (June 1977). Senate Standing Rule XXIX requires that a paperwork impact statement be prepared on all proposed legislation.

55. See generally Herbert Kaufman, *Red Tape: Its Origins, Uses, and Abuses* (Washington, D.C.: Brookings Institution, 1977) 56–58.

56. See chapter 5.

57. After the capital gain debacle in 1978, it may be a long time before this route is politically feasible. See Surrey, "Reflections," note 1 above. But see Joseph J. Minarik, "Full Taxation of Capital Gains: Who Wins and Who Loses," 5 *Tax Notes* 3 (Nov. 28, 1977), whose analysis indicates that in 1977 the winners would have far outnumbered the losers in such an exchange.

58. See Kurtz, "Tax Simplification," note 52 above; Stanley S. Surrey, "Complexity and the Internal Revenue Code: The Problem of the Management of Tax Detail," 34 *Law & Contemporary Problems* 673, 683 (1969); John S. Nolan, "A New Tax Structure for the United States—Problems of Implemen-

tation of the Political Process," University of Michigan Key Issues Lecture Series (March 30, 1977) 2, 17; James S. Eustice, "Tax Complexity and the Tax Practitioner," 8 *Tax Adviser* 27, 29 (1977). See also George T. Altman, "A Simplification of the Income Tax," 22 *Taxes* 146, 185 (1944): "The [tax] law will never be simple as long as it is a mass of special allowances and special privileges."

An additional category of tax provisions, with its own set of problems, are the provisions that are really private relief bills for particular taxpayers but that masquerade as provisions of general application. See Committee on Tax Policy, New York State Bar Association, Tax Section, "A Report on Complexity and the Income Tax," 27 *Tax Law Review* 325, 337 (1977).

4. CHOOSING BETWEEN TAX EXPENDITURES AND DIRECT PROGRAMS

1. Murray Weidenbaum, *The Case For Tax Loopholes*, Center for the Study of American Business Reprint Series, no. 12 (St. Louis: Washington University, 1978) 12.

2. Quoted in Robert Havemann, "Tax Expenditures—Spending Money without Expenditures," 9 *National Journal* 1908 (Dec. 10, 1977).

3. Ibid.

4. Ibid. at 1909.

5. The payment of Medicare and Social Security benefits has some elements of a payment-first, audit-later approach. The tax expenditure for rehabilitation of historic structures includes a certification procedure through the Department of the Interior.

6. Several of these characteristics are also discussed in 1981 CBO Study.

7. Charles Clotfelter and Lester M. Salamon, *The Federal Government and the Non-Profit Sector: The Impact of the 1981 Tax Act on Individual Charitable Giving* (Washington, D.C.: Urban Institute, 1981).

8. Akihito Udagawa, "Special Tax Reliefs and Public Choice," in *Subsidies, Tax Reliefs, and Prices*, ed. Karl Hauser (Paris: Editions Cujas, 1981) 125 (first presented as a paper at the International Institute of Public Finance Varna congress in 1977).

9. See *The President's 1978 Tax Reduction and Reform Proposals: Hearings on the President's 1978 Tax Program before the House Committee on Ways and Means*, 95th Cong., 2d Sess. (1978) 5377–5417); Senate floor debate rejecting a proposal to disallow 50 percent of "business" meal deductions, 124 *Cong. Rec.* 34590–94 (1978); Senate floor debate rejecting a proposal to reduce deductions for entertainment costs, 124 *Cong. Rec.* 35263–65 (1978).

10. The current dividing line between nondeductible "entertainment" expenses and deductible business expenses is not considered a tax expenditure because it is assumed Congress has been making an effort to locate the line properly under appropriate normative tax structure criteria. But if the line is drawn on the basis of the subsidy arguments advanced to attack the proposals, then the existing rules should be classified as a tax expenditure.

11. See Statement of Assistant Secretary of the Treasury Donald Lubick, *Interrelationship between U.S. Tax Policy and Tax Energy Policy: Hearings on Tax Aspects of National Energy Policy before the Subcommittee on Commerce, Consumer, and Monetary Affairs of House Government Operations Committee,* 96th Cong., 1st Sess. (March 13, 1979); letter of Treasury Department, appendix IV, "Comptroller General Report to the Congress on a Review of the Department of Energy's Energy Tax Policy Analysis" (EMD-79-26, March 13, 1979).

12. 1982 CBO Study. See appendix B, "Illustrative Allocation of Tax Expenditures to Committees with Authorizing Jurisdiction over Related Direct Outlays."

13. A survey by *Business Week,* April 18, 1983, found that 95 percent of a sample of 600 high-level executives disapproved of direct federal subsidies to "smokestack" industries but 61 percent favored tax incentives. See "Poll Shows Executives Prefer Tax Breaks to Direct Aid for Smokestack Industries," 19 *Tax Notes* 544 (1983).

14. Jeffrey P. Owens, "Tax Expenditures and Direct Expenditures as Instruments of Social Policy," in *Comparative Tax Studies,* ed. S. Chossen (Amsterdam: North-Holland Publishing, 1983) 171, provides an interesting view of tax expenditures in the social welfare field.

15. Congressional Research Service, Report no. 82-204E (1982). A summary of the report appears in 18 *Tax Notes* 259 (1983).

16. The wage insurance tax credit proposed by the Carter administration in 1979 as part of a wage control program was structured as a refundable credit includable in income. As such, it became an assistance program properly treated for income tax purposes but administered by the IRS rather than by the Labor Department. The investment credit is the equivalent of a government contribution to capital. The basis of the assets to which the credit relates must be reduced by the amount of the credits; in effect, this requirement ensures that the credit will be includable in income over the depreciable life of the asset. For investments in machinery and equipment, basis must be reduced by only half the amount of the credit; thus only half the amount of the credit must be included in income. Interestingly, if the lessor of property elects to allow the lessee to utilize the investment under § 48(d), the lessee must include an amount equal to 50 percent of the credit in income over the depreciable life of the asset; IRC § 46(d)(5).

If the objective is to provide a government loan, the credit itself should not constitute taxable income. Here again, the proper approach would be to require that the amount of the tax credit be repaid in subsequent years, with an appropriate interest rate charged for the period during which the taxpayer had the use of the funds. The credit would have to be refundable to reach all possible loan recipients.

17. For studies questioning the effectiveness of tax expenditures, see Jane G. Gravelle, *Tax Policy and Spillover Effects: The Use of Tax Provisions to Induce Socially Desirable Activities,* Congressional Research Service, Report no. 80-186E, (1980); Congressional Research Service report, note 15 above; Harvey Galper and Eugene Steuerle, "Tax Incentives For Saving," 2 *Brookings Review*

(1983); Harvey S. Rosen, *Housing Subsidies: Effects on Housing Decisions, Efficiency, and Equity*, NBER Working Paper no. 1611 (Cambridge, Mass: National Bureau of Economic Research, 1983).

18.   An interesting question is whether the constitutional requirement that taxes be uniform throughout the United States would preclude a pilot program in only one area. Clearly a spending program would not have to meet this requirement, and it could be argued that a tax expenditure program should therefore also be free of the requirement. On the other hand, the constitutional provision may operate as a constraint, applicable to any tax expenditure, that must be met when the tax route is used. Another constraint could be the constitutional requirement that revenue bills originate in the House. This requirement has practically no force, however, since nongermane Senate amendments are allowed and there is always some House revenue measure, however minor, pending in the Senate to be used as a vehicle for tax expenditure amendments.

19.   The current tax expenditure and direct spending programs involving the military, home ownership, higher education, retirement, disability, and general-purpose assistance seem in many respects to be direct alternatives. See Senate Budget Committee, 95th Cong., 2d Sess., *Tax Expenditures: Relationships to Spending Programs and Background Material on Individual Provisions* (1978) part II, discussing tax expenditures and major spending programs with related purposes.

20.   Examples of tax expenditure and direct programs with very different approaches are those involving export promotion (DISC and Export-Import Bank credit), energy supply development, pollution control, agriculture, rental housing, child care, employment, and health. See Senate Budget Committee, *Tax Expenditures*, note 19 above.

21.   Much of the force behind the tuition tax credit proposal stemmed from a desire to aid church-affiliated private colleges and secondary and elementary schools. Direct assistance could violate the First Amendment (although student loan programs apply to religious schools), whereas supporters of the tuition tax credit presumably hoped that it could withstand constitutional attack. In this connection see chapter 5.

22.   In some situations the executive branch considered a choice but its discussions and its reasons for finally choosing the tax route were not made public. An example was the decision in 1982 to make the proposed new DISC a tax matter rather than to allocate the funds involved to the Export-Import Bank. In 1977, when the executive recommended that most of its energy programs be handled through the tax system, there were low-level discussions on which route to use. The tax system was chosen because it could use a tested administrative machinery (in contrast to the new Department of Energy) and because policymakers believed that tax credits were politically more acceptable than direct payments. See Lee Hanson and Michael S. Kaufman, "The National Energy Tax Act of 1978: Taxation without Rationalization," 3 *Harvard Environmental Law Review* (1979) 187.

23.   See Sjoroos v. Commissioner, 81 T.C. 971 (1983), upholding the tax pro-

vision exempting government employees from paying income tax on cost-of-living allowances outside the United States. The court stated that the government had a choice between increasing salaries or allowing the exemption and that the choice was a policy decision by Congress. The court denied the claim of employees in the private sector that they were denied equal protection.

5. THE TAX EXPENDITURE CONCEPT IN THE COURTS

1. See, e.g., Flast v. Cohen, 392 U.S. 83 (1968).

2. See, e.g., Evans v. Newton, 382 U.S. 296 (1966); Burton v. Wilmington Parking Authority, 365 U.S. 715 (1961).

3. Poindexter v. Louisiana Financial Assistance Commission, 275 F. Supp. 833 (E.D. La. 1967), aff'd, 389 U.S. 571 (1968).

4. See, e.g., Lemon v. Kurtzman, 403 U.S. 602 (1971).

5. See Note, "Procedural Due Process in Government-Subsidized Housing," 86 Harvard Law Review 880, 904 n. 115 (1973) and cases cited therein.

6. 1982 Special Analysis G at 203.

7. Senate Budget Committee, 97th Cong., 2d Sess., Tax Expenditures: Relationship to Spending Programs and Background Materials on Individual Provisions (1982) 1–2. See also Congressional Budget Office, 97th Cong., 1st Sess., Tax Expenditures: Current Issues and Five-Year Budget Projections for Fiscal Years 1982–1986 (1981) xiii: "Tax subsidies can also serve as alternatives to spending or loan programs. Almost any feature that is included in a spending or loan program can be duplicated in a tax subsidy."

8. Senate Budget Committee, Tax Expenditures, note 7 above at 2. Similar statements can be found in 1984 Budget at 6–17; 1983 Joint Committee Staff Estimates at 2; and 1982 CBO Study at xiii.

9. Pollock v. Farmer's Loan and Trust Company, 157 U.S. 429 (1895).

10. Brushaber v. Union Pacific Railroad Company, 240 U.S. 1 (1916).

11. Moritz v. Commissioner, 469 F.2d 466 (10th Cir. 1972).

12. Cammarano v. United States, 358 U.S. 498 (1959).

13. Brushaber v. Union Pacific, note 10 above.

14. The only successful attack has been Moritz v. Commissioner, note 11 above.

15. An exception is Moritz v. Commissioner, which involved the then child care deduction.

16. 103 S.Ct. 1997 (1983).

17. The Court of Appeals for the District of Columbia rejected both arguments; Taxation With Representation of Washington v. Regan, 676 F.2d 715 (D.C. Cir. 1982). Earlier, the Fourth Circuit had also held against TWR on both arguments; Taxation With Representation v. United States, 585 F.2d 1219 (4th Cir. 1978).

18. Note 16 above at 2000.

19. Note 12 above.

20. The disallowance of a deduction for lobbying expenses should be classified as a tax penalty. If a monetary penalty imposed on the exercise of First

Amendment rights is constitutionally valid, a fortiori the denial of a tax expenditure to subsidize the exercise is also valid.

21. Note 16 above at 2003.

22. On direct programs and constitutional challenges generally, see Thomas J. Madden, "The Right to Receive Federal Grants and Assistance," 37 *Federal Bar Journal* 17 (1978); see also Elrod v. Burns, 427 U.S. 347, 358 n.11 (1976).

23. A case whose result was doubtful to begin with but is now even more so is Big Mama Rag, Inc. v. United States, 631 F.2d 1030 (D.C. Cir. 1980). The taxpayer, a nonprofit organization publishing a monthly newspaper, had been denied tax-exempt status by the IRS on the ground that it was not an "educational" organization as defined in the Treasury Regulations. The paper was primarily devoted to information of interest to women. The denial had been based on the view that the paper had adopted a stance "so doctrinaire" that it could not meet the test of a "full and fair exposition" of the pertinent facts that would permit an individual or the public to form an independent opinion or conclusion; Treas. Reg. § 1.501(c)3-1(d)(3)(i). The court held that the regulations were so vague as to violate the First Amendment protection of free speech. The basic issue seems to be the proper interpretation of the statutory term "educational purposes" in IRC § 501(c)(3) as the test of qualification for exemption. It is doubtful that the IRS could do any more than it did with that broad term.

24. See, e.g., Pietsch v. The President of the United States, 434 F.2d 861 (2d Cir. 1970); Reimer v. Commissioner, 42 T.C. M. 518 (1981).

25. 309 F. Supp. 1127 (D.D.C. 1970). The court quickly dismissed the government's argument that the plaintiffs did not have standing to sue. The government apparently did not raise interpretative or constitutional issues.

26. Ibid. at 1131, 1134–35.

27. In the late 1960s the IRS, the Treasury, and the White House considered issuing a ruling denying exemption to private schools that practiced racial discrimination. Opinions differed on whether the law had developed far enough in this area. There was also concern that, in view of the lack of direct authority for such a ruling, the Senate Finance Committee would attack the issuance of the ruling and perhaps somehow legislate it out of application. The IRS then decided to limit its attack on racial discrimination to situations that presented state involvement. See Green v. Kennedy, note 25 above at 1130.

28. IRS news release, July 10, 1970, 707, Commerce Clearing House, *Standard Federal Tax Reporter* ¶6790 (1970).

29. Statement of Randolph W. Thrower, Commissioner of the Internal Revenue Service, *Equal Educational Opportunity Hearings before the Senate Select Committee on Equal Education Opportunity*, 91st Cong., 2d Sess. (1970) 1995. The IRS later issued a ruling to the same effect, Revenue Ruling 71-447, 1971-2 *Cumulative Bulletin* 230 (hereafter cited as *Cum. Bull.*).

30. Green v. Connally, 330 F. Supp. 1150 (D.D.C. 1971), *aff'd without opinion sub nom.* Coit. v. Green, 404 U.S. 997 (1971).

31. Ibid. at 1164.

32. Ibid. at 1164–1165 and 1169.

33. 338 F. Supp. 448 (D.D.C. 1972).

34. Ibid. at 455–456. The court appended the following footnote to "the substantiality of the benefits provided": "There is no question that allowing the deduction of charitable contributions in fact confers a benefit on the organization receiving the contribution. The court in *Green v. Kennedy* [note 25 above] described 'the impact of Federal tax ... deduction' as a 'matching grant,' *id.* at 1136, and we agree. *See generally,* Surrey, Tax Incentives as a Device for Implementing Government Policy: A Comparison with Direct Government Expenditures, 83 Harv. L. Rev. 705 (1970); Surrey, Federal Income Tax Reforms: The Varied Approaches Necessary [to] Replace Tax Expenditures with Direct Government Assistance, 84 Harv. L. Rev. 352 (1970); Stone, Federal Tax Support of Charities and Other Exempt Organizations: The Need for a National Policy, 20 So. Calif. Tax Instit. 27 (1968)."

35. Ibid. at 456.

36. Ibid. at 457.

37. The caution expressed here reflects note 11 in the Supreme Court's opinion in Bob Jones University v. Simon, 416 U.S. 725, 740 (1974): "The question of whether a segregative private school qualifies under §501(c)(3) has not received plenary review in this Court, and we do not reach that question today. Such schools have been held not to qualify under §501(c)(3) in *Green v. Connally,* 330 F. Supp. 1150 (DC) (three-judge court), *aff'd per curiam sub nom. Coit v. Green,* 404 U.S. 997 (1971). As a defendant in *Green,* the Service initially took the position that segregative private schools were entitled to tax-exempt status under §501(c)(3), but it reversed its position while the case was on appeal to this Court. Thus, the Court's affirmance in *Green* lacks the precedential weight of a case involving a truly adversary controversy."

The caution also reflects Prince Edward School Foundation v. United States, 450 U.S. 944 (1981), in which three justices dissented from the denial of certiorari in a case denying tax-exempt status because of racial discrimination. The dissent stated that the petition of certiorari raised difficult statutory and constitutional issues.

38. Revenue Procedure 75-50, 1975-2 *Cum. Bull.* 587.

39. E.g., Norwood v. Harrison, 382 F. Supp. 921 (N.D. Miss. 1974), imposing a ratification process to determine which Mississippi schools were racially discriminatory and therefore ineligible under Norwood v. Harrison, 413 U.S. 455 (1973), to receive state-owned textbooks. See also Brumfield v. Dodd, 425 F. Supp. 528 (E.D. La. 1976).

40. Internal Revenue Service news release, IR-2027, Aug. 21, 1978.

41. Internal Revenue Service news release, IR-2091, Feb. 9, 1979.

42. *Tax-Exempt Status of Private Schools: Hearings before the Subcommittee on Oversight of the House Committee on Ways and Means,* 96th Cong., 1st Sess. (1979); *Tax-Exempt Status of Private Schools: Hearings before the Subcommittee on Taxation and Debt Management Generally of the Senate Committee on Finance,* 96th Cong., 1st Sess. (1979).

43. The bills are cited in note 25 of Bob Jones University v. United States, 103 S.Ct. 2017 (1983).

44. Congress itself had recognized the courts' interpretation of the statute. Section 501(i), added in 1976, denies tax-exempt status to social clubs that discriminate against "any person on the basis of race, color, or religion." The legislative history indicated, by referring to *Green v. Connally*, that such an addition was not needed for section 501(c)(3) charitable organizations, because this rule is already implied there. See *Tax Treatment of Social Clubs and Other Membership Organizations and Certain Other Committee Amendments*, Rept. 94–1318, 94th Cong., 2d Sess. (1976) 8 n.5; *Tax Treatment of Social Clubs and Other Membership Organizations*, H.R. Rept. 94–1353, 94th Cong., 2d Sess. (1976) 8 n.5. It would be fanciful indeed to argue, as some later did, that the specific language of section 501(i) implies a contrary result in section 501(c)(3). Why would Congress require only social clubs to be nondiscriminatory? As a proponent for accepting the legislative history of section 501(1) later argued, "no explanation [is offered], and none can be imagined, why Congress would have forbidden racial discrimination by exempt social clubs—including school-related organizations like fraternities—yet sanctioned the exclusion of blacks by tax-exempt schools themselves"; brief of *amicus curiae* (at 51) in Bob Jones University v. United States, note 43 above, discussed later in the chapter.

In P.L. 96–601 (Dec. 13, 1980), Congress later amended § 501(i) to allow auxiliaries of a fraternal beneficiary society or a club to exclude prospective members on religious grounds. The provision was designed to benefit "the affiliated corporations of the unincorporated, subordinate lodges of the Knights of Columbus" and Catholic alumni clubs, but was not intended to authorize discrimination on the basis of race under the guise of religious affiliation. H. Rept. 96–545, 96th Cong., 1st Sess. (1979); 1980–2 *Cum. Bull.* 682.

45. Treasury, Postal Service, and General Government Appropriations Act, 1980, P.L. 96–74 § 614 (1979).

46. These issues are discussed in Archie Parnell, "Congressional Interference in Agency Enforcement: The IRS Experience," 89 *Yale Law Journal* 1360 (1980). See also Note, "The Judicial Role in Attacking Racial Discrimination in Tax-Exempt Private Schools," 93 *Harvard Law Review* 378, 388 (1979).

47. Green v. Miller, 80–1 USTC ¶9401 (D.D.C. 1980), supplemented the permanent injunction of Green v. Connally, note 30 above, by requiring the schools to establish certain procedures in compliance with the injunction and to require the Internal Revenue Service to make annual reports to the court specifying the steps taken to implement the injunction. The Department of Justice did not appeal the decision.

48. The provision in effect restricted the use of funds to Mississippi pursuant to Green v. Miller, note 47 above; see 126 *Cong. Rec.* H7289 (Aug. 20, 1980). See also Melissa Brown, "Slippery Justice: The Tax-Exempt Status of Private Schools," 11 *Tax Notes* 555 (1980). It is an interesting question whether the congressional action violated the geographic uniformity clause of the Constitution.

49. In Green v. Miller, note 47 above, the court refused to pass on the valid-

ity of the appropriations act provision; see 126 *Cong. Rec.* H7212 (Aug. 14, 1980).

50. 416 U.S. 725 (1974).

51. *Bob Jones University v. United States,* 468 F. Supp., 890 (D.S.C. 1978).

52. *Bob Jones University v. United States,* 639 F. 2d 147 (4th Cir. 1980).

53. Goldsboro Christian Schools, Inc. v. United States, 436 F. Supp. 1314 (E.D. N.C. 1977).

54. No. 80-1473 (4th Cir. 1981).

55. U.S. Brief, Sept. 9, 1981, at 17 in U.S. Sup. Ct., No. 81-3 and 81-1.

56. *Administration's Change in Federal Policy Regarding the Tax Status of Racially Discriminatory Private Schools: Hearings before the House Committee on Ways and Means,* 97th Cong., 2d Sess. (1982). These hearings contain most of the documents and conferences involved in the reversal of position.

57. 656 F.2d 820 (D.C. Cir. 1981).

58. Wright v. Regan, No. 80-1124, 82-1134, Sept. Term 1981, Order (per curiam).

59. 128 *Cong. Rec.* H8615 (Nov. 30, 1982).

60. Note 43 above.

61. Justice Powell concurred in the judgment but objected to the "public benefit" test. He emphasized that the balancing of public interests involved in these situations should be left to Congress, though noting that in this instance Congress had made its position clear. He quoted former Commissioner Kurtz's statement that "questions concerning religion are 'far afield from the more typical tasks of tax administrators—determining taxable income.' " But what Justice Powell failed to perceive is that Kurtz was raising a fundamental objection to tax expenditure legislation, here charitable deductions and tax exempt status, which compelled the IRS to undertake these very questions.

62. Note 43 above at 2032 n.4.

63. 413 U.S. 455 (1973).

64. Note 43 above at 2028.

65. 397 U.S. 664 (1970).

66. Ibid. at 674-676.

67. Ibid. at 704.

68. 413 U.S. 756 (1973).

69. Committee for Public Education and Religious Liberty v. Nyquist, 350 F. Supp. 655 (S.D.N.Y. 1972).

70. Note 68 at 790-791; emphasis added.

71. Ibid. at 791-794.

72. In Kirk v. Commissioner, 425 F.2d 492 (D.C. Cir. 1970), a Methodist church employee asserted that he was arbitrarily discriminated against because IRC § 107 excluded from the income tax the rental allowance paid to "a minister of the gospel." He argued that section 107 was an impermissible constitutional discrimination and a violation of the establishment clause of the First Amendment. Quoting the Tax Court, 51 T.C. 66, 72 (1968), the court of appeals acknowledged that this was "an interesting inquiry" but, like the Tax

Court, found that it could not consider the question since the taxpayer was challenging only the deficiency asserted against him. In other words, the taxpayer's petition in the Tax Court was not drafted as an action challenging federal taxing and spending programs.

The inquiry is indeed "interesting." Section 107 is not listed as a tax expenditure, presumably because of the small amount involved. Unless it can be called an extension of section 119, exempting meals or lodging furnished on the employer's premises, so that the section 107 exclusion is merely a part of excluded employee housing fringe benefits—an extension that seems doubtful since section 119 does not cover cash payments—section 107 seems unconstitutional. There appears to be no case—and probably no instance of a direct government payment—concerned with the housing of a minister of the gospel.

73. 103 St. Ct. 3063 (1983).

74. On the merits, Justice Rehnquist distinguished this case from *Nyquist* primarily on the ground that the Minnesota statute provided aid to parents of both public school and private school children, whereas the statute in *Nyquist* provided assistance only to private school children. The majority in *Mueller v. Allen*, unlike the majority in *Nyquist*, looked only to the face of the statute to test its constitutionality and did not try to determine what percentage of the tax benefits in fact went to parents of children attending sectarian schools. In this respect, the decision reaffirmed the view expressed in *Nyquist* that the property tax exemptions upheld in *Walz* were constitutional because the benefits were provided to *all* educational and charitable nonprofit institutions. Thus, the real distinction between *Mueller v. Allen* and *Nyquist* appears to be that the majority in each case adopted a different constitutional test to determine whether financial benefits provided under a state statute violate the establishment clause. In *Nyquist*, the majority looked to the underlying facts to determine whether the tax benefits went primarily to parents of children attending sectarian schools; in *Mueller v. Allen* the majority refused to make that inquiry. As Justice Marshall pointed out in his dissent, approximately 96 percent of the taxpayers who qualified for the Minnesota tax deduction sent their children to religious schools, a higher percentage than in New York, where *Nyquist* struck down the tax benefits.

75. Note 73 above at 3069.

76. Ibid. at 3067.

77. Note 68 above at 790 n.49.

78. Note 73 above at 3068 n.6.

79. Ibid. at 3073.

80. Martin Feldstein, "The Income Tax and Charitable Contributions: Part II—The Impact on Religious, Educational, and Other Organizations," 28 *National Tax Journal* 209, 312 (1975).

81. Note 43 above. For some earlier articles, see Karla Simon, "The Tax Exempt Status of Racially Discriminatory Religious Schools," 36 *Tax Law Review* 477 (1981); Douglas Laycock, "Tax Exemptions for Racially Discriminatory Religious Schools," 60 *Texas Law Review* 259 (1982).

82. Note 73 above at 2035.

83. 485 F.2d 1003 (D.C. Cir. 1973).

84. Ibid. at 1006–7.

85. Treas. Reg. § 1.162–15(c) allows a deduction for union dues, but § 1.162–20(c)(3) denies deduction of any portion of dues used for, among other matters, political campaigns.

86. Note 16 above.

87. 73-1 USTC ¶9233 (D.D.C. 1973).

88. Note 39 above.

89. Note 87 above at 80425 n.4.

90. Ibid. at 80427–429.

91. On the general concept of state action, see Laurence H. Tribe, *American Constitutional Law* (Mineola, N.Y.: Foundation Press, 1978) 1147.

92. These tests are described in Comment, "Tax Incentives as State Action," 122 *University of Pennsylvania Law Review* 414 (1973).

93. See Robert C. Brown, "State Action Analysis of Tax Expenditures," 11 *Harvard Civil Rights–Civil Liberties Law Review* 97, 113 (1976), distinguishing between state action cases involving the government and those involving private parties. Judge Friendly, dissenting in Jackson v. Statler Foundation, 496 F.2d 623, 636 (2d Cir. 1974), drew the same distinction. If such a distinction is drawn, however, it must be applied equally to tax expenditures and direct programs.

94. In New York City Jaycees, Inc. v. United States Jaycees, Inc., 512 F.2d. 856 (2d Cir. 1975), a local Jaycee organization that allowed female members sought injunctive relief against the national organization, which restricted membership to males. The national organization received federal grants for disbursement. The court held that these grants did not constitute the requisite government involvement. It reached the same conclusion at 859 with respect to the national organization's tax-exempt status (which did not carry with it qualification to receive deductible contributions): "The lack of government involvement in discriminatory internal policies is particularly clear in a case such as this where the funds provided by federal contracts and grants do not sustain the general operations of the organization but rather are funnelled directly into discrete projects from which benefits are extended to the public without discrimination of any kind.

"Similarly the grant of tax exemptions to the Jaycees does not constitute significant government involvement in the organization's exclusionary membership policy. As the Supreme Court has pointed out in the context of a First Amendment challenge to tax exemptions granted to religious organizations, a tax exemption does not constitute government "sponsorship" but instead "creates only a minimal and remote involvement." Walz v. Tax Commission, 397 U.S. 664, 675–76, 90 S.Ct. 1409, 1415, 25 L.Ed.2d 697 (1970). See also Marker v. Shultz, 158 U.S. App. D.C. 224, 485 F.2d 1003, 1005–07 (1973). No genuine nexus between the tax exemption and the complained of internal membership policies has been shown and in its absence, there is no constitutional wrong." A similar result was reached in Junior Chamber of Commerce of Rochester v. The United States Jaycees, 495 F.2d 883 (10th Cir. 1974).

An earlier Second Circuit opinion, however, supported the plaintiff against a tax-exempt foundation eligible to receive deductible contributions. In Jackson v. Statler Foundation, note 93 above, the plaintiff sued several tax-exempt organizations, alleging racial discrimination in their refusal to hire him, to give scholarships to his children, and to grant money to his foundation. The court at 634 refused a motion to dismiss the action: "In sum, we believe that if on remand the district court finds that the defendant foundations are substantially dependent upon their exempt status [the court presumably here includes both the tax-exempt status as such and eligibility to receive deductible charitable contributions], that the regulatory scheme is both detailed and intrusive, that that scheme carries connotations of government approval, that the foundations do not have a substantial claim of constitutional protection, and that they serve some public function, then a finding of 'state action' would be appropriate. Moreover, even if one of these factors is absent, a finding of 'state action' may still be appropriate. On remand, the parties may be able to point to individual circumstances which distinguish the defendants from exempt private foundations generally. Again, the anticipated joining of the Commissioner of Internal Revenue and the State Tax Commissioner should illuminate the issues." A strong dissent was entered in the case.

Several decisions involving suits by professors, who claimed to have been wrongfully dismissed, declined to find the presence of state action where the institutions both had a tax-exempt status and received direct grants. The courts did not draw a distinction between the two forms of assistance; Spark v. Catholic University of America, 510 F.2d 1277 (D.C. Cir. 1975); Greenya v. George Washington University, 512 F.2d 556 (D.C. Cir. 1975).

95. Note 33 above at 457.

96. The literature cites Burton v. Wilmington Parking Authority, note 2 above, as holding that the allowance of a tax deduction for mortgage interest did not make the federal government a joint participant in the racial discrimination practiced by a lessee who leased commercial property from a city authority. The interest involved in Burton was interest on a business loan and therefore not a tax expenditure deduction, so that the decision would be correct under the tax expenditure concept. The Court's language regarding deduction is too broad, but the decision came down before the tax expenditure concept existed and the Court decision obviously did not consider this aspect.

97. Comment, "Tax Incentives as State Action," note 92 above at 468, makes a similar error regarding the deduction for home mortgage interest. The article fails to acknowledge that tax expenditure aid is financial assistance and should thus be subject to the same tests that would be applied to direct government aid for the purchase of owner-occupied homes. The article also errs in its discussion of the tax expenditure welfare transfer provisions.

98. See Boris I. Bittker and Kenneth M. Kaufman, "Taxes and Civil Rights:

'Constitutionalizing' the Internal Revenue Code," 82 *Yale Law Journal* 51, 73 (1972); Comment, "Tax Incentives as State Action," note 92 above at 437.

99. Bittker and Kaufman, note 98 above at 61.

100. Ibid. at 86.

101. Both Comment, "Tax Incentives as State Action," note 92 above, and Brown, "State Action Analysis of Tax Expenditures," note 93 above, criticize Bittker and Kaufman along similar lines.

102. See, for example, 1985 Special Analysis G at G-2.

103. See also the discussion of tax exemption for nonprofit organizations in chapter 7.

104. See chapter 7.

105. Note 33 above at 461–462.

106. Private Letter Ruling 7923001, Commerce Clearing House, *Estate and Gift Tax Reporter* ¶12,298 (1978), allowed an estate tax charitable deduction under a will after a state court decision had reformed a racial restriction contained in the will.

107. Title IX of the Education Amendments of 1972 prohibits discrimination on the basis of sex in "any education program or activity receiving Federal financial assistance." In 1977 the Department of Health, Education and Welfare cut off Basic Educational Opportunity grants to students attending Grove City College because the college refused to execute a form certifying that it was in compliance with Title IX. In Grove City College v. Bill, 52 *United States Law Week* 4283 (Feb. 28, 1984), the Supreme Court held that the college was "receiving Federal financial assistance" by virtue of the grants to its students. As such, its student aid program was required to comply with Title IX. The Court concluded that Title IX covered all forms of federal aid to education, direct or indirect. The interesting issue, given this sweeping language, is whether the tax expenditure assistance provided by the exemption for scholarships is likewise covered by Title IX (although, as noted by the Court, there is some legislative history to indicate that Congress intended Title IX to encompass only programs providing aid through HEW). The federal direct revenue-sharing legislation contains rules to ensure that state or local governments that use these federal funds cannot infringe civil rights. The federal estate tax contains a credit against the federal tax for state death duties. This is a form of revenue sharing. The question arises whether the absence of a specific requirement under this credit, similar to the requirement under the direct legislation, should bar a suit aimed at preventing a state with an estate tax from practicing alleged unconstitutional infringements. The answer should be no, even though it may be more difficult to trace the federal assistance in the estate tax credit than in the revenue sharing assistance.

108. For a general discussion, see Tribe, *American Constitutional Law*, note 91 above at 79.

109. Egnal v. Commissioner, 65 T.C. 255 (1975), involved the contest of a deficiency on the grounds that the U.S. government acted illegally and unconstitutionally in participating in the Vietnam War and that a payment of taxes

would constitute "complicity in war crimes" in violation of the Nuremberg principles. The court held against the taxpayer. The opinion stated, however, that a "threshold question" was whether the taxpayer had "standing" and went on to mention traditional cases such as *Flast v. Cohen*, which is discussed later in the text. This inquiry seems beside the point since the taxpayer was contesting an assertion of liability against himself rather than the general imposition of a tax on all potential taxpayers.

110. Enochs v. Williams Packing & Navigation Co., 370 U.S. 1, 7 (1962). See Bob Jones University, note 43 above. In Center on Corporate Responsibility v. Shultz, 368 F. Supp. 863 (D.D.C. 1973), the court accepted an injunction proceeding in which the plaintiff alleged having been denied tax-exempt status as the result of politically motivated interference by the White House. Later legislation provided that an organization denied tax-exempt status by the Internal Revenue Service may seek a declaratory judgment on the issue; IRC § 7428.

111. Tax legislation has moved toward permitting taxpayers to obtain declaratory rulings in the Tax Court (with appeals permitted). Examples are IRC § 7428, relating to IRS denial of section 501(c)(3) charitable organization status; § 7476, relating to IRS denial of qualification of an employee retirement pension plan; § 7477, relating to IRS refusal to issue a favorable § 367 ruling permitting tax-free exchanges involving foreign corporations; and § 7478, relating to IRS denial of qualification to state and local government obligations.

112. Massachusetts v. Mellon, 262 U.S. 447 (1923).

113. Pietsch v. The President of the United States, 434 F.2d 861 (2d Cir. 1970); Autenrieth v. Cullen, 418 F.2d 586 (9th Cir. 1969).

114. Anthony v. Commissioner, 66 T.C. 367 (1976).

115. Dennison v. United States, 73-1 USTC ¶9430 (S.D.N.Y. 1973).

116. Note 1 above at 105–106. See Tribe, *American Constitutional Law*, note 91 above at 82. For a discussion of these issues in the context of direct grants, see Madden, "Right to Receive Federal Grants," note 22 above.

117. Note 25 above at 1132.

118. Note 33 above at 452–454.

119. Note 83 above.

120. Note 87 above.

121. 426 U.S. 26 (1976).

122. Revenue Ruling 69-545, 1969-2 *Cum. Bull.* 117, reversing Revenue Ruling 56-185, 1956-1 *Cum. Bull.* 202.

123. Eastern Kentucky Welfare Rights Organization v. Schultz, 370 F. Supp. 325 (D.D.C. 1973).

124. Eastern Kentucky Welfare Rights Organization v. Simon, 506 F.2d 1278 (D.C. Cir. 1974).

125. Note 121 above at 42.

126. Ibid. at 46.

127. Ibid. at 37.

128. Slip opinion no. 81-757 (U.S. Sup. Ct., July 3, 1984).

129. Ibid. at 17.

130. Ibid. at 18.
131. Ibid. at 19–20.
132. Note 30 above.
133. Note 128 above at 7–8 (dissenting opinion of Justice Stevens).
134. Note 128 above at 17 (dissenting opinion of Justice Brennan).
135. It may be difficult for a plaintiff to state a prima facie case. In Lugo v. Simon, 453 F. Supp. 677 (N.D. Ohio 1978), involving the same revenue ruling as in *Eastern Kentucky Welfare Rights Organization,* a district court upheld taxpayers' standing on the basis of the pleadings: "From a reading of the *Simon* decision, it appears that for Article III purposes, standing would have been established in the case had plaintiffs undertaken the burden of showing that the hospitals involved, or some of them were 'so financially dependent upon favorable tax treatment afforded charitable organizations that they would admit respondents if a court required such admission as a condition to receipt of that treatment.'

"Plaintiffs in this action have alleged such a dependency on favorable tax treatment by the hospitals concerned and have also undertaken to demonstrate the contention through the filing of materials in the action setting forth financial data of the hospitals concerned showing the amounts of charitable contributions received and comparisons of receipts against expenses for fiscal years 1969 through 1976.

"Plaintiff Perez was twice denied admission to Memorial Hospital of Sandusky County. The financial data filed by plaintiff demonstrates that the hospital would have operated at a loss during six of the seven years for which data was provided but for charitable contributions. Based upon the record before this Court, the contentions of plaintiffs, at least as to that hospital, as to the dependency on favorable tax treatment as a charitable organization are clearly more than speculative. The allegations of the complaint as supported by the financial data submitted are clearly sufficient to withstand the defendants' motion to dismiss for lack of standing" (p. 689).

But the Sixth Circuit Court of Appeals was dissatisfied with the pleading and data submitted, and therefore reversed: "They had not established that, in fact, 'the asserted injury was the consequence of the defendants' actions.' 426 U.S. [note 121] at 45 . . . The Court went on to observe 'in the instant case respondents' injuries might have occurred even in the absence of the IRS ruling that they challenge; whether the injuries fairly can be traced to that ruling depends upon unalleged and unknown facts about the relevant hospitals.' 426 U.S. at 45, n.25. Plaintiffs have not avoided that pitfall here by specifically alleging facts explaining how the issuance of Rev. Rul. 69-545 led to their injuries . . . There is no evidence in the record that the policy making authorities in the hospitals were even aware of the existence of the Ruling. Nor is there any evidence tending to show that the hospitals' admissions policies were altered or amended in response to the 1969 Ruling, leading to a decline in the dollar volume of services rendered to indigents . . . In sum, we see no connection between the government action and any third-party reaction . . .

"Plaintiffs argue that if the hospitals were stripped of their tax exempt status, all other factors remaining static, the charitable contributions received by the hospitals would not have been made, since the encouragement of Sec. 170 would be absent. That is, if the hospitals were not tax exempt, they would not receive charitable contributions, thereby decreasing their revenues, and concomitantly, they would at the same time incur federal income tax liability, thus increasing their liabilities to an extent that the hospitals would have operated at a deficit. Plaintiffs conclude from this calculus that the avoidance of a loss is sufficient economic incentive to convince the hospitals not to forgo preferential tax treatment.

"This conclusion of 'dependency' is too facile for acceptance. It assumes that hospitals operate in a vacuum, that if a hospital is not tax exempt it will not receive any charitable contributions. This allegation is weakened by the parties' own stipulation that '(n)either the amount of these gifts, contributions or bequests nor the degree of tax motivation on the part of the donor can be measured or determined.' The assumption of the plaintiffs that the economic benefits of gifts and contributions would be lost entirely if the hospitals' tax exempt status were taken away is not supported in the record" (Lugo v. Miller, 640 F.2d 823, 828–830 [6th Cir. 1981]).

136. For a bill proposing to allow such standing, see Statement of Senator Kennedy, 122 *Cong. Rec.* 23789–23993 (1976). There appear to be no cases involving direct grant programs in which third parties have sought solely to enjoin overgenerous application of the program to persons or groups thereby benefited by the application.

137. See William D. Popkin, "Standing to Challenge Generous Tax Rulings: The Case for Congressional Action," 6 *Tax Notes* 163 (1978); Michael Asimow, "Standing to Challenge Lenient Tax Rules: A Statutory Solution," 6 *Tax Notes* 227 (1978), also in 57 *Taxes* 483 (1979). Over the years Congress has increased the rights of taxpayers to seek declaratory judgments in the Tax Court in order to challenge IRS decisions adverse to them. See note 111 above.

138. There could be policy reasons for distinguishing between standing to challenge overgenerous interpretations of normative tax provisions and standing to challenge overgenerous interpretations of tax expenditure provisions. The policy for tax expenditures is or should be the same as for direct spending programs, and the same tests should be applied to determine standing in both types of cases. A statutory grant of standing to challenge interpretations of normative tax provisions must rest on a quite different policy ground. It is conceivable that a statute could grant standing to challenge tax expenditure interpretations but deny standing to challenge interpretations of normative provisions on the ground that, in the latter situations, the Treasury should be given great interpretative leeway (and taxpayers greater corresponding certainty). Both Tax Analysts and Advocates v. Shultz, 376 F. Supp. 889 (D.D.C. 1974), an early case involving the gift tax exclusion, in which standing was allowed, and Tax Analysts and Advocates v. Blumenthal, 566 F.2d 130 (D.C. Cir. 1977), involving the foreign tax credit, in which standing was denied, related to normative provisions.

139. 1981 Special Analysis G at 203.

140. Some advocates are finding it necessary to deny the connection. Amicus Curiae Brief of Independent Sector in Bob Jones University v. United States, U.S. Sup. Ct., No. 81-3, at 18.

141. One reason for lawyers' failure to refer to the tax expenditure list may be that, although it includes the deduction for charitable contributions to exempt organizations, it does not include the tax exemption itself. This omission should be corrected. See chapter 7.

6. INTERNATIONAL ASPECTS

1. A schedular system does not readily lend itself to the taxation of foreign-source income. A country that decides not to tax on a worldwide basis but to tax only the domestic-source income of its residents needs a set of rules to determine domestic-source income. These source rules will have a general relationship to the source rules applicable to the exercise of source jurisdiction over foreigners, but the two sets of rules need not be exactly parallel. As discussed later in connection with the determination of source rules applicable to foreigners, there is no generally accepted normative standard similar in function to the normative standard applicable in the determination of net income. However, the international rules that have grown over time do provide a set of guidelines for the establishment of source rules. The source rules followed in the taxation of residents really function as part of the basic decision of how far to extend the income tax to the income derived by its residents.

2. For a general discussion of residence jurisdiction, see Stanley S. Surrey, *United Nations Model Convention for Tax Treaties between Developed and Developing Countries* (Cambridge, Mass.: Harvard Law School, International Tax Program, 1980).

3. A country may be influenced by practical compliance considerations in not treating as a resident a person with a very limited relationship to the country.

4. Only the United States and the Philippines use citizenship as their criterion. However, most countries that apply a rule of domicile come rather close to the citizenship rule, since their citizens living abroad may often maintain their country of citizenship as the country of domicile.

Since foreigners are taxed at a lower rate than U.S. citizens on investment income from U.S. sources, the rule taxing citizens needs protection from abuse. Accordingly, if a U.S. citizen decides to live abroad (so as not to be a resident) and also gives up his citizenship with one of the principal purposes being the avoidance of income tax, then the United States for ten years treats the individual as it would a citizen with respect to the taxation of income from U.S. sources; that is, the regular progresssive rate schedule and not the lower withholding rates are used, and stricter source rules as to U.S. sources are applied than are normally applicable to foreigners. This approach, being protective of the jurisdictional rule of taxing citizens, is not a tax penalty.

5. IRC § 911. The exclusion is currently $80,000 and is scheduled to increase

to $95,000 by 1990. The treatment of earned income of U.S. citizens working abroad has shifted several times, from a very generous exemption starting in the 1920s, to a gradual reduction of the exemption in the 1960s and 1970s, to a specific list of deductible special expenses (such as housing, educating children in U.S.-type schools, higher cost of living in a particular country, and the expense of an annual trip to the United States), to the current exemption of very large amounts of compensation plus the housing allowance. An individual's investment income from abroad is fully subject to tax.

6. For differing viewpoints on the treatment of foreign compensation, see John D. Maiers, "The Foreign Earned Income Exclusion: Reinventing the Wheel," 34 *Tax Lawyer* 691 (1981); and Charles I. Kingson, "A Somewhat Different View [of the Foreign Earned Income Exclusion]," 34 *Tax Lawyer* 737 (1981). See also Jane G. Gravelle and Donald W. Kiefer, "U.S. Taxation of Citizens Working in Other Countries: An Economic Analysis," in *Studies in Taxation, Public Finance, and Related Subjects—A Compendium*, vol. 3 (Washington, D.C.: Fund for Public Policy Research, 1979) 72.

7. The result is also contrary to U.S. financial accounting practice, which combines the parent company and its foreign subsidiaries in the profit-and-loss statement and the balance sheet.

The result is also inconsistent with the U.S. rule permitting the parent corporation to obtain an indirect foreign tax credit for taxes paid by the subsidiary. Ordinarily one taxpayer cannot get a credit for taxes paid by another taxpayer. Hence the indirect foreign tax credit views the two corporations as one.

8. See, for example, U.S. Treasury Department, *The President's 1978 Tax Program, Detailed Descriptions and Supporting Analyses of the Proposals* (1978). The Subpart F tax provisions in the code do tax a U.S. parent company directly on the profits of its foreign subsidiary. These provisions are designed to limit the deferral of tax for tax haven corporations, foreign subsidiaries insuring U.S. risks, and foreign subsidiaries investing in certain U.S. assets. These limitations are not tax penalties but instead are restrictions on the deferral tax expenditure. See the discussion in chapter 7.

9. See in general C. Fred Bergsten, Thomas Horst, and Theodorett Moran, *American Multinationals and American Interests* (Washington, D.C.: Brookings Institution, 1978); Peggy B. Musgrave, *United States Taxation of Foreign Investment Income: Issues and Arguments* (Cambridge, Mass.: Harvard Law School, International Tax Program, 1969); Stanley S. Surrey, "Current Issues in the Taxation of Corporate Foreign Investment," 56 *Columbia Law Review* 815 (1956); *President's 1978 Tax Reduction and Reform Proposals: Hearings before the House Ways and Means Committee*, 95th Cong., 2d Sess. (1978); *Revenue Act of 1978: Hearings before the Senate Finance Committee*, 95th Cong., 2d Sess. (1978).

10. U.S. Treasury Department, *The Operation and Effect of the Domestic International Sales Corporation Legislation*, annual reports. See also Jane G. Gravelle, Kent Hughes, and Warren F. Farb, "The Domestic International Sales

Corporation and Its Effects on U.S. Foreign Trade and Unemployment," in *Studies in Taxation,* note 6 above, vol. 2 (1978) at 426; George D. Holliday, "Incentives and Disincentives for U.S. Exporters," ibid., vol. 3 at 471; Harry G. Gourevitch, "Tax Treatment of Export Income in the United States and Other Industrial Countries," ibid. at 146.

11. See U.S. Treasury, *The President's 1978 Tax Program,* note 8 above.

12. IRC §§ 921–927.

13. Surrey, "Current Issues," note 9 above.

14. U.S. Treasury Department, *The Operation and Effect of the Possessions Corporation System of Taxation,* annual reports.

15. For detailed descriptions of the U.S. foreign tax credit mechanism see Elisabeth A. Owens, *The Foreign Tax Credit* (Cambridge, Mass.: Harvard Law School, International Tax Program, 1961); Elisabeth A. Owens and Gerald T. Ball, *The Indirect Credit,* 2 vols. (Cambridge, Mass.: Harvard Law School, International Tax Program, 1975 and 1978).

16. This limitation allows a credit if there is income taxable by foreign country A but a loss in foreign country B. But if there is income in both countries, with the country A rate higher than the residence country rate and the country B rate lower, there is a loss of credit to the extent of the excess tax of country A.

17. This limitation allows a taxpayer to average the rates of the various foreign countries, so that it is possible to take a credit for the tax of a high-rate country if it is combined with the tax of a low-rate country. However, if there is income taxed by foreign country A and an equal loss in foreign country B, the income and loss are netted, no overall foreign-source income is taxed, and credit is lost for the tax of country A.

18. See, for example, special limitations applied in IRC § 904(d) (foreign interest income) and § 907 (foreign oil and gas income); see also § 904(f), providing for a recapture of foreign losses previously deducted when a foreign enterprise later becomes profitable, pays a foreign tax, and claims a foreign tax credit.

19. A country could decide not to impose any limitation on the amount of foreign taxes allowed as a credit, so that a high foreign tax would eliminate a part of the tax on domestic income. This approach could still be regarded as normative. Such a country has to this extent opted for the form of tax neutrality regarding foreign investment that views neutrality in terms of the tax in the foreign country as the governing tax, applicable to all investment, domestic or foreign, in that country. Under this concept of neutrality, the grant of a refund for the excess of foreign tax over the domestic tax would also be a normative approach. But apparently all countries using a capital export neutrality criterion view that criterion as referring to neutrality between domestic and foreign investment, with no inducement to invest abroad rather than at home.

20. In the United States these rules are in Treas. Reg. §§ 861-8 and 882-5. See Surrey, "Current Issues," note 9 above. Every country, whether it uses a foreign tax credit approach or exempts foreign-source income, needs some set of rules to determine the allocation of expenses to foreign-source income.

21. There are other normative rules necessary to apply a worldwide jurisdiction approach, such as the set of rules to translate gains and losses abroad measured in a foreign currency into gains and losses in terms of U.S. dollars, a complex matter currently under study by the Treasury. For an earlier study, see Donald R. Ravenscroft, *Taxation and Foreign Currency* (Cambridge, Mass.: Harvard Law School, International Tax Program, 1973).

22. Treas. Reg. § 1.861-8(e)(3). The Tax Reform Act of 1984 extended the application of the regulation until August 1, 1985.

23. See Staff of the Joint Committee on Taxation, 97th Cong., 1st Sess., *General Explanation of the Economic Recovery Tax Act of 1981* (1981) 141.

24. The credit also extends to foreign war profits and excess profits taxes, which, being based on profits, are income taxes. The credit approach also applies to the federal estate tax, which allows a credit for "any estate, inheritance, legacy, or succession taxes." There is no statutory credit for foreign gift taxes, but some treaties allow a credit.

25. See Surrey, "Current Issues," note 9 above.

26. Treas. Reg. § 1.901-2(a).

27. Treas. Reg. § 1.901-2(b).

28. However, a generally applicable withholding tax on gross income of those not engaged in business in a country is creditable as a tax in lieu of an income tax; Treas. Reg. § 1.903-1(a).

29. Treas. Reg. § 1.901-2(b)(4).

30. Treas. Reg. § 1.901-2(b)(2).

31. Treas. Reg. § 1.901-2(b)(2) credits such a tax.

32. See Owens and Ball, *The Indirect Credit*, note 15 above. As was observed in note 7 above, the tax deferral approach is in theory inconsistent with the allowance of the deemed credit for the tax on the foreign subsidiary. Deferral emphasizes separateness; the deemed credit emphasizes the economic unit.

33. For a general discussion of source jurisdiction, see Surrey, *United Nations Model Convention*, note 2 above.

34. See International Fiscal Association, *Rules for Determining Income and Expenses as Domestic or Foreign*, Cahiers de Droit Fiscal International, vol. 65b (Deventer, Netherlands: Kluwer, 1980).

35. Canada, however, does treat incentive departures from its normal withholding rate as a tax expenditure; France does not. The Reporters for the American Law Institute *Federal Income Tax Project*, "International Aspects of United States Income Taxation" (Council Draft no. 11, Nov. 24, 1982) 13-20, adopted the approach suggested in the text.

36. U.S. Treaury Department Model Income Tax Treaty (June 6, 1981).

37. *Tax Treaties: Hearings before the Senate Foreign Relations Committee,* 97th Cong., 1st Sess. (1981) 53, 494.

38. An earlier proposed treaty with Brazil extended the investment credit to U.S. investment in Brazil, although the unilateral U.S. statute applied the credit only to domestic investment. The Senate ratified the proposed treaty, but with a reservation on the article relating to the investment credit; 114 *Cong.*

Rec. 16165 (1968). The reservation implied that assistance to foreign investment should come not through tax provisions such as treaties but through direct programs. Faced with this reservation, Brazil did not ratify the treaty.

39. *Report of the Senate Foreign Relations Committee on the Tax Convention with Israel,* Exec. Rept. 25, 97th Cong., 1st Sess. (1980).

40. This classification is discussed in chapter 7.

41. Although the treaties, as part of their purpose to eliminate double taxation, contain a provision requiring the United States to allow a credit for foreign taxes, the treaty mechanism for the credit does not go beyond the unilateral credit provision.

The adoption of "tax sparing," either through a treaty or as a code provision, should be considered as a tax expenditure. Some developed countries have granted tax-sparing credits in their treaties, allowing a credit for a tax that has not in fact been paid to a developing country, because, for example, the developing country has granted a tax holiday. So far the United States has refused to allow these credits. U.S. allowance of a tax-sparing credit would have to be based on a policy of deliberate encouragement of U.S. investment in the foreign country to complement the tax incentive encouragement of the foreign country. See Stanley S. Surrey and Paul R. McDaniel, "The Tax Expenditure Concept: Current Developments and Emerging Issues," 20 *Boston College Law Review* 225, 348 (1979).

The 1978 Protocol to the U.S.–French treaty resolved the conflict that arises because both countries use a worldwide jurisdictional basis that can overlap in the case of a U.S. citizen residing in France. The Protocol changed U.S. source rules to allow the U.S. citizen to utilize as a credit a part of the French tax on what would otherwise be U.S. source income. The ultimate total tax is the higher of the French or U.S. tax, but there is no double taxation. This change in source rules, although it benefits a U.S. citizen and not a foreigner, is designed to accommodate the application of a foreign tax credit system in situations in which jurisdictional bases differ; therefore, it would not be regarded as a tax expenditure.

42. For a discussion of the tax expenditure concept as applied in the domestic setting to "corporate integration," see chapter 7.

43. Country X (the nonimputation country) might also argue that the country Y imputation system applied to domestic shareholders but denied to foreign shareholders constitutes, in effect, an increase in the dividend withholding tax applied to country X shareholders. Country Y (the imputation country) under international rules is free to set that tax at the rate level it chooses. A treaty negotiation, however, involves consideration of the rate level of withholding taxes. In this context, country X, not having an imputation system, might contend it is entitled to a lower treaty withholding rate on dividends than the treaty withholding rate specified for dividends going to country Y shareholders from country X corporations. U.S. efforts to advance this argument, however, have not met with success.

44. Two countries, each having tax expenditure lists and using tax expen-

diture analysis, could of course phrase the nondiscrimination clause to apply it only to their normative tax systems. This solution would leave open the question whether foreigners would, under the domestic law of the other country or its other treaties, such as those of friendship, commerce, and navigation, be entitled to spending assistance granted by the other country.

45. For discussions of this subject, see Hugh J. Ault, "International Issues in Corporate Tax Integration," 10 *Law & Policy in International Business* 461 (1978); George Carlson, *International Aspects of Corporation-Shareholder Tax Integration*, OTA Paper 40 (Washington, D.C.: U.S. Treasury Department, Office of Tax Analysis, 1980).

46. For a general discussion of GATT, see Shelton Hufbauer and Gary Hufbauer, *The International Discipline of Export Incentives and Countermeasures* (London: International Trade Center, 1976).

47. *General Agreement on Tariffs and Trade, United States Tax Legislation (DISC), Report of the Panel L/4422* (1976) 15–16, para. 67.

48. Ibid.

49. Ibid. at para. 68.

50. Ibid. at para. 71 (emphasis in original).

51. Ibid. at para. 72.

52. Ibid. at para. 73.

53. Ibid. at para. 74.

54. Ibid. at para. 75. See Sabino Rodriguez III, "Note on Recent Development under General Agreement on Tariffs and Trade (GATT)," 18 *Harvard International Law Journal* 706 (1977).

55. For later provisions in GATT on deferral, see note 64 below.

56. Under French law, the foreign branch must qualify as a "permanent establishment" in the other country; accordingly, its profits would be taxable by that country if the country imposed an income tax.

57. The exemption system is also presented as an alternative in the UN model treaty for treaties between developed and developing countries. See Surrey, *United Nations Model Convention*, note 2 above.

58. *General Agreement on Tariffs and Trade, Income Tax Practices Maintained by France, Report of the Panel L/4423* (1976) 11, para. 47.

59. Ibid. at para. 48.

60. Ibid. at para. 49.

61. Ibid. at para. 50.

62. *General Agreement on Tariffs and Trade, Income Tax Practices Maintained by the Netherlands, Report of the Panel L/4425* (1976); *General Agreement on Tariffs and Trade, Income Tax Practices Maintained by Belgium, Report of the Panel L/4424* (1976).

63. The panel decision does not explicitly consider the general status of the territoriality principle. The crux of its decision lies in its conclusion, quoted earlier in the text, and especially in the words "some part of export activities, belonging to an economic process originating in that country." See the article by a member of the panel, Professor A. R. Prest, "GATT and Company Taxa-

tion," 1977 *British Tax Review* 201, particularly the following statement emphasizing the rationale for the decision: "The panel found in its report that tax practices in all three countries were contrary to GATT. The essential point was that a subsidy could be seen to apply in what was really part of a linked cycle of operations originating in the home country. One link was cut off from another by the practice of setting up sales subsidiaries abroad. (It should be noted that this argument very specifically related to the divorce of a particular part of an integrated operation; it did not in any sense apply to setting up subsidiaries abroad for production purposes.) Having established that a subsidy existed then the argument was on very much the same lines as with the United States and D.I.S.C., i.e. that it was clear that there was a subsidy on exports and that it could operate either directly on export prices or by the roundabout route of making exports more profitable and hence affecting particular prices in world markets as a result of more activity being devoted to such pursuits. Given the relative size of the three countries concerned, the argument was less broad in character than with the United States but it did apply nonetheless in particular cases."

The panel decision throws an interesting light on the territoriality principle. Gourevitch, "Tax Treatment of Export Income," note 10 above at 147, states that "France's failure to rigorously enforce arm's length pricing rules was the key to the panel's findings." Although the United States stressed this matter in its argument, Professor Prest's article and the panel decision clearly indicated that the decision dealt with a much broader point and did not rest on the U.S. contention regarding French arm's-length practices, whatever may have been the factual validity of that contention.

64.   The 1979 GATT Subsidies/Countervailing Measures Agreement includes in its illustrative list of export subsidies, "the full or partial exemption, remission or deferral specifically related to exports, of direct taxes or social welfare charges paid or payable by industrial or commercial enterprises." A footnote states: "The signatories recognize that deferral need not amount to an export subsidy where, for example, appropriate interest charges are collected. The signatories further recognize that nothing in this text prejudges the disposition by the Contracting Parties of the specific issues raised in GATT document L/4422 [note 47 above]."

For discussion of the 1979 GATT changes, see Thomas Kwako, "Tax Incentives for Exports, Permissible and Proscribed: An Analysis of the Corporate Income Tax Implications of the MTA Subsidies Code," 12 *Law and Policy in International Business* 677 (1980). The author concluded that under the 1979 language a DISC-type deferral is prohibited but the territoriality system is acceptable.

65.   In a world in which tax havens abound, the territoriality principle and the exemption method offer greater encouragement to the use of the tax haven than does the foreign tax credit method. Hence, if exemption countries are willing to tolerate the unrestricted use of tax havens by their business enterprises, the suspicion would arise that there is more of subsidy present and less of historical or jurisdictional principle involved in the continued use of the ex-

emption method. Use of the foreign tax credit method is not in itself sufficient protection against tax havens if tax deferral is allowed, but the foreign tax credit may eventually exact some payment whereas the exemption method does not. French tax officials had asserted that France tries to prevent tax haven problems so that its exemption approach in practice did not promote tax haven activities, but in 1980 the French adopted an anti–tax haven measure similar to the United States' Subpart F. See International Fiscal Association, *Recourse to Tax Havens, Use and Abuse* (Deventer, Netherlands: Kluwer, 1980) 35.

The developed countries' use of the exemption approach appeals to developing countries because, in the view of the developing countries and the enterprises affected, it meshes well with the prevalent tendency of developing countries to use tax incentive devices, such as tax holidays and accelerated depreciation, to attract foreign investment. However, this inevitable effect of the exemption approach gives it an aura of subsidy rather than of tax jurisprudence. This is not to say that the foreign tax credit approach, if combined with a deferral of tax on the profits of controlled foreign subsidiaries, represents a problem-free solution. But such deferral is classified as a tax expenditure.

The exemption system is justified by some on the ground that it tends to have the same effect as source tax neutrality for foreign investment, owing to its focus on the tax system of the source country. It thereby places all enterprises with activities in that country, whether domestic or foreign owned, on the same income tax footing with regard to those activities. But such competitive neutrality can be achieved only if all residence countries utilize the exemption approach. The foreign tax credit approach focuses on residence country neutrality: resident enterprises, whether investing at home or abroad, are subject to the same income tax (as long as the source country tax does not exceed the residence country tax). This latter neutrality can be achieved by a particular country using the tax credit method regardless of the method used by other countries. Thus, given the desire of many countries to use the foreign tax credit method, the exemption method is inherently incapable of achieving source tax neutrality.

66. See Commission of the European Communities v. Federal Republic of Germany, Court of Justice of the European Communities, Case No. 70/72 (July 12, 1973), *Reports of Cases before the Court*, vol. 1973-76 at 813.

67. In addition to this consideration by international fiscal organizations, reviews of Stanley S. Surrey's *Pathways to Tax Reform* (Cambridge, Mass.: Harvard University Press, 1973), the first U.S. full-length exposition of the subject, have appeared in periodicals in several other countries, including France, Germany, Japan, and the United Kingdom. See, for example, Pierre Kerlan, "Pathways to Tax Reform," 67 *Bulletin de l'économie et des finances* 155 (July–September 1974); Hirtomi Kimura, "Pathways to Tax Reform, 48 *Hogaku Kenkyu* no. 3 (1974); F. Neumark, "Tax Expenditures," 33 *Finanzarchiv* no. 1, 139 (1974); Torao Aoki, "Pathways to Tax Reform," *Zeinoshirubi* 6 (1974); W. B. Taylor, "Pathways to Tax Reform," 1984 *British Tax Review* 189.

Discussions of the tax expenditure concept by U.S. writers in European journals include Hugh J. Ault, "Steuervergunstigungen in der Bundesrepublik Deutschland und den USA," 4 *Steuer und Wirtschaft* 335 (1974), and Paul R. McDaniel, "The Tax Expenditure Concept: Theory and Practical Operation," 45 *Maandblad Belastingbeschouwingen* 245 (1976).

68. The International Fiscal Association has a large international membership composed of practicing tax specialists (tax executives, lawyers, accountants), government officials, and academics. On each of the two subjects chosen for its annual congress it publishes a *cahier*, containing about twenty reports prepared by national reporters from the various countries in which the IFA has local branches, and a general report summarizing and analyzing the contents of the national reports. Because the national reports follow guidelines established by the IFA, they provide organized comparative material. The subject is then discussed at the annual congress and the conclusion of the congress is summarized in a resolution or précis.

69. International Fiscal Association, *General Report, Tax Incentives as an Instrument for Achievement of Governmental Goals*, Cahiers de Droit Fiscal International, vol. 61 (Deventer, Netherlands: Kluwer, 1976). Stanley S. Surrey and Emil M. Sunley, Jr., of the United States were the general reporters.

70. Ibid. at 46.

71. This organization, considerably smaller than IFA, is composed almost entirely of public finance specialists, usually academics or government officials. Its membership includes Eastern European countries. A program committee organizes the preparation of individual papers in accordance with the program agenda, and these papers are discussed at the annual congress. The papers are published in a single volume, generally about one year afterward. No resolutions are adopted. The 1977 proceedings are published in Karl Hauser, ed., *Subsidies, Tax Reliefs, and Prices* (Paris: Editions Cujas, 1981).

72. Examples are, for Canada: Roger Smith, *Tax Expenditures: An Examination of Tax Incentives and Preferences in the Canadian Federal Income Tax System* (Toronto: Canadian Tax Foundation, 1979); for the Netherlands: Victor Halberstadt and Flip de Kam, "About the Choice between Direct versus Tax Expenditures" (paper presented at the IIPF 1977 Congress); for the United Kingdom: J. R. M. Willis and P. J. W. Hardwick, *Tax Expenditures in the United Kingdom* (London: Institute of Fiscal Studies, 1978); for Tunisia: Lotfi Maktouf, "Les dépenses fiscales, en tout qu'instrument d'une politique d'investment industriels en Tunisie (manuscript, 1979); for Belgium: Max Frank and D. Meulders, "Dépenses fiscales relatives à l'impôt des personnes physiques et solutions alternatives," *Cahiers économiques de Bruxelles*, no. 83-3rd trimestre (1979) 307; for Sweden: Nils Mattsson and Sven-Ake Bergkvist, "Skattesubventiones—Ett Medel ett Uppna Offentilga Mal," 4 *Svensk Skattetidning* 383 (1983); and for India: Arnand P. Gupta, *Fiscal Policy and the Poor* (New Delhi: Oxford & IBH Publishing, 1984) 27–53.

73. See 1983 CBO Study at 23–44 for a discussion of tax expenditure budgets in other countries.

74. See Smith, Tax Expenditures, note 72 above; papers delivered at a conference on tax policy are published in 1 *Canadian Taxation* no. 2 (1979).

75. See, however, Kerlan, "Pathways to Tax Reform," note 67 above; Jacques-Henri Favier, in IFA 1976 *General Report*, note 69 above at 349.

76. *Project de Loi de Finances pour 1981* (Paris: Imprimerie Nationale, no. 73008 B89-1980).

77. Memorandum, "Control of Public Expenditure" (item 2), Feb. 1, 1978, HMSO 196 (Memoranda).

78. See the memorandum by the Fabian Society in "Testimony before the Expenditure of the House of Commons, on the Government's Expenditure Plans 1979-1980 to 1982-83," appendix 5 to *Minutes of Evidence Taken before the Expenditure Committee (General Subcommittee)*, HMSO 237 (1979).

79. See note 72 above.

80. HMSO, Cmnd 7439 (January 1979).

81. Ibid. at 17–18.

82. The discussion in Willis and Hardwick, *Tax Expenditures in the United Kingdom*, note 72 above, provides a helpful background for many of the items in the government's list.

83. *Achter Subventionsbericht*, Deutscher Bundestag, 9. Wahlperiode Drucksache 9/986 (1981).

84. Ministerio de Hacienda, *Presequesto para 1981 de los beneficios fiscales que afectan a los tubutos del estado* (1981). The first tax expenditure budget was published in 1979. Lists have been published for later years.

85. *Taxation Expenditures: Report from the House of Representatives Standing Committee on Expenditure* (August 1982).

86. For discussions of the tax expenditure concept in the Dutch system, see Halberstadt and de Kam, "Direct versus Tax Expenditures," note 71 above; Jan Christiaanse, "Tax Expenditures," 106 *Weekblad Voor Fiscal Recht* 69 (1977).

87. IFA, 1976 *General Report*, note 69 above at 40–41.

88. OECD Committee on Fiscal Affairs, DAF/CFA/79.13 (1979) 4–9. A few OECD comparative studies do take some tax preferences into account. Examples are *The 1979 Tax/Benefit Position of a Typical Worker in OECD Member Countries* (1980) and *The Tax/Benefit Position of Selected Income Groups in OECD Member Countries* (1978).

89. See Paul R. McDaniel, "The Tax Expenditure Concept in the International Context," 47 *Maanblad Belastingbeschouivingen* 115 (1978).

90. The guidelines and the tax expenditure lists of each country are contained in Paul R. McDaniel and Stanley S. Surrey, eds., *International Aspects of Tax Expenditures: A Comparative Study* (Deventer, Netherlands: Kluwer, 1985).

7. CONCEPTUAL ASPECTS OF TAX EXPENDITURE ANALYSIS

1. *Annual Report of the Secretary of the Treasury on the State of the Finances for Fiscal Year 1968* (1969) 326, 327–329.

2. Since 1975 the executive branch list has been presented in Special Analysis G of the federal budget. The congressional tax expenditure lists are in the Joint Committee Staff Estimates, annual projections for five fiscal years; and in the annual CBO Studies. See also Senate Budget Committee, 94th Cong., 2d

Sess., *Tax Expenditures: Compendium of Background Material on Individual Provisions* (1976); idem, 95th Cong., 2d Sess., *Tax Expenditures: Relationships to Spending Programs and Background Material on Individual Provisions* (1978).

3. Budget Act of 1974, P.L. 93-344. § 3(a)(3) (1974).

4. This language is from the Senate version of the act, S. 1541, 93d Cong., 2d Sess. § 3 (1974). Although the wording in the final version of the act was different, the conference committee report explained: "The Senate definition of 'tax expenditures' has been simplified although no change in meaning is intended"; H.R. Rept. 1101, 93d Cong., 2d Sess. (1974) 50. See also Statement of Senator Javits, 120 *Cong. Rec.* 7674–81 (1974); Statements of Senator Muskie, ibid. at 7900, 7935. In general see Paul R. McDaniel and Stanley S. Surrey, "Tax Expenditures: How to Identify Them; How to Control Them," 15 *Tax Notes* 595 (1982).

5. See Richard Goode, "The Economic Definition of Income," in *Comprehensive Income Taxation,* ed. Joseph Pechman (Washington, D.C.: Brookings Institution, 1977) 1; Emil Sunley, "Summary of the Conference Discussion," ibid. at 261; E. Carey Brown and Jeremy I. Bulow, "The Definition of Taxable Business Income," ibid. at 241, utilizing the Haig-Simons approach to define income for business firms, whereby "income . . . consist[s] of accrued changes in net worth, plus distributions and less net contributions of capital" (ibid. at 243).

6. Henry Simons, *Personal Income Taxation* (Chicago: University of Chicago Press, 1938) 50. For a recent discussion of Simons's views on taxation and economic systems, see Walter Hettich, "Henry Simons on Taxation and the Economic System," 32 *National Tax Journal* 1 (1979).

7. 252 U.S. 189, 207 (1920).

8. Helvering v. Bruun, 309 U.S. 461, 468–469 (1940); United States v. Kirby Lumber Co., 284 U.S. 1, 3 (1931).

9. Commissioner v. Glenshaw Glass Co., 348 U.S. 426, 431 (1955).

10. Haig-Simons is described as "ideal" in U.S. General Accounting Office, *Tax Expenditures: A Primer* (PAD80-26,1979) 28; and in Roger Smith, *Tax Expenditures: An Examination of Tax Incentives and Tax Preferences in the Canadian Federal Income Tax System* (Toronto: Canadian Tax Foundation, 1970) 5. The 1981 Special Analysis G describes it as a "theoretically pure treatment" and as a "theoretically pure income tax structure" at 208.

11. This conclusion has been reached by others writing on the tax expenditure concept, including Smith, *Tax Expenditures* at 3–7, and GAO, *Tax Expenditures* at 7; both in note 10 above.

The analysis in the *Government of Canada Tax Expenditure Account* (1979) 4, though using different terminology, essentially follows the U.S. approach. Instead of S-H-S, it uses a "benchmark tax structure" based on "neutrality." Instead of a "generally accepted structure of an income tax" it uses a "pragmatic criterion" to produce a workable tax expenditure list.

12. See the discussion of this point with reference to medical expenses in

Stanley S. Surrey, *Pathways to Tax Reform* (Cambridge, Mass.: Harvard University Press, 1973) 21–23. If ability to pay is used as a criterion, it is impossible to distinguish among the reasons for an individual's inability to pay—to distinguish, say, between a medical illness and a mania for gambling but with unsuccessful results. See also John F. Due, "Personal Deductions," in *Comprehensive Income Taxation,* note 5 above at 38; but see Charles E. McLure, Jr., "Comments," ibid. at 69.

Those who stress an "inability to pay" approach on horizontal equity grounds—claiming that those with equal ability to pay should pay equal taxes—must of course define ability to pay, which by their reasoning is different from income. Although ability to pay may be the general reason for a country's adoption of an income tax, those structuring that tax must concern themselves with defining income.

13. See Smith, *Tax Expenditures,* note 10 above at 26. See also Gerard M. Brannon, "Tax Expenditures and Income Distribution: A Theoretical Analysis of the Upside-Down Subsidy Argument," in *The Economics of Taxation,* ed. Henry Aaron and Michael J. Boskin (Washington, D.C.: Brookings Institution, 1980) 87.

Using "standard of living" as a basis for applying an income tax also does not seem helpful. The term is used in U.S. Treasury Department, *Blueprints for Basic Tax Reform* (1977) 36, in contrast to "ability to pay," as a means of determining whether gifts should be deductible by the donor and includible in income by the donee. The Treasury asserted that the answer was yes for both the donor and donee under a "standard of living" basis and no for the donor under an "ability to pay" basis.

14. See *Annual Report of the Secretary of the Treasury,* note 1 above at 327.

15. The Asprey Committee, appointed to review the Australian tax system, concluded: "The adoption of a compulsory family unit basis must be rejected on grounds of general social principle. The right to be taxed as an individual has always been accorded in Australia. At a time when women are playing an ever greater role in the economic and other affairs of society, the withdrawal of this right would certainly be regarded as a retrograde step. And objections would come not only from women; men too might take exception to a universal and compulsory commingling of their tax affairs with those of their wives. This would, in the Committee's view, make a change in this direction politically unacceptable irrespective of whether married women (or married men) paid more or less tax after the change than they do now; social attitudes to the separate status of the sexes, rather than purely economic considerations, are involved here"; Taxation Review Committee, *Full Report* (Canberra: Australian Government Publication Service, 1975) 134.

For a discussion of comparative tax treatment of the family, illustrating the issues involved, see OECD Committee on Fiscal Affairs, *The Tax/Benefit Position of Selected Income Groups in OECD Member Countries, 1974–1978* (1980) and *The 1979 Tax/Benefit Position of a Typical Worker in OECD Member Countries* (1980).

16. Numerous studies presenting many differing viewpoints demonstrate the difficulties policymakers face in making these decisions; it therefore seems clear that the issue lies outside tax expenditure analysis. See, for example, Michael J. McIntyre and Oliver Oldman, "Treatment of the Family," in *Comprehensive Income Taxation*, note 5 above at 205; the several articles on the subject in Aaron and Boskin, *The Economics of Taxation*, note 13 above, and in 1 *Canadian Taxation* no. 4 (1979); Michael J. McIntyre, "Individual Filing in the Personal Income Tax: Prolegomena to Future Discussion," 58 *North Carolina Law Review* 470 (1980); Peggy B. Musgrave, "Women and Taxation," in *Reforms of Tax Systems*, ed. Karl W. Roskamp and Francesca Furte (Detroit: Wayne State University Press, 1979); International Fiscal Association, *The Income Fortune, and Estate Tax Treatment of Household Units*, Cahiers de Droit Fiscal International, vol. 67a (Deventer, Netherlands: Kluwer, 1972); Boris I. Bittker, "Federal Income Taxation and the Family," 27 *Stanford Law Review* 1389 (1975).

17. See McDaniel and Surrey, "Tax Expenditures," note 4 above, for detailed discussion.

18. 1983 Special Analysis G at 4–5.

19. 1985 Special Analysis G at G-5.

20. IRC § 1256, for example, requires that unrealized appreciation in commodity futures contracts determined as of the end of the taxable year be included in income.

21. See Kul Bhatia, "Capital Gains, the Distribution of Income, and Taxation," 27 *National Tax Journal* 319 (1974).

22. Michael F. Duhl, "Like-Kind Exchanges under Section 1031: Multiparty Exchanges, Nonsimultaneous Exchanges, and Exchanges of Partnership Interests," 58 *Taxes* 949 (1980).

23. The 1981 Special Analysis G stated at 211 that the exclusion of gifts and bequests from income is not a tax expenditure, because the "tax system subjects gifts and bequests to taxes separate from the income tax." This, however, is only a partial explanation of the policies and attitudes supporting the exclusion of gifts and bequests from taxable income and is irrelevant to the classification of the rule under an income tax.

24. IRC §§ 118 and 362. Presumably the same result would follow for individuals or partnerships engaged in business activities.

25. The Revenue Rulings generally exclude such transfer payments as "in the nature of disbursements made in furtherance of the social welfare objectives of the Federal government."

26. See, for example, Richard A. Musgrave and Peggy B. Musgrave, *Public Finance in Theory and Practice*, 3d. ed. (New York: McGraw-Hill, 1980) 347; Emil M. Sunley, Jr., "Employee Benefits and Transfer Payments," in *Comprehensive Income Taxation*, note 5 above at 75, 92; idem, "Conference Discussion," ibid. at 266–267, 281; Joseph A. Pechman, *Federal Tax Policy*, 3d ed. (Washington, D.C.: Brookings Institution, 1977) table B-1 at 321; cf. Richard Goode, *The Individual Income Tax* (Washington, D.C.: Brookings Institution,

1976) 100; idem, "The Economic Definition of Income," in *Comprehensive Income Taxation*, note 5 above at 17; and Henry J. Aaron, "Comments," ibid. at 31. The Treasury also adopted this view in its exposition of a comprehensive income tax; see *Blueprints for Basic Tax Reform*, note 13 above at 61. It is sometimes argued that inclusion of transfer payments in income would produce national personal income in excess of the stock of goods and services, since the payment of the taxes by which the transfer payments are financed, such as individual income tax, is not a deductible item. But Musgrave and Musgrave, *Public Finance* at 272, answer this argument: "From the economist's point of view, national income is the sum of factor earnings during the period, reflecting in turn the value of output which the factors have produced. Transfers received from government or private sources (such as gifts or bequests) are not components of income in the national income sense. But it does not follow that they should be excluded from taxable income. Choosing a suitable definition of taxable income is an issue in tax equity, not in national income accounting. A person's taxable income need not be the same as his share in national income; nor need total taxable income equal total national income."

27. 1985 Special analysis G at G-11.

28. Ibid. at G-13 and G-14.

29. 1982 Special Analysis G at 206–207.

30. See, for example, Goode, "The Economic Definition of Income," note 5 above at 17; and Aaron, "Comments," note 26 above at 31.

31. This position was adopted by the group of fiscal scholars from six OECD countries participating in a comparative study of tax expenditures. See Paul R. McDaniel and Stanley S. Surrey, eds., *International Aspects of Tax Expenditures: A Comparative Study* (Deventer, Netherlands: Kluwer, 1985). See also Congressional Budget Office, 97th Cong., 2d Sess., *Interactions among Programs Providing Benefits to Individuals: Secondary Effects on the Budget* (1982). In determining whether individuals are above or below the poverty line, the government includes only cash grants, not noncash food, housing, and medical benefits. However, Reagan administration statements that there are fewer poverty-level individuals than is generally believed do depend on inclusion of both cash and in-kind transfers. Some welfare programs using minimum income eligibility levels also include benefits under other programs in the measurement of income; thus determinations of eligibility for AFDC benefits and housing subsidies include the dollar value of food stamps. Different countries provide welfare benefits through various sources, such as government, employers, and other institutions. Clearly, whether the recipient is or is not subject to tax on those benefits is important to comparative analyses. In the absence of tax expenditure tables, the analyses cannot allow for this effect on the comparative measurements.

For estimates of poverty that include noncash benefits, see U.S. Department of Commerce, Bureau of the Census, *Estimates of Poverty Including the Value of Non-Cash Benefits; 1979 to 1982*, Technical Paper 51 (1984).

32. Thus Professor William D. Andrews, though accepting the validity of

the tax expenditure concept, objected to the inclusion of these items in the tax expenditure list; "Personal Deductions in an Ideal Income Tax," 86 *Harvard Law Review* 309 (1972). To support his argument, Professor Andrews in effect converted the normative structure of the tax system from one based on the production of income to one based on the expenditure or consumption of economic resources, excluding savings. He then argued that under a consumption-type tax, deductions for charitable contributions and medical expenses should not be regarded as tax expenditures. These arguments might be open to question even if the United States were to adopt a consumption tax. In an income tax system, however, the basic question must be whether expenditures for charitable contributions and medical expenses are costs of producing income. Professor Andrews did not address this issue.

Moreover, under Professor Andrews's approach, it would seem essential that a deduction for charitable contributions be accompanied by a requirement that beneficiaries include the charitable gifts in income; otherwise the nontaxation of the recipients would constitute a tax expenditure. What is manifestly clear is that under either Professor Andrews's or the traditional approach, a tax expenditure is involved in the existing rules. Either the charitable deduction itself or the nontaxation of the beneficiaries of charitable gifts is a tax expenditure. See Surrey, *Pathways to Tax Reform,* note 12 above at 19–23, for further analysis of this issue and for discussion of the "ability to pay" justification for the medical expense deduction. See also Mark G. Kelman, "Personal Deductions Revisited: Why They Fit Poorly in an 'Ideal' Income Tax and Why They Fit Worse in a Far from Ideal World," 31 *Stanford Law Review* 831 (1979).

Other critics of the tax expenditure concept also take the view that a tax on consumption is preferable to a tax on income. Thus Joseph E. Stiglitz and Michael J. Boskin state that "the tax expenditure concept suffers from a further defect: the legislation implicitly assumed that the 'natural' tax base is income, broadly defined . . . there is little justification for this [assumption] . . . to know what is being 'exempted' from taxation one needs to know what 'ought' to be taxed"; "Some Lessons from the New Public Finance," 67 *American Economic Review* 295, 297 (February 1977). The article then discusses whether consumption is a more appropriate tax base than income. It may or may not be, but since the United States uses income as its base, it is appropriate to structure a tax expenditure list accordingly. A tax using consumption as the base would result in a different tax expenditure list; contrary to the assumptions of many who prefer the consumption base, the legislature would undoubtedly also work into such a tax a large number of incentive and relief exceptions.

33. See, for example, Goode, "The Economic Definition of Income," note 5 above at 16; Due, "Personal Deductions," note 12 above at 38, 45, 47. Interestingly, Henry Simons did not elaborate on his use of the term "consumption." He stated: "Consumption as a quantity denotes the value of rights exercised in a certain way (in destruction of economic goods) . . ." See *Personal Income Taxation,* note 6 above at 49, 50, 96. But at 52 he mentioned leisure as con-

sumption (though not to be taxed), and at 139 he included gifts as consumption to the donor and therefore not to be deductible by the donor. He implied at 54 that the dichotomy is between business expenses and personal consumption.

Brannon, "Tax Expenditures and Income Distribution," note 13 above, appears to be an exception in that he seems not to regard the wealthy as purchasing services with their charitable contributions, though he does consider the poor as in part buying services through their religious contributions. He concludes that it is therefore socially desirable to subsidize the contributions of the wealthy more than those of the poor. For this reason (and because he believes that the elasticity of tax-induced giving is greater than one) he is satisfied with the upside-down aspect of the charitable contribution deduction. In real life, however, the wealthy do seem to have some consumption motives in their choice of gifts. See Kirtzman and Shephard, "Letters Indicate Miller Suggested 'Free Enterprise' Wharton Dean," *Daily Pennsylvanian* (1980), referring to a $1.5 million *negotiated gift* to the Wharton School. See also Simons, note 6 above at 57. Henry B. Hansmann, "The Role of Nonprofit Enterprise," 89 *Yale Law Journal* 835 (1980), in analyzing the factors that make for the utilization of nonprofit organizations, is clear that those who support such organizations are making payments for services to be rendered to the supporters. This is the case whether the contribution is to the performing arts or to an organization such as CARE.

34. It is interesting that most observers of the national economic scene treat medical expenses as consumption items. Thus *Morgan Guaranty Survey* 5–8 (June 1980) classified medical expenses as essential consumer outlays. Medical expenses are also treated as consumption in the national income accounts.

35. Due, "Personal Deductions," note 12 above at 45, regards casualty losses as negative incomes that reduce net wealth without yielding consumer satisfaction. But this view should not mean that the allowance of the deduction is not a tax expenditure. The items that can be involved, such as an automobile, are consumption items and therefore are not deductible when purchased. Loss through casualty can in one sense be considered as rapid consumption, although admittedly there is no satisfaction from the rapidity.

36. Moreover, even if a casualty loss can be considered to be a cost of producing income, it is not a cost of producing *taxable* income; a personal casualty loss is associated with the net imputed rental value of a consumer durable. Even if one does not view a casualty loss as consumption, classification of the deduction as a tax expenditure is appropriate since, under general tax principles, deductions should not be allowed for costs of producing income that are not included in the tax base. See IRC § 265. McDaniel and Surrey, *International Aspects of Tax Expenditures,* note 31 above, reached the same conclusion with respect to similar tax provisions in the countries involved in the study.

37. The current code provision, § 274(b), denying an employer a deduction in excess of $25 for items claimed by an employee to be excluded as a gift (ex-

cept for certain awards costing the employer less than $400), is a simpler administrative method of handling these items than seeking to tax the employee.

38. *President's 1978 Tax Reduction and Reform Proposals: Hearings before the House Ways and Means Committee*, 95th Cong., 2d Sess. (1978) 5219.

39. For the variety of viewpoints on the proper treatment of fringe benefits, see *Tax Treatment of Employee Fringe Benefits: Hearings Before a Task Force of the House Ways and Means Committee*, 95th Cong., 2d Sess. (1978).

40. IRC § 132.

41. For a general overview of the subject, see Henry J. Aaron, ed., *Inflation and the Income Tax* (Washington, D.C.: Brookings Institution, 1976). See also Emil Sunley, "Indexing the Income Tax for Inflation," 32 *National Tax Journal* 328 (1979); Martin Feldstein, "Taxes, Inflation, and Capital Formation," 32 *National Tax Journal* 347 (1979); and Congressional Budget Office, 96th Cong., 2d Sess., *Indexing the Individual Income Tax for Inflation* (1980).

42. For a comparison of the extent to which various countries have indexed their tax system for inflation and the various reasons for doing so or not doing so, see International Fiscal Association, *Inflation and Taxation*, Cahiers de Droit Fiscal International, vol. 67a (Deventer, Netherlands: Kluwer, 1977); OECD, *The Adjustment of Personal Income Tax Systems for Inflation* (1976): and P. Massone, "Adjustments of Profits for Inflation," 35 *Bulletin for Fiscal Documentation* 3, 51 (1981), relating to Latin America.

43. Some interpret the Haig-Simons definition as requiring tax base indexation; see, for example, Roger Brinner, "Inflation and the Definition of Taxable Personal Income," in Aaron, *Inflation and the Income Tax*, note 41 above at 121, 122. Others disagree; see, for example, Goode, "The Economic Definition of Income," note 5 above at 13. The position adopted in the text is the same as that adopted in McDaniel and Surrey, *International Aspects of Tax Expenditures*, note 31 above.

44. See House Ways and Means Committee, Revenue Act of 1978. H.R. Rept. 1445, 95th Cong., 2d Sess. (1978) 125.

45. In this respect the tax depreciation rules differ from the tax inventory rules, which permit the use of last-in, first-out (LIFO) accounting instead of first-in, first-out (FIFO) accounting for inventories only if the taxpayer uses LIFO in reporting to shareholders and creditors (IRC § 472). Although the use of LIFO can reduce taxable profits and hence tax liabilities for a given year, its use in financial statements also reduces book profits. Hence whereas a corporation under general accounting rules has a choice between using LIFO or FIFO in its financial statements, the choice involves a real financial decision. The condition attached to the tax law prevents the taxpayer from having a tax profit that differs from the financial profit.

46. Staff of the Joint Committee on Taxation, 97th Cong., 1st Sess., *General Explanation of the Economic Recovery Tax Act of 1981* (1981) 75.

47. It is sometimes said that economic depreciation is too elusive to determine, so that any statutory method of accounting for a capital expenditure

cannot be a tax expenditure. But economists and accountants acknowledge the validity of a concept of economic depreciation—appropriately spreading the cost of an asset over its useful life—even though there can be problems in the actual measurement. Accountants must pass on the depreciation methods used by companies in preparing financial statements. Economists have intensively studied the determination of useful lives. See, for example, Charles R. Hulten and Frank C. Wykoff, "The Measurement of Economic Depreciation," in *Depreciation, Inflation, and the Taxation of Income from Capital,* ed. Charles R. Hulten (Washington, D.C.: Urban Institute, 1981) 81; Dale W. Jorgenson and Sullivan, "Inflation and Corporate Capital Recovery," ibid. at 171. The Auerbach-Jorgenson plan for immediate expensing of the discounted present value of depreciation deductions was based on economic lives; Alan J. Auerbach and Dale W. Jorgenson, "Inflation-Proof Depreciation of Assets," 58 *Harvard Business Review* 113 (September–October 1980). The reserve ratio test, developed in the 1960s by the Treasury, was an accurate device to test whether the economic lives claimed by taxpayers accorded with their actual use of the assets. Consequently, it is a tax expenditure to substitute a depreciation method—such as ACRS—that does not claim even to attempt a correspondence with economic depreciation.

48. *Economic Report of the President* (1982) 31. For a later study showing the effect of the 1982 act changes, see Eugene Steuerle, *Interpretation of Effective Tax Rates on New Depreciable Assets* (Washington, D.C.: U.S. Treasury Department, Office of Tax Analysis, 1982).

49. JCT Staff, *Explanation of Economic Recovery Act,* note 46 above at 33–34.

50. Because there are differing views on how to treat corporations, the GAO study, *Tax Expenditures,* note 10 above at 33, overstated the matter when it asserted that "in the world of *ideal* tax systems corporations do not exist. Only individuals exist; and if they happen to band together to create a business enterprise, the profits and losses should be attributed to the individuals" (emphasis added). See Stanley S. Surrey, "Reflections on Integration of Corporation and Individual Income Taxes," 28 *National Tax Journal* 335 (1975).

51. For a complete discussion of this subject see Charles E. McLure, Jr., *Must Corporate Income Be Taxed Twice?* (Washington, D.C.: Brookings Institution, 1979). See also Charles E. McLure, Jr., and Stanley S. Surrey, "Integration of Income Taxes: Issues for Debate," 55 *Harvard Business Review* 169 (September–October 1977); *The President's 1978 Tax Reduction and Reform Proposals: Hearings before the House Ways and Means Committee,* 95th Cong., 2d Sess. (1978); Marshall E. Blume, Dean Crockett, and Irwin Friend, *Financial Effects of Capital Tax Reforms* (1978); Charles E. McLure, Jr., "A Status Report on Tax Integration in the United States," 31 *National Tax Journal* 313 (1978); Alvin C. Warren, Jr., "The Relation and Integration of Individual and Corporate Income Taxes," 94 *Harvard Law Review* 717 (1981).

52. Although the differing treatments in the U.S., German, and Canadian

tax expenditure lists are appropriate for each country's list, international comparisons are difficult when they involve countries that have adopted different fundamental policy approaches to the corporate-shareholder tax issue. Accordingly, we concluded in *International Aspects of Tax Expenditures*, note 31 above, that sufficiently generalized partial integration approaches such as those used in Canada and Germany would be considered neither tax expenditures nor tax penalties. This approach seems essential to meaningful international comparisons of tax expenditures and tax penalties.

53. Before passage of the Revenue Act of 1978, corporate taxable income above $50,000 was taxed at a 48 percent rate; taxable income below $50,000—the surtax exemption range—was taxed in two brackets of 20 and 22 percent.

54. H.R. Rept. 1445, note 44 above at 143. The Senate Finance Committee took the same position; *Revenue Act of 1978*, S. Rept. 1263, 95th Cong., 2d Sess. (1978) 253.

55. H.R. Rept. 1445, note 44 above at 79.

56. Ibid. The Senate Finance Committee report emphasized the "small business" thrust of the new rate schedule even more heavily; S. Rept. 1263, note 54 above at 110.

57. H.R. Rept. 1445, note 44 above at 144; S. Rept. 1263, note 54 above at 262.

58. IRC § 162(f).

59. Tank Truck Rentals v. Commissioner, 356 U.S. 30 (1958).

60. IRC § 162(e).

61. Professor Carl Shoup has pointed out: "The listing of tax expenditures will no doubt be 'incomplete' (or overcomplete), but if publication were to be denied to any listing that was sure to be incomplete, on the grounds that incompleteness is 'potentially misleading' . . . as indeed it is, national income accounts would never have appeared and no censuses would have been taken"; "Surrey's *Pathways to Tax Reform*: A Review Article," 30 *Journal of Finance* 1329, 1334 (1975).

62. 1982 Special Analysis G at 209–210.

63. Ibid.

64. Michael J. Graetz, "Assessing the Distributional Effects of Income Tax Revision: Some Lessons from Incidence Analysis," 4 *Journal of Legal Studies* 351 (1975), appears to take somewhat this view by stressing the importance of determining the precise economic effects in the economy if a tax expenditure were granted or dropped—that is, the ultimate consequences in terms of who benefits and who loses under the tax expenditure and under an elimination of that expenditure. See also Nicholaw Le Par, "Measurement of the Revenues and Distributive Effects of Tax Expenditures," 2 *Canadian Taxation* 220 (1980); Allan M. Maslove, "The Distributive Effects of Tax Expenditures: A Suggested Methodology and an Example," ibid. at 225: George Fallis, "The Incidence of Tax Expenditures: A Framework for Analysis," ibid. at 228; Boris I. Bittker, *Federal Taxation of Income, Estates, and Gifts* (1981) 3–67.

65. *Tax Expenditures: A Primer*, note 10 above at 26–27. See also Congressional Budget Office, 97th Cong., 2d Sess., *How Changes in Fiscal Policy Affect*

the Budget: The Feedback Issue, (1982). See also appendix to Statement of Honorable W. Michael Blumenthal, in Revenue Act of 1978: Hearings before the Senate Committee on Finance on H.R. 1351, 95th Cong., 2d Sess. (1978) 183, 200–201; Congressional Budget Office, 97th Cong., 1st Sess., A Review of the Accuracy of Treasury Revenue Forecasts, 1963–1978, vol. 9 (1981) 29.

66. 1981 Special Analysis G at 215.

67. See 1985 Special Analysis G at G-15. Paul R. McDaniel, "Tax Expenditures and Federal Spending Limitations," 10 Tax Notes 475, 479 (1980) points out that "direct loan programs are actually treated [in] three different ways for budget purposes: For some loan programs, the gross funds loaned in a year are included in outlays and repayments are included in revenue receipts. For some loan programs, funds loaned and amounts repaid are netted and only the net expenditure figure (if any) is shown as an outlay. A third group of loan programs is completely 'off budget' and has no effect on outlays at all."

68. The 1981 Special Analysis F used the "present value" method at 191 in estimating the current revenue loss from the tax exemption for interest on state and local government bonds. For this purpose the analysis used a discount based on the Aaa corporate bond rate on a maturity of eighteen years—a period said to be consistent with the average maturity (fifteen to eighteen years) of securities in the tax-exempt market.

69. For example, 1981 Special Analysis G at 211–12. This advice is also repeated in the CBO and JCT lists.

70. Congressional Budget Office, 94th Cong., 2d Sess., Budget Options for Fiscal Year 1977: A Report to the Senate and House Committees on the Budget (1976) 382. See also 1985 Special Analysis G at G-16.

71. For a study on interactions among direct budget programs, see Congressional Budget Office, 97th Cong., 2d Sess., Interactions among Programs Providing Benefits to Individuals: Secondary Effects on the Budget (1982).

72. 1985 Special Analysis G at G-12.

73. See California 1979–80 Governor's Budget Summary, A-83; Maryland Tax Expenditure Report, Fiscal Year 1980–2; but see also Wisconsin Summary of Tax Exemption Devices, 1979–81 Biennium at 99.

74. Statement of Senator Kennedy, in Revision of Federal Estate Tax Law: Hearings before the Senate Finance Committee, 94th Cong., 2d Sess. (1976) 45. The list was prepared by the authors.

75. Stanley S. Surrey, William C. Warren, Paul R. McDaniel, and Harry L. Gutman, Federal Wealth Transfer Taxation, 2d ed. (Minneola, N.Y.: Foundation Press, 1982) 765. See pages 766–768 for a discussion of specific items included in or excluded from the list, and the revenue estimating procedures employed. The discussion in this chapter is based on the discussion there. The French tax expenditure list covers both its wealth transfer taxes and its net wealth tax. McDaniel and Surrey, International Aspects of Tax Expenditures, note 31 above, includes tax expenditure items and estimates for both the wealth transfer and net wealth taxes of the countries involved in the study.

76. Senator Edmund Muskie, later Chairman of the Senate Budget Committee, stated during the floor consideration of the Budget Reform Act of 1974: "The use of the words 'income tax' in the definition [of tax expenditures] should not preclude consideration of tax expenditures in the gift and estate tax systems. Generation-skipping under the estate tax, for instance, has an estimated cost of well over $250 million annually, and the charitable deduction under the estate tax, including deductions for family foundations, has a much larger annual cost, well over $1 billion annually"; 120 *Cong. Rec.* 7935 (1974).

The House Ways and Means Committee report on the Estate and Gift Tax Reform Act of 1976 stated: "The estate and gift tax provisions of [pre-1977] law may be regarded as tax expenditures, although they have not been included in past tax expenditure budgets. The revenue loss from [pre-1977] law estate tax provisions is estimated currently as $4.9 billion per year for estates above the $60,000 [basic] exemption. Under this bill, the provisions for raising the limitation on the marital deduction, revising the valuation of certain real property devoted to farming or closely held businesses, the extension of time for payment of estate tax, the tax on generation-skipping transfers and the increased exclusion for property passing to orphans together would increase tax expenditures, i.e., reduce budget receipts, by $187 million in fiscal year 1978, $201 million in 1979, $215 million in 1980, and $231 million in 1981. There would be no change in revenues in fiscal year 1977"; *Estate and Gift Tax Reform Act of 1976, House Ways and Means Committee,* H.R. Rept. 1380, 94th Cong., 2d Sess. (1976) 73.

77. H.R. Rept. 1380, note 76 above at 46.

78. Ibid.

79. The Tax Reform Act of 1984 limited the availability of the alternate valuation date to situations in which the assets have declined in value since the date of death. This change was designed to prevent post-mortem tax planning involving a trade-off between a higher estate tax value in exchange for a higher income tax basis granted for property transferred at death.

80. The Office of Management and Budget does not require any specific statutory authority to expand its tax expenditure list to include the wealth transfer taxes. See Statement of Senator Muskie, note 76 above.

The House Ways and Means Committee report on the Estate and Gift Tax Reform Act of 1976, note 76 above, acknowledged that the estate and gift tax provisions contain tax expenditures. In its list of these tax expenditures, however, the report included not only true tax expenditures but also some items that lie outside the tax expenditure concept as applied to a transfer tax (such as the marital deduction). This kind of confusion illustrates the need for a careful and clear distinction between the normative and tax expenditure provisions in the wealth transfer taxes.

81. McDaniel and Surrey, *International Aspects of Tax Expenditures*, note 31 above, identifies and qualifies tax expenditures in the value-added taxes and national sales taxes employed by the countries involved in the study.

82. See *California 1979–80 Governor's Budget Summary*, note 73 above, at A-81 to A-85.

83. William M. Hildred, "Passive Tax Expenditures in State Income Taxes," reproduced in 123 *Cong. Rec.* 25121 (1977).

84. Commonwealth of Massachusetts, *The Tax Expenditure Budget* (1984).

INDEX